TAROT AS A WAY OF LIFE

TAROT AS A WAY OF LIFE

A JUNGIAN APPROACH TO THE TAROT

Karen Hamaker-Zondag

SAMUEL WEISER, INC.

York Beach, Maine

First published in 1997 by
Samuel Weiser, Inc.
Box 612
York Beach, ME 03910-0612

Library of Congress Cataloging-in-Publication Data

Hamaker-Zondag, Karen.
    [Tarot als levensweg. English]
    Tarot as a way of life : a Jungian approach to the tarot /
Karen Hamaker-Zondag.
        p. cm.
    Includes bibliographical references and index.
    ISBN 0-87728-878-X (pbk. : alk. paper)
    1. Tarot. 2. Jung, C. G. (Carl Gustav), 1875-1961.
I. Title.
BF1879.T2H33613   1997
133.3'2424--dc21   97-1920
                                      CIP

ISBN 0-87728-878-X
BJ

Typeset in 10 point Galliard with Herculaneum display
Cover design by Ray Rue

PRINTED IN THE UNITED STATES OF AMERICA
04 03 02 01 00
10 9 8 7 6 5 4 3 2

For Ton and Paul

CONTENTS

ACKNOWLEDGMENTS

THE CHAPTER TITLED "The Major Arcana and the Way of the Hero" forms part of the Bona Futura project on the tarot and is included in this book by kind permission of Bona Futura BV. Part of the chapter called "The Tarot and Astrology" has already appeared in the book *Astrology and the Tarot: A Survey*, by Karen Hamaker-Zondag (in a single limited edition issued by Symbolon in Amstelveen, Holland), and is included in this book by kind permission.

Illustrations from the Universal Waite Tarot reproduced by permission of U.S. Games Systems, Inc. Stamford, CT 06902, USA. Copyright © 1990 by U. S. Games, Inc. Further reproduction prohibited.

Illustrations from the Morgan-Greer Tarot reproduced by permission of U.S. Games Systems, Inc. Stamford, CT 06902, USA. Copyright © 1979 by U. S. Games, Inc. Further reproduction prohibited.

Illustrations from the Hanson Roberts Tarot reproduced by permission of U.S. Games Systems, Inc. Stamford, CT 06902, USA. Copyright © 1985 by U. S. Games, Inc. Further reproduction prohibited.

Illustrations from the Haindl Tarot reproduced by permission of U.S. Games Systems, Inc. Stamford, CT 06902, USA. Copyright © 1991 by U. S. Games, Inc. Further reproduction prohibited.

Illustrations from the Tarot of the Witches Tarot reproduced by permission of U.S. Games Systems, Inc. Stamford, CT 06902,

USA. Copyright © 1974 by U. S. Games, Inc. Further reproduction prohibited.

Illustrations from the Pierpont Morgan Visconti-Sforza Tarocchi reproduced by permission of U.S. Games Systems, Inc. Stamford, CT 06902, USA. Copyright © 1975, 1984 by U. S. Games, Inc. Further reproduction prohibited.

Illustrations from the Tarot of Marseille Deck reproduced by permission of U.S. Games Systems, Inc./Carta Mundi. Copyright © 1996 by U. S. Games, Inc./Carta Mundi. Further reproduction prohibited.

Illustrations from the Sola Busca Tarot Deck reproduced from *The Encyclopedia of Tarot*, Volume III. Copyright © 1990 U. S. Games, Inc. Further reproduction prohibited.

Illustrations from the Arcus Arcanum Tarot reproduced by permission of AGM AGMüller, CH-8212 Neuhausen, Switzerland. Copyright © 1986 AGM AGMüller. Further reproduction prohibited.

PREFACE

WHEN I STARTED to study the tarot more seriously in 1972, I did as so many others do: thinking that the cards themselves were rather fanciful, I let the pictures take second place to what was said about them in the books. I would ask a question, would deal the cards in accordance with a certain system, and then as quickly as possible I would look up the meaning in some book.

Initially this worked well; and, after trying out various decks, I chose one that seemed to suit me best. But there came a time when I was no longer satisfied. In the first place, I wanted to know why the meanings assigned to the cards were what they were. I had carefully memorized them, but how were they determined? This question became more crucial when, on delving still deeper into the literature on the subject, I came across conflicting meanings for the same card. I was perplexed.

Also, when I started to take a closer look at the pictures in different tarot decks, more and more discrepancies came to light. Some people swore by the Marseilles deck, others swore by Waite's deck. These were the most influential traditions I encountered. But there are countless other decks, some of them derived from Waite but with different or more artistic designs. Meanwhile I had a acquired a taste for the tarot and enjoyed working with it. My interest was intensified when I saw a deck in which the fifth card of the Major Arcana, the Pope (or Hierophant) was depicted as Bacchus! Such a spiritual and religious card, and then Bacchus: how was that possible? What is the tarot really?

Because I was also very busy working with astrology, the I Ching, and Jungian psychology in addition to the tarot, I began to gain insights from a non-tarot point of view.

I put the cards under the archetypal magnifying glass, and studied their symbolism in the light of Jungian psychology and the archetypes. It soon became apparent that the symbolism of a great many tarot decks is totally inadequate: the depth psychological aspect has, in many cases, been sacrificed to prettiness of design.

It also became clear that the spirit of the age in which a deck is designed will permeate the symbolism of that deck. And the psychological state of the designer plays a considerable part in the presentation. The effect of these influences should not be underestimated: they mean that every deck has some deficiencies. A card showing Bacchus instead of the Pope as the embodiment of spirituality: what does that tell us about the designer?

Furthermore, the difference between the Major and Minor Arcana began to be more apparent. It is true that this difference is mentioned in all the books; unfortunately, where complex spreads are concerned, the authors seem to lose sight of it.

Through working with dreams, with drawings, and other aspects of the imagination—in short with the spontaneous symbolic language of the unconscious, I realized that the cards of the Major Arcana represent the individuation process, i.e., the process of development and becoming whole, with all the problems and pitfalls of this. In every age and culture this process has given rise to myths and legends—a collective expression of the wisdom lying hidden deep inside each one of us. The tremendous diversity of these myths tends to obscure their underlying pattern, but in Joseph Campbell's splendid book, *The Hero with a Thousand Faces*,[1] we can see how closely the process of becoming a complete individual follows specific patterns. Jung called them archetypal. It is the Major Arcana that reflect the general course of individuation.

The Minor Arcana appear to show how we express, or fail to express, these underlying patterns in everyday life, how they affect us, and what we make of them. Thus they are *applications* of the patterns of the Major Arcana, but they do not have anything like the range of

---

1. Joseph Campbell, *The Hero with a Thousand Faces*, rev. ed. (Princeton: Princeton University Press, 1990).

the latter: they are more specialized. If several cards of the Minor Arcana appear in a spread which also contains a card belonging to the Major Arcana, the Minor Arcana are drawn into the sphere of influence of the Major Arcana!

Like astrological signs, the Minor Arcana are often allocated to the elements. However, in spite of the similarities, there are also differences. These will be discussed in a separate chapter.

The sequence in the suits of the Minor Arcana from 1 (the ace) through 10, is often given a numerological treatment. I myself have experimented with this concept and have had a certain amount of success, but it was not completely satisfactory. I discovered that sometimes there is more to a card than might be expected from its numerological meaning. And yet I knew from Jungian psychology that numbers are very important. Jung called numbers "the archetype of order."

Therefore I became interested in learning the significance of numbers in dreams, visions or visualizations, drawings, and anything else that is a spontaneous manifestation of individual consciousness. I also wanted to know what part numbers played in myths, legends, fairy tales, folklore and other collective traditions of the past and present. By combining these I gained fresh insights into the role of several numbers, and these insights seemed to agree better with what I had gleaned from certain cards when I actually had been working with these cards.

And so I combined the archetypal meanings of numbers (including their paradoxes) with the basic meanings of the four suits as given by the court cards of the Minor Arcana. As a result, my insight into the meanings of the numbers and suits considerably deepened my understanding of the possibilities and problems of each card; it also clarified and solved the contradictory interpretations in various books on the subject. With this insight it is not necessary to commit to memory the meanings of the cards in a whole deck; you can learn to understand them by analyzing their composition.

It is this analytical approach that I am going to describe. You can then start to gain your own elementary insights into the cards. Every card—certainly those of the Major Arcana—can contain a world of meaning. Once you grasp the principle, you can derive and understand all the possibilities for yourself. In this way, the tarot becomes a powerful tool for gaining insight into your psychic situation, as well as into the time pattern in which you find yourself. The tarot becomes a life-path, the Way of the Hero in yourself.

I have already shared a large part of my own life-path with my husband Hans, who has sorted out and recorded all my discoveries and all my brainwaves, subjected them to constructive criticism, and supported them where possible. I am very grateful to him for this.

—KAREN HAMAKER-ZONDAG

Chapter One

WHAT IS THE TAROT?

T HE CLASSICAL TAROT deck contains 78 cards, which are subdivided into two groups:

- The Major Arcana: consisting of 22 cards; and,
- The Minor Arcana: consisting of 56 cards.

That the Major Arcana contains fewer cards than the Minor Arcana seems at first sight to imply a contradiction in terms: but "Major" and "Minor" do not refer to the quantities of the cards, but to their importance. The 22 cards of the Major Arcana correspond to things that lie very deep in our psyche. They are often likened to a way of initiation, and not without good reason, as we shall shortly see. The 56 cards of the Minor Arcana have more to do with how this works out in daily life.

The cards of the Major Arcana are called "trumps"; those of the Minor Arcana have no special name. The Minor Arcana are divided into four sets or suits: Wands (Scepters), Swords, Pentacles, and Cups.

Each suit consists of a series of cards numbered from 1 through 10. There are also four court cards: Page (Knave), Knight, Queen, and King. So we have the following structure:

- Major Arcana: 22 trumps
- Minor Arcana: four suits: Wands, Swords, Pentacles and Cups, each consisting of ten numbered cards and four court cards.

As far as we know, the tarot cards have always been used to gain insight into situations and activities, and to study future trends. Therefore, the tarot has gained a reputation as one of the "mantic" or predictive methods. And it is generally used for predicting the future. In a fit of curiosity, you purchase a tarot deck and an explanatory booklet; then you ask a question, deal one or more cards as instructed, and simply look up "what will happen."

The tarot lends itself very well to this approach, even though the result depends partly on how you interpret your book. However, by setting to work in this way, we fail to do the tarot justice. We are not taking into account that each card is a picture, a picture with a symbolic value built around a whole range of symbols, each with its own meaning, and together giving the necessary depth to the card. When we make an insightful approach to the analysis of its symbolism, it can become a source of inner enrichment and psychological growth, and prediction will take second place to accurate and clear self-insight.

Working with the tarot can become a way of completely accepting yourself and your life, and of learning to cope with the ups and downs. The tarot, itself, will point you in the direction of a proper outlook on life: working with the symbolism and hidden depths of the tarot is nothing less than learning to dance to the rhythms of the cosmos.

The Power of Symbolism

NOW THAT WE ARE on the subject of symbolism, we are faced with the question of which tarot deck is the best to use. There are very many, including the old ones, like the Visconti-Sforza, and Marseilles decks; popular ones, like the Rider-Waite deck (or the new version, the Universal Waite deck), and very difficult or controversial ones, like the Crowley Thoth Tarot, etc.

Plenty of people have designed their own tarots, or have produced variants of existing versions. Each design inevitably evokes certain associations in us. It resonates, in fact, with the contents of our unconscious, which are activated by the sight of pictures. Specific emotions can be aroused by it so that, for example, one finds a given picture so beautiful that one is scarcely able to take one's eyes off it. This emotion reveals what is one's actual preoccupation. Another picture or part of a picture may produce horror, or something less specific, like uneasiness, or nameless fear.

We are not always very aware of these things, but visual images, whether in the tarot or on TV, activate all sorts of things in our unconscious and can therefore be a wonderful mirror to reflect what is going on inside us. All we need is eyes to see.

The tarot, however, has an added dimension. In a deck with a good symbolic design we are fascinated not only by the pictures, but by the symbols, which awaken something in us that shows us how a certain problem can be resolved. This very important process takes place mostly in our unconscious, out of sight of our rationalizing conscious. Often, therefore, we do not fully realize how helpful good symbolic pictures can be. Their role is similar to that played for children by fairy tales.

Fairy tales are packed with pictures having a symbolic basis. Most children take them for granted, and most adults think of fairy tales as quaint little stories. The underlying message conveyed in the imagery supports the child in his or her development. The story of Little Red Riding Hood, for example, tells of a small girl who, heedless of her mother's warnings, takes a wolf's advice and, leaving the forest path, goes deeper into the forest in order to pick the prettiest flowers. Meanwhile, the wolf hastens to the tiny cottage of the grandmother Red Riding Hood intends to visit. He gobbles up the old lady, and the same fate awaits Red Riding Hood when she arrives. Fortunately, a hunter comes along in the nick of time, cuts open the wolf's stomach, and Red Riding Hood and her grandmother step out unharmed. Red Riding Hood and her mother are reunited.

I have met many children who, at a certain stage (not infrequently around their third year), treasured this story as their favorite fairy tale. Their parents had to read it to them over and over again. In the course of time, often after many months, they were suddenly satisfied and did not need the story so compulsively.

What do we see in this fairy tale? Red Riding Hood is disobedient, listens to an instinct (the wolf) and does impulsive things (picks flowers), and has to face the consequences (being eaten by the wolf). But, for all that, everything turns out fine in the end. This reflects the position of the child in the defiant stage: it wants its own way, but is still unable to fend for itself. It experiences a conflict between obedience, which brings it positive attention (staying on the forest path and doing as one is told), and what it really wants, what gives it the most fun (picking the pretty flowers). In everyday life this can express itself, for example, in turning the knobs on the stove when forbidden to do so, and in similar unruly behavior. The child knows that he or she will be scolded or punished, and that the punishment will not be pleasant.

But the fairy tale says, "Don't be afraid! Although you experiment and occasionally go your own way, everything will come right again, and you are not going to forfeit your secure parental environment." The fairy tale emphasizes that this conflict is a general human pattern, and shows the child the way in symbolic picture-language. As long as the story is a "must," we know that the child needs it as a constructive guide. (Of course, like so many products of the unconscious, the fairy tale may be interpreted in several ways. I have chosen this way because it is seen so clearly in young children.)

Just as a fairy tale provides a child with unconscious guidance and helps the child cope with problems in ordinary daily life, so the pictures in various tarot decks work in us. We are not even half aware of how much one of the little tarot images can activate! There is an enormous variation in the way the different tarot decks are designed; therefore what is activated in our unconscious has, or will have, varying resonances. The greater the agreement between the pictures and the symbolism with which we have become familiar through depth psychology, the greater will be the impact made by the pictures on our unconscious. So your choice of deck will certainly have an effect on your way of working, on what you can do with the tarot, on what it releases within you, and on what you feel.

Choosing a Deck

IF YOU USE THE tarot only as a means of prediction, and the symbolism of the pictures is subordinate (as far as you are concerned) to the readings in the explanatory booklet, it hardly matters what deck you use. But if you intend to use the tarot in a deeper manner, and want to take account of its symbolism, then, as we have just seen, differences in design become particularly important. Although each deck, in its main features, points in the same direction, some decks have a much richer and more harmonious symbolic pattern than others, even though the latter may have superior artwork. Thus you can go considerably further with one deck than you can with another. In chapter 3, I shall elucidate this by making a number of comparisons.

After analyzing a number of the different decks, my current thinking is that Waite's tarot is the best from a symbolic point of view, and I shall constantly refer to it in this book. However, if another deck activates important emotions in you, and speaks to you, or gives you a good feeling, do not hesitate to work with it! That deck may well strike a sympathetic chord in you and may be able to help you on your way. Working with imagery and with the unconscious has many irrational aspects, so let your feelings guide you in your choice of cards.

Symbols in the Tarot

PICTURES AND SYMBOLS help to express the language of the unconscious. The unconscious is extremely creative and playful, having a logic of its own, which is nothing like logic as we know it. It is the very playfulness and creativity of the tarot that turns it into a mirror we can use infinitely in many situations. But this requires that the user be prepared to be creative and playful, too, when handling the tarot, and to be ready to come to terms with the working of the unconscious. Whereas the conscious has to do with order, the unconscious is connected with chaos—in which great potential lies hidden. Whereas the conscious obeys rules and regulations in order to make situations more manageable and easier to grasp, the unconscious functions best when there is a degree of freedom, especially in situations that are chaotic or illogical. Controlling and pressurizing are deadly to the inspired and intuitive creativity of the unconscious.

This idea has important consequences for it affects the way we handle the tarot. To satisfy our conscious minds, we tend to turn to lucidly written books in which each card is interpreted along the lines of: what card "X" means, and how it is to be interpreted when it falls in such-and-such a place. And what the best layouts are.

WHEN THE UNCONSCIOUS is put first, we usually concentrate on the actual cards. We look for a layout that appeals to us, and we venture to empathize with and meditate on the symbolic picture, to pay attention to what it evokes in us, and to see what transpires. If we stick to the standard interpretations found in books, we deprive ourselves of the opportunity to handle the multi-layered symbolism of the cards freely and with inspiration. This symbolism can have much more personal significance for us than can be found within the covers of a book. All that books can do is to list the general meanings; they can never inform us how the symbolism relates to our individual lives.

It may be helpful to compare this with dreams. The symbols in your dreams may very well have generally valid meanings as recorded in the dream books, but in your own case a certain symbol could mean something entirely different. In Jungian dream analysis, we always look for the personal significance, adding if need be the collective symbolic meaning.

If we treat the pictures of the tarot as collective symbols, it is certainly possible to make a splendid general description of them; but each one who works with the tarot possesses a unique emotional make-up and has highly personal reactions. The tarot can latch onto our individual use of symbolism in such a way that the meanings of certain cards can include something extra for us (sometimes temporarily), or certain cards have something special to say to us. That little bit extra varies from person to person.

The secret of understanding the cards is to be receptive and to let their symbolism work in you. For this purpose, you should go beyond the "meanings of the cards" whenever you feel the urge to do so. However, this entails stepping into an unstructured inner world where you, yourself, are the sole guide. And yet, by taking this step, you will be rewarded with the experience that you can plunge deeper and more intensely into yourself than you had thought possible; and, as an individual, you will increase your ability to support others. The creativity and inspiration of the unconscious can enrich your life, provided you take care to avoid psychological projections, in which a wish or fear can be the father of the thought.

To some extent this book is different from the many systematic workbooks and keys in this area. On the basis of their symbolism, the cards are treated as representatives of psychic mechanisms (the Major Arcana) and of the way in which these mechanisms express themselves in everyday life (the Minor Arcana), but there is no grand synopsis spelling out exactly what the cards mean in every department.

Instead, I try to show by reference to psychic mechanisms how you can learn to adapt the interpretation according to the insights you have gained into the symbolism.

Chapter Two

THE HISTORY AND BACKGROUND OF THE TAROT

THE ORIGINS OF the tarot lie in obscurity. According to some, we have to look for them in the initiatory rites of ancient Egypt. Others see connections with India. There are also those who regard the cards as repositories of the occult lore of the nomadic Romanies (or Gypsies), and so on. We just do not know, and historical references to the tarot are very late: it is only at the end of the Middle Ages that we hear of the tarot. However, many people feel, after studying the cards in depth, that they are older than this.

It may be that at one time the tarot was something different from the pack of cards we know today, or perhaps the pack was called by another name. For example, it is known that certain pictures with a small format (cards!) once played a part in religious instruction and initiation in Eastern countries. These symbolic pictures were in essence a sort of secret language, a code with an accompanying dogma or insight which could be understood by none but initiates.

This method of conveying occult knowledge is also seen elsewhere in the world. Universally, from the Maya to Pythagoras, we find symbols, either abstract or in picture form, that have a deeper meaning than is apparent at first sight. Nevertheless, what is important in connection with the tarot is that cards were actually in use in the East in addition to paintings and murals. Also there does seem to be a link between Oriental tradition and tarot symbolism.

The Suits

ON EXAMINING THE Minor Arcana, we see that it is composed of
four groups (or suits): Cups, Wands, Pentacles, and Swords. Each of
these four suits has its own basic meaning and is subdivided into the
numbered cards, 1 (ace) through 10, and the four court cards: Page,
Knight, Queen, and King.

Many attempts have been made to link the suits to the four elements. Although there is an unmistakable correspondence between
these groups and the elements, there are differences, too. This suggests that we should not confine our attention to the elements but
should dig deeper. For why are we presented with these symbols
rather than others? Why do these four symbols also lie on the
Magician's (or Juggler's) worktable in the first card of the Minor
Arcana? The four symbols are often encountered in mythology, but
we want to know when they first made their appearance in the deck.

The *Larousse World Mythology*[1] shows a cup, a scepter, a ring,
and a sword being held in the hands of the four-armed androgynous
(half-male and half-female) divinity, Ardhanarisvara. This divinity is a
combination of Kali and Shiva. (See figure 1, page 11.)

The Greek goddess of fate, Nemesis, carried the same symbols:
a cup, the bough of an apple tree, a wheel, and a sword. And other
gods elsewhere, such as the Indonesian monkey god Hanuman, seem
to have this quartet as their attributes.

Clearly these four symbols have a deep significance, and have
been understood in the same way at different times in different parts
of the world. The cups are everywhere the same, the wands (rods)
take the form of a scepter, or of the bough of an apple tree. The pentacles, where are represented as circles or as coins, are also seen as
rings or wheels, and the swords, like the cups, are always the same.

The cup, and related hollow forms, are an age-old symbol of
the receptive principle of the cosmos, interpreted today as a facet of
yin, or the female factor. The sword has always and universally been
recognized as the cosmic principle that has to do with separation and
differentiation: a facet of the yang, or male factor. Circular forms, like
the pentacles, are female, too, and vertical forms, like the wands
(scepters), are male.

---

1. *Larousse World Mythology,* Pierre Grimal, ed. (London: Hamlyn, 1965).

Figure 1. The four-armed androgynous god Ardhanarisvara, with his/her four emblems: cup, scepter, ring, and sword. From Isaac Myer: Qabbalah: The Philosophical Writings of Solomon Ben Yehudeh Ibn Gebirol or Avicebron *(New York: Samuel Weiser, 1974).*

It is very noticeable that, in various myths, these four attributes of different divinities can be reduced to various forms of duality, the primeval polarity, yang-yin or male-female. Even in the Christian Church we encounter this symbolism in the form of the chalice and the cross.

The very fact that an androgynous divinity, itself symbolic of the fusion of male and female, possesses these four attributes, reveals even more clearly that the suits of the Minor Arcana and the objects on the Magician's table in the Major Arcana are meant to point us to the primary polarity of the cosmos, which expresses itself in the opposites of light and darkness, day and night, activity and passivity, creation and reception, male and female. We each need to find a way of bringing this polarity into equilibrium in ourselves. This is our way and our fate. Not to find the way will be literally or figuratively "fatal" for us. That is why these symbols are also the attributes of Nemesis. The Stoics worshipped her because they saw her as the principle governing the course of the world and of nature. Even Zeus feared Nemesis: she was relentless and inescapable.

If there is a lack of balance between yin and yang in our daily lives, we shall inevitably reap the consequences, either in the form of external problems, or in the form of fears and nightmares, and either as physical illness, or as mental problems, such as neuroses (or worse).

There is nothing new about this, but in ancient times it was expressed in the form of symbols. Such symbols are found in pairs in the tarot. By recognizing them in the layouts we can determine which side of the balance takes precedence in our lives. Given the close correlation between the themes of the Major Arcana and those of the old myths, it seems hardly likely that toward the end of the Middle Ages someone just sat down one afternoon and produced the basic designs of the cards.

The symbolism of the tarot looks more like the precipitation of original knowledge which we have all been carrying around inside us from time immemorial, and have expressed in countless ways in myths and pictures. This knowledge could have been enshrined gradually in these 78 cards. The cards strike me as the result of a process of growth in which various designers have put part of themselves— designers who, being products of their times, were unconsciously influenced by them. Thus certain tarot decks have become dated because they are too strongly connected to the period in which they were produced. In chapter 3, I shall give some examples of this.

The Numerological Aspects

WHAT IS MORE, the numbering of the cards does not seem arbitrary, although the numbers 22, 56, and 78 convey little to most people. As a matter of fact, the structure is worth studying. Numbers have always played an important role in symbolism, quite apart from their place in numerological systems.

Here I will confine my attention to old symbols that are met with universally. C. G. Jung said, at the end of his life, that numbers might well be primary archetypes.

Take the number two: it occurs wherever there is duality, and therefore stands out as the number of duality, of yang and yin, male and female.

The numbers three and seven have always been regarded as significant, and not only in Christendom. Think of the Holy Trinity, or more simply of the creative relationship and state of equilibrium between man and woman. The process involved in this fecund meeting of opposites is represented by the number three, and the everyday symbol of this creativity is the child.

Three, however, is an idea; the number four stands for its realization in everyday life. Consider the child: the life of the child still has to take shape. It is the start of something new and the symbol of the creative impulse which can initiate a fresh process. It leads to reification and realization in the number four; which is why four has to do with matter, and also with mandalas. An idea is useful and creativity makes sense only when applied to life, itself.

Jung observed in his work how tremendously significant the number four is: he discovered the four manners of psychological orientation (the four functions), while the number four in dreams, imagination, and fantasies often indicates that things are falling into place and that processes are having a good outcome. We can think of the four points of the compass, the four rivers of paradise (where two trees stood!).

So far we have:

1) Unity;
2) Primary polarity;
3) The idea resulting from an encounter, the start of a process;
4) Formation in the concrete world.

Thus there is a close connection between the numbers three and four: they represent the translation of an idea into reality. The success of this translation is liked with the number seven, which is 3 + 4.

Now let us turn to the numbers of the tarot:

$$2 \times 7 = 14$$

Each suit or group of the Minor Arcana consists of fourteen cards, which express both the male and female sides (number two) of the number seven.

$$3 \times 7 = 21$$

The multiplication of these two key numbers gives the number of Major Arcana minus 1. For the Major Arcana consists of 22 cards but is numbered only as far as 21! The Fool bears the cipher 0. He is everything and nothing. A fantastic "invention," because without The Fool, the series produced by 3 x 7, would always remain static.

Three is a form of rounding off, and seven is a form of rounding off. In three, there is a field of tension between becoming concrete in four or in dropping back to two. In seven there is also a field of tension, with which I shall deal in chapter 5. Seven appears to be involved in a living paradox. The potential of creation is contained in three and seven, but that in itself is not enough. A creative impulse or spark is required to initiate the process.

And it is the 0, The Fool, who can spring in everywhere and make breakthroughs. Even in the ordinary card readings, The Fool signifies, "Be prepared to take a leap in the dark, life is secretly taking a new turn for you." Besides 21 cards of the Major Arcana, we have the 22nd card as number 0; a card that belongs everywhere and nowhere, which imparts dynamism and cranks up processes.

The number of Major Arcana (3 x 7), again leaving out The Fool, is said to represent an ancient Egyptian doctrine to which Pythagoras alludes. In this, the three is a perfect number and the seven is a mystical number. If we discard The Fool from the whole deck we are left with 77 cards, and that is 11 x 7. Now when we think of the number eleven in connection with carnival, we see that the idea of The Fool comes to the fore in the number eleven, and that it is manifested in the tarot seven times, although more covertly than on the individual card.

8 x 7 = 56

The Minor Arcana amount to 8 x 7 = 56 cards. Eight often refers to "form," and it is the Minor Arcana that confront us with the outcome of situations in the material world, the world of form. Three is the idea that seeks concrete fulfillment: 3 x 7 is the Major Arcana. And the great Zero, The Fool, is, in all cases, the completing primary impulse, the will to live, the urge to do something creative. It is, in short, the human need for individuation, the process set in motion by the Major Arcana (the 3 x 7), and elaborated in the Minor Arcana as reflected in matter: the 8 x 7.

The numbers seven and fourteen also play a symbolic role in other respects. Each in its own way has to do with order. Thus, ideally, the phases of the Moon have a cycle of 4 x 7 = 28 days. If we call the day of the New Moon (our starting point) day 0, then we have the first quarter on the 7th day, Full Moon on the 14th, the last quarter 7 days after Full Moon, and New Moon 14 days after Full Moon.

So there are four phases (and we have already seen how important the number 4 is) of seven days each. In Buddhism, we find something similar in the tradition that the Buddha took his first fifty-six steps in the four main directions: in each direction he took 7 steps out and 7 back, or 14 steps per direction, and 4 x 14 = 56, the total number of cards in the Minor Arcana.

The number fourteen plays a part in other myths, too—in the 14 steps of the heavenly ladder of Osiris, to mention one example. Thus the design of the subset known as the Minor Arcana is based on numerological symbolism, and the cards are grouped in four suits analogous to a mandala, which expresses concrete realization. The four suits themselves have symbols that direct our attention to the primary polarity of life, yang and yin, which seek to maintain a balance by eternal interaction.

What is more, it turns out that a great deal of insight and knowledge has been incorporated in certain card allocations. It is not by accident that The Moon is Card 18 and The Sun is Card 19. The orbital planes of the Sun and Moon are set at a small angle to one another, with the result that the solar and lunar eclipses occur in cycles. One such cycle lasts for about nineteen years. Astrologers will understand that this has to do with the revolution of the North Node around the zodiac. But note: two nineteen-year periods and one eighteen-year period bring the Sun and Moon back to their starting point precisely. This is called the Great Year. The number of cards of the Minor Arcana is 19 + 19 + 18 = 56. Symbolically, the Sun is always one step ahead of the Moon, therefore The Moon is Card 18 and The Sun is Card 19. And so we will find astronomical knowledge, or rather a knowledge of celestial cycles, enshrined in the tarot.

Pictographic Relationship to the Alphabet

MORE THAN ONE author has pointed out the resemblance of the 22 letters of the Hebrew alphabet to the 22 cards of the Major Arcana, and searchers for similarities have been encouraged by the fact that the letters of the Hebrew alphabet have their own symbolic values. The question whether the Major Arcana might not have been developed out of early alphabets has also been raised.

Although this is not inconceivable, my own impression is that the meanings of the letters in ancient (usually pictographic) alphabets, and the wealth of symbolic imagery encountered all over the world, spring from some profound source within ourselves, a form of "hidden knowledge" located by Jung in the deepest layers of the collective unconscious.

It is in the latter that the archetypes have their origin and they serve as relay points of psychic energy in which the "hidden knowledge" is converted into symbols and images before its psychic energy impinges on the conscious. This transformation can occur individually in dreams, visions, doodles, and spontaneous dances; it can occur collectively in myths, fairy tales, folklore, and legends. This leads me to believe that what we have is not just what has been handed down from our own culture. Analogous expressions all over the world, in the form of independently arising systems and processes, each in its own way is a reflection of the latent knowledge of humankind, and each is unconsciously helping us to find our bearings in the world of phenomena.

Early Card Games

IN MY OPINION, the origin of the tarot goes back a long way. In essence, the tarot is anchored in our unconscious and represents self-knowledge. However, it is only between A.D. 1300 and 1500 that we come across references to what sound like actual tarot cards, although they are not called by that name. The earliest mentions are more of the existence of playing cards in decks of various designs.

In 1377, a German monk, Brother Johannes, wrote about the *ludus cartarum* (game of cards). This contained only 52 cards and there is no suggestion of the existence of the Major Arcana. However, the good brother pointed out how valuable these card games were for the promotion of morals and education! In 1423, St. Bernard of Sienna preached a fierce sermon against playing cards in the church of San Petronio in Bologna. The deck he named consisted of 56 cards. Incidentally, the Church has often set its face against card games; therefore the views of Brother Johannes are all the more remarkable.

It looks as if the Major and Minor Arcana developed separately and were merged at a particular moment. Only after card games have proliferated and they begin to be named in sermons, in decrees forbidding their use, and even in poems, does the word *tarocchi* (pronounced "tarock-key") occur for the first time. The oldest list describing the cards of the Major Arcana dates from ca. 1500 and is found in a Latin manuscript titled *Sermones de Ludo Cumalis.* Although exhibiting some variations in card sequence and design, the description is already quite close to that of the cards we have today.

The Classic Tarot

THE EARLIEST ALMOST completely preserved set of tarot cards is the world-famous Visconti-Sforza deck, which was produced in the middle of the 15th century. Several different versions are known to exist. The originals are genuine works of art, so beautifully have they been designed and painted. The cards have been dispersed into various museums around the world. We fumble in the dark over such questions as: How were they used? Why were they made at that particular time?

It is generally accepted that members of the Visconti-Sforza family posed as models for the pictures on the 22 cards of the Major Arcana. You will see their heraldic symbols and coats of arms. According to some people, the cards also represent, in a highly symbolic form, persons and events belonging to 15th-century Milan.

A number of experts state that the "tarocchi" were used for centuries, both as a game and as portraits of noble families. This assumption has been made chiefly because there are no indications that the tarot was used for prediction. Such indications certainly exist for the ordinary playing cards: ca. 1487 there appeared the *Mainzer Kartenlosbuch* [The Mainz Fortune Telling Book], apparently the work of a book illustrator in Ulm, in which the ordinary playing cards are illustrated together with their meanings.[2] But there is not a word in it concerning the Major Arcana.

Personally I doubt that the main purpose of the Visconti-Sforza tarot was to portray this aristocratic family. Of course family members

---

2. See Stuart R. Kaplan, *The Encyclopedia of Tarot,* Vol. 1 (Stamford, CT: U.S. Games Systems, 1978), p. 348.

may have served as models; but it strikes me as improbable that people would include such cards as The Hanged Man and The Devil in a series meant to glorify the family. Admittedly, four cards are lacking from the Visconti-Sforza deck as we now have it: two suit cards and, from the Major Arcana, The Devil and The Tower. However, these would originally have been present as we can tell from their existence in comparable decks of the era. In one reproduction of these cards, The Devil and The Tower have been reconstructed in the style of the other cards belonging to the same period.

The deck also contains many Christian scenes. Thus The Devil is said to be a warning against the temptations of the "world, the flesh, and . . .," and it is conjectured that The Hanged Man represents St. Peter, who, according to tradition, asked to be placed head downward when he was being crucified. Again, there are cards, such as the poverty-stricken and ragged Fool, and I cannot imagine that any high-born person would consent to serve as a model. The skeleton of Death is even less palatable. No, I think that the order of the cards and their symbolism had already been settled, and that aristocratic families had personalized decks made for themselves. But were these considered a game or were the cards intended to give insights? We do not know.

After they had been current for some centuries, the cards suddenly became the center of attention at the end of the 18th century, when the Frenchman, Court de Gebelin, published his *Monde Primitif* in 1781. He asserted in that book that the compilation of cards in the Major Arcana was the ancient and magical *Book of Thoth*, which had been rescued from the great fire of Alexandria. His contention was that this book was the synthesis of all human knowledge combined with a profound mysticism. For Thoth was the Egyptian god of wisdom, science, and occultism.

Another Frenchman, Eliphas Levi (the pen-name of Alphonse Louis Constant) who, in the 19th century, was know for his books on magic, pointed out numerous correspondences between the tarot and the Kabbalah. All this interest, and the allusions to deeper mysteries and the links with occultism, made the tarot very popular in magical orders, occult groups, theosophical societies, etc. And then, in the 20th century, the tarot caught the attention of the general public, and is now regularly used by many people for the purpose of divination, or simply to gain insight into situations.

Many different tarot decks have been published and one of the more popular decks is the Tarot de Marseilles because it looks so authentic. But there are others of importance, and the encyclopedic work of the collector and tarot expert Stuart R. Kaplan shows how great the number of different decks has become.[3]

Among these are the beautifully designed deck created through Aleister Crowley's vision. He wrote a book to go with it. A. E. Waite's deck was published in 1910 by Rider & Co., in London (which is why it is known as the Rider-Waite Tarot). It very quickly gained the enormous popularity it still enjoys.[4]

The symbolic pictures in the Rider-Waite deck were drawn by Pamela Coleman Smith, following Waite's directions. He was unusually knowledgeable about symbolism but, owing to his membership in the occult societies in existence at that time, he found it necessary to keep silent about what he knew. From his own mouth we have scarcely any details about his purposes or insights, but analysis of the symbolism of the cards reveals that Waite was an authority or must have possessed great insight (intuitive or otherwise).

However, the artist Pamela Coleman Smith must also have had great insight in order to reproduce Waite's rough outlines so subtly and symbolically. Waite adapted the tarot symbolism and altered certain pictures: he wished to bring it more into agreement with the understanding of occultism and symbolism current in his own day. Therefore he called it the "revised tarot."

He also took another important step: he changed the Minor Arcana. Until the early 20th century, the number cards of the Minor Arcana (with one exception) had no real pictures on them. They contained nothing but a symbol and the card number; thus the Seven of Wands had seven wands on it and nothing more. Waite made recognizable pictures for each of the 56 cards of the Minor Arcana. Admittedly he also upheld the old method by giving the number of that symbol a place somewhere on the card, but usually as an integral part of the design.

---

3. See Stuart R. Kaplan, *The Encyclopedia of Tarot,* in three volumes (Stamford, CT: U.S. Games Systems, 1978, 1985, 1990).
4. This book is illustrated using the Universal Waite deck. The original A. E. Waite deck has been repainted, using softer colors, and the deck may be of interest to people familiar with the Rider-Waite deck.

Figure 2. Top: The Fool (Waite Tarot) and Five of Cups (Sola-Busca Tarot); Bottom: Ten of Wands (Waite Tarot) and Ten of Swords (Sola-Busca Tarot). From Stuart R. Kaplan, The Encyclopedia of Tarot, Vol. III *(Stamford, CT: U.S. Games Systems, Inc., 1990).*

Figure 3. Top: Seven of Swords (Waite Tarot and Sola-Busca Tarot);
Bottom: Six of Wands (Waite Tarot) and King of Cups (Sola-Busca
Tarot). From Stuart R. Kaplan, The Encyclopedia of Tarot, Vol. III
(Stamford, CT: U.S. Games Systems, Inc., 1990).

Figure 4. Top: *Queen of Swords (Sola-Busca Tarot); Queen of Wands (Sola-Busca Tarot).* Bottom: *Queen of Swords (Waite). From Stuart R. Kaplan,* The Encyclopedia of Tarot, Vol. III *(Stamford, CT: U.S. Games Systems, Inc., 1990).*

Figure 4 (continued). Top: King of Wands (Waite Tarot and Sola-Busca Tarot). From Stuart R. Kaplan, The Encyclopedia of Tarot, Vol. III *(Stamford, CT: U.S. Games Systems, Inc., 1990).*

Thus all 78 cards in the Rider-Waite deck have a broad symbolism, which is somewhat deeper and richer in the Major Arcana than it is in the Minor Arcana. There are strong indications that Pamela Coleman Smith had in front of her the one tarot deck (or photos of it anyway) that does have actual pictures in the Minor Arcana and probably dates from the 15th century. There are one or two striking resemblances between the old *Sola-Busca Tarot* and A. E. Waite's Minor Arcana, even though the differences are more numerous (see figures 2 through 4 on pages 20-23).

In the next chapter we shall see why the Rider-Waite deck has rightly become the tarot of today, and how it relates in terms of symbolism to other decks.

Chapter Three

A COMPARATIVE STUDY OF THE SYMBOLISM IN A FEW DECKS

OUT OF THE GREAT number of different decks I have selected seven that are among the most popular. They include the already mentioned Rider-Waite deck, which is highly regarded, and the very authentic-looking Tarot de Marseilles, thought by some to be a genuine product of the Middle Ages.

I am compelled to observe that, as far as is known, no cards of the Tarot de Marseilles have survived from the Middle Ages. This deck cannot be traced further back than 1784, the year when Grimaud published his first deck of cards. And just as currently there are numerous versions of Rider-Waite, so in the 18th century there were numerous versions of the Tarot de Marseilles. In the following comparative study I shall make use of the Tarot de Marseilles as reproduced on the cards of Grimaud.

The decks from which I am going to select a few cards for the purpose of comparing their symbolism are as follows:

1. Tarot de Marseilles
2. Rider-Waite Tarot
3. Hanson-Roberts Tarot
4. Morgan-Greer Tarot
5. Arcus Arcanum Tarot
6. Haindl Tarot
7. Tarot of the Witches

Because the Tarot de Marseilles was the most popular deck before the Rider-Waite came along, and the latter was in a certain sense a reaction to the former, I shall begin by comparing these two. Afterward supplementary material will be introduced from other decks, some of which are very artistic interpretations of the Rider-Waite deck, while others are completely original.

I have chosen four cards from the Major Arcana—The Fool, The Magician, The Lovers, and Death. I shall first give the general principles and their associated psychological mechanisms. Second I will discuss the way in which the different cards express these principles and mechanisms.

The same thing will be done with one card from the Minor Arcana (the Seven of Cups): I shall explain how this card works in practice, and how its meaning has been incorporated in the pictures on the cards in the various decks.

The Fool

THE PSYCHIC MECHANISM associated with The Fool is our innate desire (potentially capable of fulfillment) to develop our personality. Self-knowledge is central to this. The Fool is the mechanism that tends to keep us from stagnating and ceasing to grow inwardly. Therefore, it is always when we are at the start of something new that The Fool appears; often it seems to us that we are about to take a leap in the dark, but into a situation or activity that is very important for us.

In many respects this leap is hard: we are leaving the known and have no idea how things will turn out. Thus it is very important to have a good relationship with our inner world, so that we can experience or feel how to react.

• The Direction in Which the Fool is Walking

In the Tarot de Marseilles, The Fool is waking toward the right-hand side of the card, this being generally considered the Yang or male side. In the Rider-Waite Tarot, The Fool is walking toward the left-hand side of the card, the yin or female side. Figure 5 on pages 28 and 29 shows The Fool from the various tarot decks we discuss here.

In the Middle Ages, and also for some centuries afterward (in contrast to the state of affairs in our own times), an enormous development of thought and reason still lay ahead. Medieval people had to come out from under the shadow of the saying, *Memento Mori* ("remember you must die"), to learn that they were more than units in a collective. As the Renaissance dawns, we see a tendency in the direction of *Memento Vivere* ("remember you must live"), we see the introduction of perspective into art, and the growth of individualism—which led historically to the French Revolution and the American War of Independence.

The development of the yang side in both men and women was then of the highest importance.

Even if the Tarot de Marseilles belongs to a later date, for example, to the 17th or 18th century, the foregoing remarks are still largely valid. We must not forget that the rate of change of the collective mentality was much slower during these centuries than it is now. To give but one example, an 18th-century farmer still worked in exactly the same way as his counterpart in the 12th century. Today, life is very different, and it would be a mistake to think that our contemporary techniques and developments were available in former centuries.

In the present century we are often left facing the consequences of an overemphasis on rationality and efficiency. We no longer know the meaning of receptivity, femininity, or yin. We have assumed for too long that we can find an answer to any problem with our logic and technology.

But now we are starting to wake up to the one-sidedness of this approach. Science is increasingly encountering the irrational in its experiments, and chaos theory has made its bow. Yin is once more knocking at the gate of the bastions of reason, soft though that knock may be.

Our times call for a renewed awareness of female values, of yin, of receptivity and of an acceptance of the role of the "not-rational." A positive response to this call is required from human beings not only as a species, but as individuals, as each of us strives to become more balanced personally and to give the community its proper place. Therefore in our day and age The Fool must really walk to the left....

In the Hanson-Roberts and Morgan-Greer decks, The Fool walks to the left, too, and in the Haindl deck The Fool faces left.

Tarot de Marseilles

Waite Tarot

Hanson-Roberts Tarot

Morgan-Greer Tarot

Figure 5. Different versions of The Fool. These are tarot decks that are all available today.

Arcus Arcanum Tarot

Tarot of the Witches

Haindl Tarot

However, in the Arcus Arcanum Tarot, and in the Tarot of the Witches, The Fool is walking to the right—which, from the point of view of symbolism, is against the trend of our times.

• *The Dog ("Either the Dog or the Cat will Bite You . . .")*

The part played by the dog in the Tarot de Marseilles is not the same as that played by the dog in the Rider-Waite deck. In the Rider-Waite deck, it is drawn as a playful quadruped jumping up at its owner. In the Tarot de Marseilles, the dog springs at The Fool from behind and tears a hole in his pants.

The dog often occurs in symbolism (in dreams, for example) and depicts instinctive forces in the unconscious. Animals can represent these forces on different levels: the fiercer or older the animal, the more remote is this factor from our conscious. It makes a big difference if you dream of a cat, or dream of a lynx. The cat has been domesticated for centuries, and has close ties with human beings and human culture. Symbolically its significance is not hard to grasp.

Exactly the same is true of the dog: it represents a part of our instinctive world. It symbolizes helping forces that are waiting until we learn to use them, for they are associated with the dog. In common with many other factors in the unconscious, the dog can draw our attention to matters of which the conscious mind is not very aware. We have only to think of the helping and warning role of animals in fairy tales! It is important to train ourselves to pay attention to them, and to not reject them as being nonsensical or irrational. For then the same instinctive forces will indirectly cling to our coattails, for in the end they will not allow themselves to be driven away.

In the Tarot de Marseilles, the dog springs at The Fool from behind, and an important detail is that the pants of The Fool are torn at the top of the leg where the buttocks begin—not a place one would particularly wish to have exposed.

The Fool walks toward the right in this deck; his orientation is in the direction of the further development of consciousness. Characteristic of this development is often (temporarily or otherwise) a thrusting to one side of premonitions and of other apparently illogical, non-rational things. But this means running the risk of being thrown off balance and of becoming so one-sided that, like The Fool, we "get caught with our pants down"!

That is the danger depicted by the dog in the Tarot de Marseilles. The existence of the helping and warning powers of our instincts is usually not seen (the dog is behind The Fool), and their presence is not felt until they pounce.

How different the Rider-Waite deck is! There the dog is the companion of The Fool. Not that the latter can see the animal properly while gazing upward, but potentially the dog is closer to his field of awareness. What is more, although the dog is jumping up, it is doing so at the side of The Fool without tearing his clothing. In the 20th century, especially with our advances in (depth) psychology, we have gained more insight into the workings of the unconscious and into its contents.

There is also a growing desire (as evidenced by the various new age movements) to learn to understand the language of the unconscious again, to study symbolism, to restore to their rightful place (as irrational facts) dreams and synchronistic events, etc. That the dog is displaying companionship says as much. If we are willing to see and understand our faithful companion, it can prevent us from falling into the abyss that seems to be facing us. In the Tarot de Marseilles there is no precipice. Then the great advance was the development of consciousness with all the ups and downs of that. In our own day and age, the required step is to make our psyches whole by relearning to see, understand, and use the language of the unconscious.

In the Hanson-Roberts deck the dog is missing, but a precipice is visible in the background. Now, symbolically, the dog as a helping power is of the greatest importance, and its absence deprives The Fool of an essential feature. He can successfully leap into the abyss only to the extent that he has a friendly relationship with his instinctive world! The Morgan-Greer deck does show a friendly dog; the precipice is there, too, but it is not very obvious.

The Arcus Arcanum deck displays a cat, instead of a dog, as the companion of The Fool, and the animal in the Tarot of the Witches is halfway between a dog and a cat. Given the fact that cats occur everywhere else in the Major Arcana of this pack, it is most likely that here, too, the animal with The Fool is a cat.

Now a cat, just as much as a dog, is a symbol of instinctive and warning factors in the unconscious; but, at the same time, a cat has a significance of its own. The cat is more willful, and in fairy tales it is well-known as the witch's animal. The cat is not as docile as the dog, but goes its own way. Traditionally, the cat is often associated with night: a cat has an outstanding ability to hunt in the dark, and therefore various cultures have imagined it as a being in league with the powers of darkness.

The cat is thought of as cunning and sly (we have only to picture the way it creeps up on its prey to see the reason for this), and as a representative of the dark feminine (like the wicked witch in folk stories). Although the term "dark feminine" is a judgment made within a certain culture-context, and this irrational and nature-oriented side of femininity does have very positive aspects, it is a fact that the yin side has been little understood in our social situation over the centuries. These are some of the ways in which this image differs from that of the dog, and so it matters a great deal whether it is the cat or the dog which helps you (or tears your clothes).

In the Arcus Arcanum deck, this free-spirited animal of the night goes on ahead and stands at the edge of the precipice. The incomprehensible (and thus the often reputedly dark) side of the feminine can certainly attend The Fool in our own times, especially when he moves toward the right in the direction that leads away from the irrational side. For, in the shape of the cat, he possesses this aspect of human nature which is in need of integration today. But the Arcus Arcanum deck does not show convincingly that the cat is giving a warning; it seems more interested in watching what The Fool is going to do.

The Tarot of the Witches also exhibits a Fool who is walking to the right, The Fool who wants to leave the irrational behind. But now, as was done to him by the dog in the Tarot de Marseilles, he is attacked from behind by the cat, which tears a hole in his pants. It is the instinctive nocturnal feminine, the dark irrational side, that claws The Fool. In everyday life the assailant can be, for example, a highly charged atmosphere, intense emotion, and perhaps even depression. These hold The Fool back from the path that is leading him to the brink of disaster. Instead of assistance from the unconscious being given The Fool as he travels in the yin direction, and protection from falling into the abyss, as we saw in the Rider-Waite deck, it is the dark yin-forces that are trying here to restrain the yang-Fool from going any further along his one-sided path—a world of difference in symbolism!

The Haindl Tarot differs totally from the foregoing pictures. There is no precipice, no warning dog or cat, but a swan with a supple curved neck and broad outspread wings and a wounded breast.

According to the accompanying booklet, the injured swan stands for the Fall and the expulsion of humanity from the Garden of Eden. Looked at from the point of view of collective symbolism, the wound on the bird's breast seems to have a connection with the old fable that the pelican pecks its breast in order to feed its young with its own blood. An analogy drawn from this belief makes the pelican a symbol for the death of Christ and His eternal offering on the cross for humanity. The same symbolism occurs in alchemy, in which the pelican is associated with the selfless labor of distillation or purification. So the bloodstain could refer to this symbol. However, the card does not show a pelican, but a swan.

The swan used to be seen (except in the Middle Ages) as a symbol of purity, and it was said to have prophetic powers. Nevertheless, to the best of my knowledge, a swan with a wounded breast has no part to play in the collective symbolism of mythology. Therefore, at this point, we are studying a piece of personal symbolism. As a creature accompanying The Fool, the swan might indicate the need to undergo the individuation process as a cleansing, but strictly speaking, the swan in this picture does not represent help from the unconscious. Therefore in the version found in the Haindl deck, it is the idea of the Fall that is prominent in the action of The Fool.

The Magician

BOTH IN THE TAROT de Marseilles and in the Rider-Waite deck, we see a man with a wand in his hand, a lemniscate over his head (this shape forms part of his hat in the Tarot de Marseilles), and a table in front of him containing various items. But there are clearly differences of design and thus of symbolic meaning. In psychological terms, the general meaning of The Magician is the urge to give our lives directed activity. Energetic action, target-setting, and self-realization for the sake of gaining insight into reality form the basic meaning of this card. This insight can involve the physical world, the behavior of matter and of the psyche, and the activity of the spirit. So we have to take a very broad view.

• *Matter*

In the Tarot de Marseilles, The Magician is holding the wand in his left hand. In the Rider-Waite deck it is the right hand that is used.

Traditionally, the left hand stands for reception, for anticipation, for every facet of our unconscious, both positive and negative. The right hand, in contrast, stands for guiding, acting, and doing, and for our conscious. Readers may want to compare the various decks. See figure 6, pages 36-37. The older deck, the Tarot de Marseilles, seems to represent deliberate activity as originating much more in the unconscious than the Rider-Waite deck shows it to be. In the Rider-Waite deck, conscious guidance and target-setting is much more clearly represented by the right side. A rod (or a wand) is often the symbol of the directing or controlling of energy (one example being a blackboard pointer), or of keeping it within measure (as is done with a conductor's baton). This directing, controlling, or keeping within measure is still, in the Tarot de Marseilles, largely an affair of the unconscious; the advantage being that the helpful side of the unconscious can emerge more easily, and the disadvantage that conscious understanding and wise guidance are not so much in evidence. But it is inquiry and comprehension, direction and guidance, that The Magician is supposed to express! His wand has two ends, one pointing to spirit, the other to matter—the two poles of existence—both very important, and needing to be held in balance. Both the Tarot de Marseilles and the Rider-Waite deck depict a wand with identical ends, thus alluding to the fact that the polarities in our lives are equal in value.

The Morgan-Greer, Hanson-Roberts, and Arcus Arcanum decks, and the Tarot of the Witches, all have The Magician holding the wand in his right hand, signifying the need to develop conscious insight into the world of phenomena. However, the wands vary in shape. The Morgan-Greer deck has a wand similar to the one in the Rider-Waite deck, with ends that look alike.

The Hanson-Roberts deck has an interesting design in which the wand is held high and has ends that obviously differ. The upper end is not even completely in the picture: a fact that is full of significance. If you become involved in art therapy, you will observe that patients who are finding it difficult to face a certain facet of themselves, or who are insufficiently aware of it, or who do not pay enough attention to it, will very often draw in such a way that their sheet of paper does not seem big enough. In other words, the object does not (quite) fit into their picture. The top of the wand in the Hanson-Roberts deck, the yang side, falls just outside the picture.

Perhaps this Magician is not so investigative as he should be? And the yin side, the bottom tip of the wand, has not crystallized into a distinct knob. So there seems to be a lot of work left to be done by this Magician.

In the Arcus Arcanum deck we see a beautiful wand with dissimilar ends: the top is crowned, but the bottom is not. Therefore there is no expression of equal values here, but the difference could be explained by the need to distinguish between male (top) and female (bottom).

The Tarot of the Witches shows a small wand which is held at the bottom, thus leaving only the top visible. In contrast to the other decks, the wand is held downward (and seems to be pointing at the crystal ball on the table). Now the position of the arms in the Rider-Waite deck, namely with the right arm raised to heaven, and the left arm directed downward in order to preserve contact with the Earth, reinforces the message of the similar ends of the wand—that the primary poles, yin and yang, heaven and earth, etc., must be in balance. This symbolism is absent from the Tarot of the Witches, and the wand seems to be no more than one a conjurer might use.

In the Haindl deck, the wand is completely missing from The Magician card. This is an important signal; especially as the wand emphasizes the active side of The Magician, since it is an image of the desire to direct and control. Instead, the Haindl deck shows crystals streaming out of The Magician's eye on the left, which must be interpreted as the ability to perceive the pure forms of existence. This ability can be disturbed by unintegrated, somber emotions, as represented by the dark figure rising out of the tiara on the head of the pale figure. Therefore the Haindl deck does not present us with an active Magician in its symbolism, but a contemplative one, a Magician who has more yin qualities than allowed for by the original tarot ideas.

• The Magician's Table and its Contents

In the Rider-Waite deck the objects on The Magician's table symbolize the four suits of the Minor Arcana. As we saw in the previous chapter, these represent well-established categories in our lives. The employment of these categories and the effort to deepen our insight into them, improves our capacity to function in a better and more balanced way in everyday life and to set ourselves more realistic goals.

Tarot de Marseilles

Waite Tarot

Hanson-Roberts Tarot

Morgan-Greer Tarot

Figure 6. Different versions of The Magician. These tarot decks are all being used today.

Arcus Arcanum Tarot

Tarot of the Witches

Haindl Tarot

What is more, there is a link here between the Major Arcana, of which The Magician forms a part, and the protean phenomenal world of the Minor Arcana.

In the Tarot de Marseilles we see a much more arbitrary assortment of objects on the table, such as a knife, dice, a bag or satchel, and a beaker—in short nothing that would indicate a desire to employ definite categories. As much as anything, the card seems to be depicting a juggler. Although The Magician reflects our need to discover the creative principles behind the world of appearances, both in the Tarot de Marseilles and in the Rider-Waite deck, the design of this card is much more clear-cut in the latter.

The other decks, with the exception of the Tarot of the Witches, are like the Rider-Waite deck in making open reference to the four suits. The Hanson-Roberts deck, the Morgan-Greer deck, and the Arcus Arcanum deck, show the four symbolic items lying on the table in various arrangements.

In the Haindl deck, the objects are standing in the foreground without any means of support. The way in which they are grouped is rather striking: the scepter has become a sort of spear, which seems to be thrust through the cup, and the sword impales the stone that serves as a pentacle. From a symbolic point of view this makes a tremendous difference: whereas on the other cards the four objects from the Minor Arcana are separate, the Haindl deck groups them in pairs in which the yin symbols (the stone and the cup) are pierced by the yang symbols (the spear and the sword). Symbolically, this must signify that the four factors representing our reality (the four elements, the four suits of the Minor Arcana) are reduced to two pairs that cannot be treated apart from one another.

Although it does look very attractive, I cannot reconcile this particular symbolism with my own experience.

The objects on The Magician's table in the Tarot of the Witches are not the same as those on the other cards. There are no symbols borrowed from the Minor Arcana, and therefore no suggestion of any desire on the part of The Magician to understand the controlling factors of everyday life. The cat, the dice, and the crystal ball indicate a very intuitive approach without any planning in the accepted sense of the word.

This Magician gives priority to the subjective, irrational, and experiential processes in his approach to the world. These are not intrinsically bad, on the contrary, they form a valuable addition to the rationalism of our Western society. But the original meaning of The Magician is not brought out here: The Magician is much more yin than his status really allows.

The Lovers

THE PICTURES ON the cards of the Rider-Waite deck, and on the Tarot de Marseilles are, surprisingly enough, quite different! People who have just started to study the tarot often imagine that this card represents true love, and that it predicts a happy relationship when dealt, but the truth is often otherwise. Figure 7 (pages 40-41) shows the different versions of The Lovers in the decks we discuss here.

Primarily, The Lovers card represents an inner urge to reconcile the opposites in life, and especially the major opposites of conscious and unconscious. This can be learned by confrontation with the outside world, and by the formation of relationships with it. Through our own reactions and those of others, we learn to experience what is going on in our unconscious. Only then are we in a position to function honestly and level-headedly in a loving relationship. And it helps to make clear and independent choices: it is always up to us to learn how to relate to others.

The Tarot de Marseilles has the picture of a man standing between two women: an older one on the left of the card (who is holding his attention) and a younger one on the right. Over his head Cupid or Eros is about to shoot an arrow, more or less in the direction of the younger woman.

The entire picture breathes a duality which can be interpreted in different ways. It could represent a man who has to choose between his ties with his mother (at whom he is looking) and a (possibly erotic) relationship with the woman at whom Eros is pointing his arrow. This is an unconscious process we all pass through, whether we are men or women: we have to disengage ourselves from our parents in order to deepen and give shape to our relationship with our life partner.

The older woman can also stand for the wise and spiritual feminine factor in the man, and the younger woman for the physical and sensual side. These two facets are often seen as conflicting, but the fact is that sexuality and spirituality are very closely connected. Learning to unite the two in ourselves instigates clear psychic growth.

L'AMOUREUX
THE LOVER

Tarot de Marseilles

THE LOVERS.

Waite Tarot

Hanson-Roberts Tarot

Morgan-Greer Tarot

Figure 7. Different versions of The Lovers. Here we have also included the Visconti-Sforza Tarot.

Arcus Arcanum Tarot

Tarot of the Witches

Haindl Tarot

Visconti-Sforza Tarot

The Rider-Waite deck does not depict Eros on The Lovers card, but an angel performing a benediction. It also shows a man and woman reaching toward one another, with the two trees of paradise in the background: the "tree of life" behind the man and the "tree of the knowledge of good and evil" behind the woman.

This tree symbolism in the background indicates the necessity of learning to be discriminating, in respect to both ourselves and the outside world. It is not enough to come to terms with "Life" and "Knowledge" (the two trees), a special effort has to be made in our intimacy with the opposite sex to recognize the "other" in ourselves.

Incidentally, the above has nothing to do with marriage. In the unconscious of every woman slumbers a male aspect (C. G. Jung called it the *animus*), and a female aspect (the *anima*) in the unconscious of every man. Only if the woman learns to accept and develop her inner purposefulness and executive powers will she grow less dependent on male figures outside herself. And only when the man dares to accept that he carries within himself the emotional and irrational as valuable foils to his sense of purpose, will he learn to accept and appreciate the world of the feminine and of yin.

It is this meaning that we find in The Lovers: with the blessing of Heaven it is our primary task to unite the two poles of yin and yang within ourselves, with a view to being able to distinguish more clearly and to live more harmoniously in our total situation—male and female, social and environmental. In order to initiate this process, we have to make various choices and leave our sheltered environment. In practice, the card often turns up for young people who are leaving the parental home and standing on their own two feet, or who are taking responsibility for themselves in some other way. The card does not always represent a love affair!

When comparing the Rider-Waite deck with the Tarot de Marseilles, we see that in the Tarot de Marseilles there is an obvious field of tension between attachment to parents and protection (the old woman), and the desire for an independent relationship and sexuality (the young woman).

In the Rider-Waite deck some depth has been added to this theme: breaking free from the parents is symbolized by the decision to form a new relationship: the man and woman are reaching out toward one another. However, more generally, what is being shown is not just a choice between the parents and a potential partner, but a move toward independence from the parental images that are always active in us. By getting these into proper perspective, the originating primary energies become energies that keep alive the connection with the creative (yang, father, man) and the receptive (yin, mother, woman) in each man and woman.

Thus in the Rider-Waite deck we find a multiple process with a corresponding number of choices symbolized, not so much concerned with one individual (as we suggested by Cupid's arrow in the Tarot de Marseilles) as concerned with the relationship of the inquirer to self and world, both materially and spiritually. In this respect, the Rider-Waite deck offers a picture that is more in harmony with our times.

In the previous chapter I mentioned the Visconti-Sforza deck, and I want to make a brief comparison of this deck with the Tarot de Marseilles. It is remarkable that in the 15th-century Visconti-Sforza deck, the mother figure encountered in the Tarot de Marseilles does not appear. Instead we see a man and a woman shaking hands with each other, and overhead a young blindfolded Cupid who is not shooting an arrow.

In their symbolism, the young man and woman shaking hands have more in common with the couple in the Rider-Waite deck. However, the blindfolded Cupid alludes to the blindness of the projections made by those who fall in love, and so has less to do with taking—into the outside world—a deliberate step that involves making choices. Therefore, although the Visconti-Sforza deck does show the step into the outside world, the choice seems, even so, to be determined by fate and the unconscious.

In regard to this card in particular, it would be interesting to know if the Tarot de Marseilles is a genuine product of the Middle Ages or not, for then we would be seeing two processes side by side. If the Tarot de Marseilles is a more recent deck, we could well be looking at the influence of the designer's psyche, who would have imported his own conflicts into the cards in defiance of what the symbolism should have been!

In the Hanson-Roberts, Morgan-Greer, and Tarot of the Witches decks, there is a strong emphasis on the love relationship. In the Hanson-Roberts deck, a heavenly figure halfway between an angel and a young Cupid still plays a role, but the deeper symbolism of the Rider-Waite deck in the form of the two trees in the background is missing. Another danger of this design is that the card may be interpreted with too much emphasis on love between the sexes, whereas its true scope is much wider.

The same applies to the Morgan-Greer deck, in which the angel is missing as well as the trees. The phallic-looking arum lilies occupy the foreground here, and can symbolize the sexual attraction between man and woman, among other things. The plate hardly permits other associations, therefore its symbolism points very much in one direction: love (including physical love) between the sexes. One cannot make it symbolize children leaving home and taking their first independent step into the world, which is certainly one aspect of The Lovers (venturing to become involved with the world).

In the same sphere lies the Tarot of the Witches, in which the physical aspect is even more uncompromising. The tree symbolism of the Rider-Waite deck can be supplied here by treating the two lovemakers as a "tree trunk," entwined by black hair in a way that is reminiscent of the serpent in Adam and Eve (it is shown coiled round the left-hand tree in the Rider-Waite deck).

The contraries are expressed by the Sun and Moon in this card, but this is a recurrent theme in the Tarot of the Witches. Indeed, it appears to be one of the deck's basic motifs, and keeps reminding us that the tarot is grounded in the eternal field of tension between yin and yang.

The Arcus Arcanum deck presents a completely different picture. We see a young, romantic pair who wish to come together to strengthen their relationship, but are standing still at a crossroad near the "World Tree." A second couple, walking along different paths, are about to meet at the World Tree, and these express another form of relationship. So we are offered a choice in this area.

According to the accompanying booklet, the designer wanted to express, among other things, that there is a conflict between different forms of attraction, and that a choice must often be made, not on rational grounds but on the basis of other values or inclinations. However, irrespective of the intentions of the designer, you should, when contemplating this picture, be able to see, for example, that the young people have reached an important turning point in their relationship in regard to their parental images!

In the Haindl deck we again see a man and a woman, and the two trees on either side of them are meant to be the two trees of paradise, just as in the Rider-Waite deck. But where the angel stands in the Rider-Waite deck, we now have a spear, a cup, a rose, and a unicorn. The unicorn and the rose were meant by the designer to represent the mystical qualities of love, the ground is the earthly side of love, and the woman's fossilized hair shows the great age of human sexual traditions. The spear and the cup can be interpreted as male and female symbols.

In this deck, the emphasis is more on the earthly and the mystical side of the sexual relationship between man and woman, and less on the more general "step into the outside world."

Death

AS A PSYCHOLOGICAL STAGE, Death represents the removal of everything we no longer need. This includes old attitudes and patterns of behavior, masks behind which we hide, and all the things that obstruct our free development. The decision to jettison our ballast is often fraught with anxiety: the old is familiar, the new is not. When the old disappears, it can feel as if we are falling into a black hole: it is sort of like a dying process. But, at the very same time, the new can arise. Figure 8 (pages 46-47) shows various versions of Death we will discuss.

It comes as no surprise that a skeleton appears so frequently on the cards representing Death. In the Tarot de Marseilles we see it holding a scythe, a widespread symbol of irrevocable cutting off. Mown limbs lie scattered over the field. On the left, Death is standing on a severed head, and on the right we see a crowned head: even princes do not escape Death. The whole symbolism of the card points to the absolute end, inevitable and irrevocable.

In the Rider-Waite deck this is represented in another manner. The figure of Death, seated on a white horse, is riding to meet us. The king has already fallen, and although the prelate is praying, he will not escape death either. A maiden on the right seems about to collapse. The only one who can do anything is the little child in blue, who is offering Death a bunch of flowers.

A highly important lesson lies hidden in this detail, namely: no one can escape the need to adjust and change in life. There comes a

Tarot de Marseilles

Waite Tarot

Hanson-Roberts Tarot

Morgan-Greer Tarot

Figure 8. Different versions of the Death card.

Arcus Arcanum Tarot

Tarot of the Witches

Haindl Tarot

time for each of us when we must take our leave of stagnant situations and obsolete attitudes. There is no point in copying the king, who tried to resist it by main force. Life will bring it on our path either from without or within. One can accept it through religion (like the prelate) but cannot ward it off. Youthful innocence is also no guarantee that it will pass us by. The only sensible attitude is that of the little child who goes to meet this energy openly and freely as something to be taken for granted in life, and not as a threat (the tiny bunch of flowers!).

And so, after this step has been taken, your limitations can be handled much more easily, and the encounter with Death does not involve a definite end, but a hopeful beginning, even if you do not know in advance where the new will lead you! The small boat is heading for a distant port: it sets sail up the river, not knowing whether it will encounter storms or calm. But it does set sail—and life goes on. By means of all this symbolism, this card presents us with much less of a definite end than its counterpart does in the Tarot de Marseilles, and, in addition, it reveals the best way to tackle this psychic process.

The Hanson-Roberts deck has a stylized version of the card in the Rider-Waite deck, but there are several important variations: there is no cleric trying to fit the event into a religious framework, and the child in blue (who is holding a posy in the Rider-Waite deck)—is dead! In the background, there is no small boat on the river, and, in short, the hopeful symbolism and indications of how to cope with this stage of life are absent from this card.

The same can be said of the Arcus Arcanum deck: there is a pretty picture of a skeleton, holding a scythe, and riding on a white horse under a red evening sky, but all the people are dead. In the Morgan-Greer deck there are no people at all, only the skeleton with the scythe. In the distance, the sun is setting over a river. There is a white rose with clearly defined thorns in the foreground, but in this context a rose, on its own, carries no thought of a new beginning, nor does it suggest how one should approach death.

The Tarot of the Witches also features a skeleton with a scythe, but no people. Green snakes are crawling out of the skull through the fontanel, an eye-socket, and the mouth. The psychic energy (the snakes) is leaving the skeleton and is, so to speak, ebbing away. Once more it is dying that is emphasized, and there is no comforting symbolism showing the way out of this dilemma in life.

Now the Haindl deck does have a boat. The boat here is meant to be a symbol of life and death. According to the designer, the peacock's eye in the middle symbolizes standing eye to eye with the truth when you are facing death. The bird represents the soul and the divine potential in humanity. The scythe-carrying skeleton, itself, announces that this is the card of Death. With this picture the Haindl deck indicates, first and foremost, the process of taking an honest look at everything, and at the same time, by means of the symbolism of the boat, shows the connection between life and death. The unconcerned acceptance exhibited by the child (which we have interpreted as a piece of good advice in the Rider-Waite deck) is missing here, just as it is missing from the other decks.

A Minor Arcana Card: The Seven of Cups

Not all tarot decks have full pictorial illustrations in the Minor Arcana. The Tarot de Marseilles, the Haindl deck, and the Tarot of the Witches show, each in its own way, seven emblematic cups. The advantage of this neutral form of representation is that the symbolism can be studied from all sides. And that is also the disadvantage: the plates give us too little to go on. The Seven of Cups confronts us with the strength of our emotions and imagination, and with the danger of confusing dreams with reality. In a positive sense, dreams, wishes, and longings can stimulate us in daily life—but they can also be a distraction. The Seven of Cups alerts us to the risks and advantages of the world of illusions. Figure 9 (pages 50-51) shows the Seven of Cups from seven different decks.

A. E. Waite has made this point by wrapping the seven cups in clouds to place them in the realm of imagination. The cups are set out in two rows: four in the bottom row and three in the top. This division is deliberate; the lower four cups express the danger, and the upper three suggest fruitful psychic development.

Looking at the cups in the bottom row from left to right, we see a castle on a mountain—a symbol of might; a pile of jewels—a symbol of possessions; a laurel wreath—a symbol of fame and ambition; and a monster—a symbol of assertiveness that too quickly spills over into aggression. It is all very well to dream of power, glory, rich-

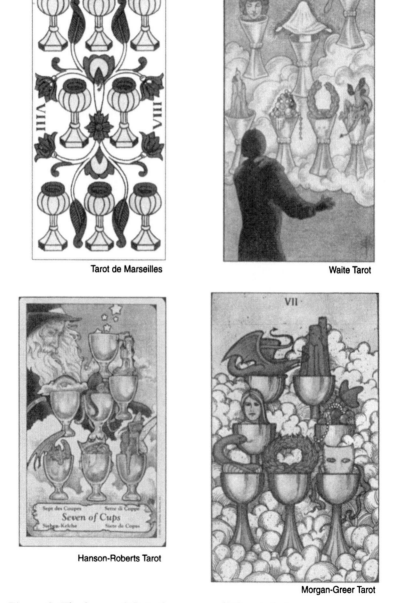

Tarot de Marseilles

Waite Tarot

Hanson-Roberts Tarot

Morgan-Greer Tarot

Figure 9. The Seven of Cups from seven different decks.

Arcus Arcanum Tarot

Tarot of the Witches

Haindl Tarot

es, and the ability to do whatever enters one's head, but everyday life is not like that; and if we confuse dreams with reality, this will have far-reaching and mainly negative consequences for our character development.

The top row contains a head—a symbol of our unconscious "other side." In a Jungian sense, this is the animus and anima, from which we can draw great support and inner equilibrium when we make contact with it. The serpent in the right-hand cup is a symbol of the flow of psychic energy. This is important because stagnation leads to mental logjams, and the formation of complexes.

The middle cup contains a person standing with outstretched arms and covered by a sheet, but radiating light through it. This is a symbol of our true, divine center. In the Jungian sense, it is the Self. Thus the lower row has seductive, but dangerous, symbols, and the upper row has symbols of wholeness and growth.

Turning to the other decks, we see that all sorts of things have happened to the contents of the cups, and there is no division into two as in the Rider-Waite deck.

In the Morgan-Greer deck, for example, we have a bottom row of three and two rows of two above that. The image of the Self, the shining figure under the sheet, has been replaced by a mask! The bottom row has the flow of psychic energy (the serpent), the craving for fame and honor (the laurel crown), and the mask, which can be interpreted only as a defense against the outside world, or as carnival attire. There is no way it can be interpreted as a center of wholeness in oneself.

In the row above, we have the animus (or anima) and the desire for possessions, side by side; and the whole is crowned by power (mountain and castle) and assertiveness-aggression (the monster). However, because of the dragon-like form of the monster, it could also refer to the devouring forces of the unconscious. Looking at these details and their arrangement, I am not very happy with them as a piece of symbolism.

We encounter the same problem in the other cards. The Hanson-Roberts deck also has several rows of cups. The laurel wreath, the serpent, and the Self have disappeared. The animus (or anima) has had to make way for a fairy (!), and the serpent has become a sort of squid. The laurel wreath has been replaced by a rainbow and the Self would appear to have been replaced by stars.

The whole duality of the seven (see elsewhere in the interpretation of the Seven of Cups in the Minor Arcana) is definitely not represented in this card, and the division into warning and integrating symbols given in the Rider-Waite deck is missing.

In the Arcus Arcanum deck, a dark figure sitting in the foreground beholds in a mirror a tender scene of a man and a woman who are jointly holding the cup containing the symbol of the Self or divine inner center. This is a first-rate feature of this card. But the division of the cups on the table into two rows does not correspond to the twofold division into dangers and gifts. On the left we see the dangers of power, aggression (or the devouring unconscious), and honor; on the right we see the serpent as a positive factor which must represent the flow of psychic energy. However, the serpent is lying still and is not active as in the Rider-Waite deck.

The animus (or anima) has now become a framed portrait, which rather suggests a picture of the past (whether recent or remote is unimportant here), instead of a reality to which we must address ourselves. The jewels in this row refer to the danger lurking in covetousness. So here a rather muddled symbolism replaces the clear-cut symbolism of the Rider-Waite card.

FROM THESE FEW examples it would seem that when a serious effort is made to come to grips with the symbolism, the choice of tarot deck is very important. Pictures always stimulate our feelings and emotions, and bring to life any associated personal symbolism. I frequently observe tarot users paying scant attention to the plates, and quickly turning to the interpretations given in some book. Often they have memorized pages of so-called "meanings" without ever asking themselves if these really fit the pictures.

For quick queries this may not be bad; but if the tarot is to be used in greater depth (e.g., by meditating on the illustrations), it is vital to look out for what the symbolism can release in us.

From what has been said so far, it will no doubt be obvious that my own preference is for the symbolism of the Rider-Waite deck, which suits the spirit of our age and represents the meanings of the cards very aptly. Perhaps, in days to come, some new inspired deck will appear, which will be more representative of the developments, needs, and dynamics of some future century.

The psychic processes of human beings remain the same in their deepest sense, but at various stages they lead to different wants and images. Above all, the Major Arcana represent our attainment of full status as human beings or, as Jung put it, our individuation process, a process encountered everywhere in myths and cultures as "The Way of the Hero," as the next chapter will show.

Chapter Four

THE MAJOR ARCANA AND THE WAY OF THE HERO

IN NUMEROUS MYTHS and sagas throughout the world, we discover the self-same themes, themes which seem to be common to humanity. C. G. Jung called them archetypes. They are themes which mark, portray, and symbolize stages in our psychic (of the psyche) growth, for the fundamental quest of the hero is to become a balanced and integrated person.[1]

This hero lives in each of us, or rather we are the hero of our own lives. And, like all heroes, we have to go through caves and pits, face adversity, perform labors, make hard decisions, and fight dragons and other terrifying creatures which symbolize certain forces in our unconscious. Each step of the way (of the individuation process) brings us, whether we like it or not, into specific situations in life, or is associated with psychic developments that make themselves known in dreams and fantasies, fears and upsets, new desires and visions, doodles, and so on.

Notes on the Psychic Process

WE SHOULD CERTAINLY not categorize inner developments as good or evil. Some processes can be experienced and regarded as negative at one stage, while at another stage they can be important and even necessary. For example, The Devil does not strike a particularly bright note for many of us. Nevertheless, this card symbolizes the

---

1. When I speak of "psychic" here, I am referring to "the psyche" and not to the development of ESP, as in a psychic or a fortune-teller.

confrontation with our drives, and, indeed, with the risk of being drowned in self-gratification, hedonism, greed, lust for power, etc.

Yet one sees children at the age of puberty drawing this very card. For them, experiencing the pull—this way and that—of these inner forces, and of sexuality, is inevitable. Because of the uncertainty experienced in puberty, young people can push their way to the front rather too provocatively and insistently, can make a big issue out of being independent, and can find themselves on a collision course with society. They have to go through the process symbolized by The Devil in order to reach a new state of balance that can give them a sense of their own worth—without having to wear the "right" clothes, and without feeling the need to resist being told what to do.

Thus, in this context, The Devil is neither good nor bad; it simply represents a development phase. However, if a businessman draws the card in answer to a statement, "Give me a deeper insight into my business relations with so-and-so," then, putting it mildly, he needs to stop and think about his readiness to take advantage of the other party. In which connection, I would say that some situations in life bring people on your path who can "release" certain forms of behavior in you, through which you get to know your shadow better (and even to integrate it) by confronting the more uncivilized side of yourself. And The Devil can initiate this development if you are willing to recognize what the card is telling you.

None of the cards contains a judgment. Each card is essentially neutral, and has both constructive and destructive sides, as well as its own form of stagnation. Or, to put it another way, you can get bogged down in a certain psychic process and can persist in patterns of behavior that are inadequate and dated. In working with the cards, and especially in studying their connection with these common human drives and processes, it has become increasingly clear to me that the Major Arcana can be divided into three groups:

- The basic drives (cards 0–V);

- The construction of the ego (cards VI–XII);

- The integration of conscious and unconscious (cards XIII–XXI).

The Basic Drives (Cards 0–V)

EACH OF US HAS a deep-seated urge to develop into a full-fledged individual. Over and over, at different times in our lives, this urge raises its head, stimulates us, becomes an incentive to action, sets us on fresh paths, and confronts us with hard choices. Due to this perennial urge, we are able to break fresh ground and avoid getting stuck in a rut. Under its influence, we often take steps that initially seem difficult or productive of uncertainty, but afterward are seen as important turning points in our lives.

This urge is symbolized by Card 0: The Fool. He is the absolute beginning of everything even before it becomes tangible. Wherever The Fool falls in a spread, there can be a breakthrough which feels like a leap into the unknown. But there is also a great potential for growth in it.

Heaven and earth, day and night, male and female, are all forms of expression of the primary polarity called yang and yin in the East. Under the yang, or male, principle comes the active element, the creative capacity, the daylight period in the space of twenty-four hours. The passive element, the receptive, the skill to deal creatively with what we meet on our path, and the nocturnal period in the space of twenty-four hours come under the yin, or female, principle. As we saw in chapter 2, the mutual interaction of yin and yang, of male and female, is fundamental to the tarot. These principles are heavily emphasized in Cards I through IV: yang in The Magician and The Emperor, and yin in The High Priestess and The Empress.

Of the male principle, The Magician gives mainly the (inner) active facet and the setting of inner goals, whereas The Emperor expresses mainly the urge to arrange and to produce external structure—he tends to represent activities in a socially ordered framework.

In The Magician there is a visible beginning, and, as a psychic tendency, he also represents our desire to be occupied with all sorts of things. The Emperor, on the other hand, stresses clear-cut action. This means stripping away all the irrational and chaotic aspects until an effective, efficient, and ordered whole remains. Here, too, we have the two sides, the advantages and disadvantages of the yang principle. Activity can be important, but must not run to excess. The same applies to the making of rules: they are good for efficient functioning, but creativity must not be paralyzed by them.

Figure 10. Cards 0 to V in the Major Arcana (Waite deck).

As a yin card, The High Priestess expresses supreme passivity, and at the same time a state of rest in complete but unconscious knowledge—she is serene, quiet, and mystical. The other yin card, The Empress, is the vivacious and creative side of the female pole. She indicates the urge to enter into life to the full in the here and now, without troubling to find out if what we are doing is logical or reasonable. She listens to an inner logic of a completely different order.

So now we see two faces of both yang and yin: each has an inward-looking face—The Magician and The High Priestess—and an outward-looking face—The Emperor and The Empress.

Yin and yang are complementary, but they are also natural opposites in many respects, and this can set up fields of tension. Their eternal and continual functioning requires a bridging mechanism, a psychic factor (of the psyche) that can help balance this tension in an acceptable way.

A perspective is provided by our religious function, represented by The Pope or Hierophant. This innate religious sentiment, which should not be identified with church-going or adherence to a specific religious belief, causes us to look for an extra dimension in life, the dimension of inquiry into the meaning of things. Some find this meaning by belonging to a community of believers sharing a common faith, others look within themselves and also have a deep sense of unity with living things, or they may have mystical experiences.

The cards for these basic drives are shown in figure 10 (page 58). We can summarize the basic drives as follows:

- The Fool is the (vital) urge that aims at maintaining our process of growth;

- The Magician and The Emperor are two aspects of yang, and The High Priestess and The Empress are two aspects of yin, through which yang-yin expresses the vital male-female and day-night polarity;

- The Hierophant is the innate religious drive that aims at bridging the life-polarity and adding a dimension to it.

With this initial package we enter the inner world and encounter the series of Cards VI through XII.

The Construction of the Ego (Cards VI–XII)

WE COME TO KNOW the basic drives and discover what forms of expression to give them in our contacts with life and the world around us. Figure 11 (page 62) illustrates Cards VI to XII and shows us how the next phase will go. We have to venture out to relate to other people, to animals, things, and to the world outside us; and we inevitably make choices as we do so. This is the phase of The Lovers, a card which in principle need not have anything to do with falling in love. More often it refers to having the courage to become involved in life and with others, and to having the courage to make choices. It projects yang and yin on the outside world. Such projections can be seen particularly clearly in partnerships of course.

Through the emotions and experiences produced in contacts with others, we come to know our own unconscious drives. In this way we can also learn to see ourselves more clearly, to consciously improve the choices we make and to conduct ourselves better—the phase of The Chariot.

The Chariot has no reference to military triumphs. We see a charioteer whose "horses" are two sphinxes facing different ways: the conscious must make a self-controlled effort to manage opposing unconscious processes and forces in order to get its "chariot" moving forward and to advance socially. Decisions are always being made:; certain desires and inner processes can greatly impede our functioning in our environment, and so we do our best to suppress them. The outer world and the inner world are easily at odds with one another. It is frustrating not to be able to rid ourselves of things we would prefer not to see, and therefore would gladly suppress. The contents of our unconscious lead a life of their own and pop up uninvited in our deeds, in our dreams, and in our anxieties. It is of the utmost importance to keep an eye on the factors we would like to prevent from playing a role.

Thus we ought to listen to what our unconscious has to say, and we should listen to our instincts. Then, with our conscious mind, we need to decide what we will do with the message: this is where the card Strength comes in. It depicts a woman (symbolizing receptivity) who can open and shut the mouth of a lion (unconscious forces): there are times when the unconscious can be heard and times when it must be silent. In this open exchange between conscious and unconscious we shall gradually come to see our lives in a different light, and be able to see ourselves in broader perspective. There is more to life than merely existing. We set out on a quest, like The Hermit.

What is the meaning of events? Why do they happen to me? Who am I? In the phase of The Hermit, we ask questions that have no clear-cut or predetermined answers. We need the freedom, space, and independence to be able to discover our own answers and to gain insights that can lead us to our own truth, whether it is spiritual, philosophical, or social. These are hard questions, especially when they concern the meaning of things, for everyday life brims with a concurrence of circumstances, things that seem to happen to us by chance, or by some stroke of fate. All this is a painful psychic process which leads us to the insight that there is a connection between our own psyche and what we endure. It is important to note that, although the connection is there, it is present at a level where we cannot immediately blame someone else for our situation. Often we repeat the same patterns, only to have the same events recur, possibly with slight variations.

It is the phase of The Wheel of Fortune that brings these facts home to us. Take a look at what you are really doing, look at the unintentional side effects of your activities. Are things turning out as well as you intended? And do you not find yourself getting embroiled in the very situations you so anxiously try to avoid? In The Wheel of Fortune we can learn to feel responsible for ourselves and our lives, and not to lean on others, or put the blame on others when things go wrong. If we stay where we are, we shall just go around and around in the same old way. An open and honest assessment of our activities and behavior in the outside world (including our intentions toward, and our relationships with, others) is logically involved in taking responsibility for our own lives.

And that brings us to Justice. It is through the insight into repetitive patterns in our lives, gained by what we discover in the phase of The Wheel of Fortune, and also through an honest analysis of this insight under the eye of Justice, that we are encouraged (on the basis of our self-analysis) to become more balanced. We see a clearer connection between our inner and outer lives, between the ego and the conscious on one hand, and the pros and cons of the unconscious on the other. We catch sight of our limitations and inhi-

Figure 11. Cards VI to XII from the Major Arcana of the Waite deck.

bitions (including those that are carried over from the past) and can gradually jettison our superfluous cargo—not by repression, but by assimilation. It disposes us to be more modest; it is the phase of The Hanged Man.

Assimilation often means, first and foremost, having a good cry over old grief and being prepared to dwell on your inner pain. Withdrawal into yourself to look at your repressions with insight and understanding, and without self-pity (which, naturally enough, will try hard to assert itself), belongs to the phase of The Hanged Man.

Keeping up appearances is not important—inner processes matter most. It is like a pupating caterpillar; the butterfly will eventually emerge, but the process goes on under the surface, invisibly, away from the world. Like Odin, who (in the same way as other mythological figures) hung upside down from a tree, so The Hanged Man is involved in the process of attaining a certain form of wisdom.

Not knowledge from books, but union with something inner (hard to describe, but not hard to experience) can form an unshakable basis for positive "knowing" and "feeling" in the future. Making a clean sweep, and having a high degree of reserve belong to this phase, which can give us the insight into the changes ahead. Maybe we need to abandon a certain behavior, or change a certain way of life that is not (or is no longer) appropriate. And this brings us to the next group of cards.

Integration of Conscious and Unconscious (Cards XIII–XXI)

WHAT IS HOLDING you back? What are you afraid of? What are your typical reactions when hiding your uncertainty? How fretful are you? In the phase of Death we are confronted with these questions, and also with feelings and experiences of inhibition and pain. Figure 12 (page 64) shows the Major Arcana cards involved in this next phase. Sometimes, through a crisis, we are obliged to endure a confrontation with ourselves in order to lay aside old patterns and disguises. And it is funny—when once you have put it behind you completely (or at least as best you can), you suddenly feel a tranquillity, a serene

Figure 12. Cards XIII to XXI in the Major Arcana from the Waite deck.

tranquillity. All at once you do not need to keep plunging into various activities, but can adopt a more detached attitude to emotions and events—the phase of Temperance.

Temperance provides a measure of balance. Not total equilibrium, but a new feeling of rest after labor, enabling us to get ourselves and the world more easily into perspective. In this phase, we will also observe that we are able to respond to others more cordially, honestly, and lovingly. However, as newly acquired behavior, it can still easily "fly away," and we see an angel, not a human being, in the picture. That is a warning that we can allow ourselves to be seized by the heady feeling that we have already arrived. If we persist in this illusion, repressed factors and things we thought had already been assimilated will gradually resurface and bring us into the situation represented by The Devil.

Are you really as nice as you make out? And if you profess a certain philosophy of life, how far do your behavior and your life style agree with what you say? To what extent is your helpfulness a bid for power? How far have egotistic motives crept into your noble behavior?

These are painful questions which we all often manage to avoid. By specious reasoning we prove to our own satisfaction that it is others who have these faults; and this is absolutely characteristic of the phase of The Devil! He prepares the way for the confrontation with our Shadow, that is to say, with our less pleasant side.

If we handle this confrontation honestly, we can suddenly change a great deal. But if we avoid it, we shall suddenly, and unexpectedly, receive an emotional shock, as illustrated by The Tower. The process of The Tower includes a flash of renewal and substantial demolition, whether initiated consciously or not. As if a thunderbolt had been hurled from a cloudless sky, life seems completely different all at once. Rapid changes, often accompanied by stress (for example, through illness or dismissal from a job) are typical of The Tower. Life seems to be giving us a kick to get us moving forward along the path that belongs to our inner being and our total psyche, so that we have to stop living within the narrow borders of security or remain bogged down in certain ideas and theories.

The Tower is the phase in which we are, so to speak, thrown back into life. The time for hiding away is past, even though we may still skulk behind complaints about things that are wrong, about setbacks and the like.

However, if we welcome this renewal, after this phase is over a period of rest will arrive. We will have the big confrontation with the unconscious behind us and will have a better idea of the difference between ourselves and the outside world. This means that we realize we are both individuals and human beings, that although we share human characteristics with others, we are unique, and that we are responsible for our own actions, but not for the sorrows of the world. This results in tranquillity and an internalization—The Star. Out of an inner peace with ourselves and the world, and a certain acceptance that things can take a different course than we had planned, we can be filled with a calmness that makes us less open to being influenced. We no longer pay so much heed to what people think and say; for example, we are not so likely to be taken in by slanted advertising and catchy slogans. We are at the start of a turning inward that conducts us to the deeper layers of ourselves. Habits and masks are largely laid aside and we take a close look at what remains. We are also in a position to dig down and to have the courage to admit that there is still much that is hidden and repressed that, unconsciously and unobserved, adversely affects our everyday life.

Thus, The Star prepares for the stage of The Moon. Incomprehensible, odd (and often alarming) deep-rooted factors, now visit us in dreams, symbols, feelings, emotions, and projections. How often we see that, after so much has already been assimilated, some more intense events or emotions come across our path? Old problems crop up again, but now on a deeper level and under a new guise. It is like taking an unnerving examination in which we are faced by something with which we feel we can do nothing.

However, what is important in the stage of The Moon is to let imaginings, fears, and feelings speak. Give these factors a place in yourself and accept them as part of your personality. They belong to a world that can help and warn you, just as animals in fairy tales can play a warning role. Accept, too, that you have no hold on these irrational and capricious factors living deep inside yourself and others. Dare to have dealings with them. Only then will you proceed in the direction of truly becoming whole, and reach the phase of The Sun.

The Sun says, "Learn to have a proper love of yourself, a love that is not egotistical. Embrace life and it will embrace you. Go to meet it with a spring in your step, openly and gladly! Be joyful." This joy does not mean that you have lost all sense of responsibility; even less that you have no individuality, or that you are still nothing but a child. However, do discover the child in yourself and dare to play. For many of us this is still a hard task, but a necessary step if we would genuinely go further. Only if you like yourself, and are able to accept yourself as you are, can you also like others and appreciate their value. This makes an opening for a deep feeling of love for your fellow human beings and for life: the phase of The Judgement.

Although there are other phases in which you can get a sense of a higher order, in which you can experience a certain inner repose, the card of The Judgement may be said to represent a phase that is more significant than any of these. What you experience here is a sense of life, and of your own life in particular, that can no longer be put into words. You experience, know, and feel these inner connections, and the relationship between yourself and the world. It brings its own feeling of spirituality and, with the availability of this deeper inner knowledge, you are in a much better position to live the life that really belongs to you.

In this phase, too, you discover that, without realizing it, you have already had a certain "infilling" of life and have already begun to assimilate it. Now you are ready to pick up the thread consciously. Usually this is associated with a deep feeling of fulfillment. The process eventually overflows into what the last card of the Major Arcana expresses—The World.

Because you are able to see your inner life in a wider context, you know that life has both day and night sides, in which joy and sorrow each have a natural place. In the phase of The World you are able to accept life as it comes and to take things in your stride. You can say "yes" to whatever you meet on your path, and can dare to plunge into the pain and emotions which are a part of life. With The World you are a well-rounded individual and do not lose yourself in grief or joy. You can accept them without allowing yourself to be fazed by tiresome experiences, or having your head turned by any successes you experience. You dance through life, go with the flow, and know that it is good. What is more, even though you wish that some things were different, you just know that your total psyche has something different in store for you than what your conscious will might want to choose.

Heed the rhythm of the whole, and dance along with the changes in the energy of The World—whether these are rehearsed or not. Needless to say, this will help you to stay happy through storm and shine, and you will feel a deep love for life and for all that lives. You will be at one with the world.

We are all traveling this Way of the Hero, even though we all come to a standstill from time to time, and our individuation process breaks down. These are the moments when The Fool can re-enter in order to give us a prod—perhaps from within, but quite possibly from an unforeseen concurrence of circumstances. Each inner situation is connected with external circumstances and events—incidentally, without necessarily causing them—for what happens is more a kind of mirror effect.

The cards of the tarot hold up to us a similar mirror in our continually moving and changing lives. And if we draw the card of The World, even then we have not yet arrived. Each card of the Major Arcana represents a primary pattern, a part of the way that we, as human beings, must walk in order to find ourselves. The card says nothing about level. When we have completed one cycle, we have to start all over again, so that we can do something fresh with our new attainments. New experiences come along, too, not to mention new problems. If, for example, in the phase of The World, we have achieved a measure of genuine serenity and have felt love for life flowing through us, then in the course of time The Empress can bubble up inside, and the urge to pause in middle life in order to express our inner creativity in a new way begins to stir, and becomes a source of fresh problems.

The tarot cycles will never cease to perform a mirror function for any of us as long as we live.

Chapter Five

THE NUMBER CARDS OF THE MINOR ARCANA

THE MINOR ARCANA, consisting of 56 cards, are very different in form and meaning from the Major Arcana. When you work with cards from the Major and Minor Arcana simultaneously, the Major Arcana cards supply the main motifs, the leading emphases, and the direction; these are then refined, amplified and filled in by the cards of the Minor Arcana. But do not underestimate the Minor Arcana for all that!

Just as the Major Arcana depict The Way of the Hero, our individuation process, so the Minor Arcana depict the processes and dynamics of the psyche. But, as has already been shown, the pattern is different.

In chapter 2, we saw that the structure of the tarot is anything but arbitrary, and that The Magician (Card I) has on his table items representing the four suits of the Minor Arcana. It is The Magician who wants a broad understanding of the world, of the way in which matter coheres (the motive for such studies as physics and chemistry), though not to the exclusion of psychic dynamics. On his table lie symbols suggesting a determination to embrace reality as it presents itself in daily life—from gravitation through economics, from frivolity through lovesickness.

It is these facets of life that we find in the cards of the Minor Arcana. Although life throws up an inconceivable variety of phenomena, events, conditions, and ideas, a single structure underlies it. In a subtle manner, this, too, is indicated by the Minor Arcana. If we aim to examine these 56 cards in depth, we must first understand the underlying structure.

The Minor Arcana comprise four groups of fourteen cards each. We saw in chapter 2 that the number fourteen often occurs symbolically in the context of religion. The number seven is a special number in many parts of the world; indeed it is a sacred number in many cultures. In its twofold manifestation, seven makes fourteen. We can think of the fourteen rungs of the ladder of Osiris, the ladder that joins Heaven and Earth, for it brings together spirituality and everyday life.

This numerical product hints subtly at the fact that there is something higher, something more meaningful, in all that we look on as ordinary in our lives.

The division of the Minor Arcana into four suits is also highly significant in itself. Various authors have tried to tie them into the four elements (see also chapter 8). For a satisfactory understanding of the interpretation of the Minor Arcana, the following indications will provide a good basis.

Wands

WANDS HAVE TO DO with movement and action, initiatives, and the launching of new ideas. Therefore Wands are characterized by powerful performance, capable of supporting various activities and original ideas, but are also capable in a negative sense of counterproductivity through rashness.

Swords

SWORDS REPRESENT THE power of discrimination as expressed in thinking and logic. The Swords are also active, meaning that they make distinctions on their own initiative, and in a negative sense, cause separation.

Pentacles

PENTACLES STAND FOR the world of what is tangible, and of genuine form-production in matter, working toward positive results; also for the experiencing of the manifest world. Therefore Pentacles are connected with what we can perceive with our senses and translate into form. This can find a useful outlet in concrete creativity, and in the enjoyment of the physical world, but can less helpfully involve clinging to the past, greed, and the pursuit of pleasure.

Cups

CUPS STAND FOR the world of experience and feeling in the broadest sense of the word. Therefore Cups have to do with displays of emotion, giving shape to the emotions, and the role of emotions in relation to others. They also have to do with susceptibility, fantasy, dreams, and the irrational in general. In a positive sense, this gives a feeling of peace and fulfillment, but in a negative sense, they can indicate unrealistic expectations and fantasizing, capriciousness, and so on.

WANDS AND SWORDS FORM the yang principle; Pentacles and Cups are two aspects of the yin principle.

Each of the four suits of the Minor Arcana contains four court cards: Page, Knight, Queen and King, and ten other cards from the ace through ten. Numbers play an important part here, and we could look at them from a numerological point of view; there would be nothing absurd in that. However, in my opinion, because the tarot is such a tremendous psychological mirror, it is preferable to investigate how certain numbers are employed in the world of mythology, fairy tales, symbolism and dreams. Dreams are always an individual expression of the unconscious, and mythology is its collective expression.

Analysis of this particular role of numbers can help us to gain a psychological insight into certain of them; this insight can then be applied to the analysis of the Minor Arcana. So our first step will be to take a quick look at the world of numbers in psychology.

All imaginable things in the variegated cosmos belong to one and the same underlying reality. This is nothing we can perceive with the senses, but a single world embedded deep down in our psyche beyond the borders of time and space, a world in which all things are one.

In his *Mysterium Coniunctionis,* Jung called this world *Unus Mundus.*[1] In the depths of the *Unus Mundus,* mind and matter are one. (Similar findings are being voiced by modern physicists.) The *Unus Mundus* is best seen as a transcendental background which, in the deepest sense, is the basis or source of our total reality, both material and spiritual. What in our consciousness and experience presents itself as two completely separate domains, is actually fully united.

In synchronistic phenomena, we sometimes obtain a striking glimpse of the way in which mind and matter are intertwined. For an outstanding treatment of "prediction and synchronicity" I can warmly recommend the book *On Divination and Synchronicity* by the Jungian analyst Marie-Louise von Franz.[2]

According to C. G. Jung, numbers have to do both with the world of matter and with the psyche. As far as matter is concerned, this is clear enough: science and technology could not exist without numbers and the manipulation of numbers. The modern world would be unthinkable without mathematics, which was such a difficult tool to handle for early mankind to handle. Primitive tribes could not get beyond the series "one, two, three, many." But that changed, and now we are aware that each form and each physical phenomenon has a mathematical aspect. We employ numbers every day without stopping to think that they could have a *meaning.*

We encounter numbers in the psyche, too. They may be featured in individual dreams; and certain numbers constantly recur as images in specific psychic circumstances. Thus Jung established that when people with mental problems produce dreams or drawings containing mandala forms with their fourfold divisions, the way to healing has been taken, and the psyche is once more in a position to make sense of itself. As a matter of fact, this result was so striking that Jung concluded that the mandala is the ultimate unit of all archetypes, and also of the multiplicity in the world of phenomena. Therefore, in a certain sense, the mandala is an equivalent of the *Unus Mundus.* Jung called the resultant central force

---

1. C. G. Jung, *Mysterium Coniunctionis, The Collected Works,* vol. 14, R. F. C. Hull, trans., Bollingen Series No. XX. (Princeton: Princeton University Press, 1963).
2. M. L. von Franz, *On Divination and Synchronicity* (Toronto: Inner City Books, 1980).

and central structure in our psyche the Self—a kind of superordinate archetype.

The number four also seems to be prominent in fairy tales; for example, in the shape of four tasks which the main character has to perform in order to escape a certain fate, or of a king with three sons (four people in all), and so on.

Although myths, fairy tales, and legends must originally have spring from the brain of some individual, the fact that they have been preserved for so long (no doubt being reworked and polished over the years) is an indication that they have appealed to large groups of people. And if for so many folk they are, or have been, somehow significant in an imaginative or emotional way, then they must address a layer in the psyche that is part of the collective unconscious.

Therefore the themes in myths, legends, and fairy tales belong to the psyche, too, and we can analyze the manner in which numbers play a role in them. Now these numbers are seldom formally stated figures, but are more often quantities. We have to extract them from the narrative: for example, by counting the number of main characters, of animal helpers, of tasks, of wicked fairies, and so forth. And, as we do so, universally analogous patterns suddenly jump out at us!

Some natural numbers and their multiples have an important connection with psychic factors. C. G. Jung said that numbers are the most primitive form of the spirit![3] Elsewhere he said that the natural numbers are the archetype of ordering that has become conscious. By which he meant that we have an unconscious knowledge of natural order, and at the moment we become aware of any ordering, we perceive or comprehend it in the form of, or with the help of, natural numbers. In the exact sciences we do no more than just that.

Ordering plays a role in the psyche, too, but so far this has received insufficient attention. The ordering that exists inside and

---

3. See, for example, C. G. Jung, *Civilization in Transition, The Collected Works.* Vol. 10, R. F. C. Hull, trans., Bollingen Series No. XX (Princeton: Princeton University Press, 1964), ¶ 776, where he says, "Now if we conceive numbers as having been *discovered*, and not merely *invented* as an instrument for counting, then on account of their mythological nature they belong to the realm of the "godlike" human and animal figures and are just as archetypal as they." And in ¶777, "[N]umbers can be vehicles for psychic processes in the unconscious."

outside us appears in thoughts and concepts, in external forms and structures, in dreams and works of art, and practically anything one cares to mention. And the knowledge of order is also given shape in the tarot in its own way.

Since numbers are symbols in the world of the psyche, and therefore much richer in content than words can express, we can only hint at their nature. But there need not be very many numbers to which the structures of life can be reduced. Nor do we have to assume a logical sequence.

Jung impressed on his students that the unconscious did not take account of time and space, and that it had its own form of logic, which did not in any way resemble the logic of the conscious. Thus three does not need to issue from two; it might do so, but again it might not. Each number is a world in itself, with its own right to exist, its own significance, and its own manifestation in relation to life. And, as a result of psychic dynamics, it flows in its own time out of the *Unus Mundus* or Self. It seems odd at first that things as "logical" as the numbers we use in our calculations should suddenly have to be considered as self-subsisting psychic factors with a deeper symbolic meaning incapable of expression in the language of conscious logic.

While we are on the subject, it is intriguing to note that in the religion of the Maya, numbers and symbols are incorporated in their gods. Psychologically speaking, each god is a certain specifically significant symbol in us. For the Maya, almost all the gods had their own numbers, and the supreme god, the god who was over the whole of creation, had the number one. He was known as Hunabku, the One Who is Alone. That the Maya knew that, in the final analysis, not everything in the unconscious is numerable, was expressed by them symbolically—the last five days of their year were unnumbered. The gods of chaos and of the underworld belonged to those days— gods who bore no numbers and no names. There are other cultures, too, where gods and numbers were connected.

Nevertheless, although numbers have their own unique meanings, and can surface in the psyche completely independently, we earn from the analysis of myths and the order of the events narrated in them, and also from the analysis of individual psychic material, that certain themes tend to appear in certain sequences or to be marshalled in certain ways. The links between numbers and these themes allow us to see how numerical sequences unfold in time.

Jung observed on his travels that as soon as three persons come together, a fourth person will join the company, as if the set of three cannot, or will not, continue to exist, but is looking for completion. Hence numbers seem to be closely involved in the manner in which one's psyche unfolds and the manner in which experiences are acquired—or, as Jung put it, with how the archetypes arise and behave in the conscious.

Because numbers have to do with the psyche as well as with matter, they seem to represent, in both worlds, a dynamic that operates in time. By observing a certain temporal quality, we can glimpse the archetype (or archetypes) at work inside it. The associated numbers have an ordering function.

Now it would be an error to think that we can simply say that "one" stands for everything, and "two" stands for duality, etc. Yes, we can say this; but we must also realize that when we treat these numbers as a dynamics of the psyche and of matter, it is not possible to put into words much of their meaning. But numbers do have very specific individual properties, which should undoubtedly be open to symbolic interpretation, and in my opinion there is a lot of ground lying fallow here.

In the light of experiences with dreams, drawings, and other symbolism, we shall now take a look at several numbers, and see how what we learn about them illuminates the corresponding cards of the Minor Arcana.

The Ace of One

WHENEVER WE MULTIPLY any number by itself, the product is always a larger number. In the case of two, 2 x 2 is equal to 2 + 2, which is 4; but above that, the square of a number is always greater than the sum of its addition to itself. In the case of one, on the other hand, the result of multiplying it by itself is smaller than the result of adding it to itself. One multiplied by itself always remains one. Does that imply that one is always utterly itself? That one is divine perfection, which remains itself during division by itself and multiplication by itself?

But when it reflects itself by addition of itself, the other, the two comes into being. Thus the one that is all, does not see itself and is not conscious of itself. Only by mirroring in the other, the two, and the experience of duality, can the one become conscious of itself. But this mirroring evokes confrontations and tension as in every process of true awareness. Symbolically, therefore, the one is a state of unity and wholeness, yet is in fact unaware of itself. Therefore there is an enormous potential within it that keeps striving for realization.

When we examine the four aces we see the same symbol in each: a divine hand coming out of a cloud and holding the suit emblem. All Aces have essentially the same meaning, due to the fact that they are the first cards, and in this respect, they represent the whole potential of their suit. We are meant to accept this potential as a gift and to do something with it; to derive from the knowledge that "everything is already there" an impulse to set to work and actualize it. Then the future will be ours.

This is emphasized in the symbolism of the four suits: Wands, Swords, Cups, and Pentacles. The Wands (or Rods) are in bud and are not dead. The Swords on the cards are everywhere true Swords, but in the ace, the weapon is crowned and draped with greenery—a symbol of fruitfulness, even here. The Pentacles are shown in fruitful surroundings, and water is flowing from the cup in the Ace Card. All are fruitful symbols bearing a promise of growth, even in the Ace of Swords. It is here that power lies, but you must grasp it. Therefore the aces have to do with opportunities, each in its own sphere of influence.

It is remarkable that the number one seldom occurs in dreams, at least as far as my own experience goes, and Paneth makes the same observation in his book, *Zahlensymbolik im Unbewusstsein* [Number Symbolism in the Unconscious].[4] Perhaps the one in dreams is none other than ourselves as the chief actor in those dreams, and we can mirror this one only when we start dreaming of one or more other persons. But then a number that is not the number one is immediately produced.

---

4. Ludwig Paneth, *Zahlensymbolik im Unbewusstsein* (Zurich: Rascher, 1952).

ACE OF WANDS
(Yang)

Fresh creative ideas and impulses break through which greatly appeal to you. They are well worth the trouble of putting into effect. You are facing new challenges, which bubble up from within, or come from outside on your path. You are on the threshold of some new enterprise or some new direction in life, and can proceed with enthusiasm and energy. Although everything seems to be going your way, do not be in too much of a rush.

ACE OF SWORDS
(Yang)

You can now come to grips with what was chaotic and can reduce it to some form of order; calmly, yet to an extent, rather remotely. You feel a need to make orderly arrangements of things, and may become involved with hobbies or studies in which the use of your intellect and understanding comes to the fore. The positive side of this card is a clear head, which, on the basis of sound insight, can be decisive and cut the Gordian knot; an added advantage being a strengthening of your self-confidence. The negative side can be an accompanying coolness and remoteness; there is little warmth or fervor in the Ace of Swords.

ACE OF PENTACLES
(Yin)

Although the Ace of Pentacles suggests activity, this activity is not the same as that engaged in by the Ace of Wands. The Ace of Pentacles does not come up with an idea to be realized (that is the role of Wands), but reveals that the time is ripe to give concrete expression to innate or developed gifts and talents and maybe to achieve something with them. With the Ace of Pentacles it is good to concentrate on one or two facets of reality and give yourself wholly to them. If you consider devoting yourself to some project for which you have a gift, quite often it will crop up on your path, or circumstances will encourage you to make a start on it. It seems to be a regular occurrence that the Ace of Pentacles favors the start of a relationship and introduces a feel-good factor even before anything has taken place on the concrete plane.

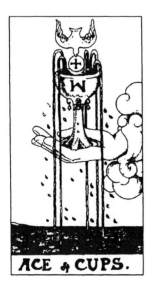

ACE OF CUPS
(Yin)

Gladness, a feeling of good luck, and a sense of fulfillment belong to the Ace of Cups. Not because of anything concrete (that is the Ace of Pentacles), but because we are in a position to tap into deeper strata of the emotions where there is an almost religious dimension left unexplored below the pavement of everyday life. The Ace of Cups makes us receptive to other values, to the world of the irrational and dreams, to symbolism and subtlety. The usual "ace" characteristic of setting to work is not always so prominent in the Ace of Cups, or so it would seem. For withdrawal into the world of dream and fantasy, of doodling and imagination, though possibly less "useful" from a social point of view, are for the Ace of Cups a great way of gaining permanent access to that deeper emotional source that gives a sense of happiness and satisfaction leading indirectly to self-acceptance. Therefore, the Ace of Cups can represent a potential for love in a broad sense: a love of ourselves and of life. The danger of the Ace of Cups is that of getting hung up on feelings and failing to take part in daily life.

Two

TWO IS ONE LOOKING at its own reflection. It is the polarity of one with itself that is initially experienced as something "other." What do you do about this polarity? Do you involve yourself in it? Does it evoke doubts? Do you try to fight it? All these are questions that are tied up with the theme of duality, and the four suits tackle them in their own way. In this context two also means discord, or things about which you are uncertain. Two disturbs unity and dislodges it. When two appears in dreams, there is often a question of duality in various forms, and the situation is dynamic. Two is not self-sufficient and cries out for a solution.

As I said in chapter 2 in reference to the picture of The Magician, the cup and the pentacle on the juggler's table are representatives of the feminine in the cosmos, or yin, and the baton and sword are representatives of the male principle, or yang. Yin and yang have to do with duality each in their own way. As is well known, yin tries to mingle with everything it encounters and endeavors to yield to life. Yang, on the other hand, tries to distinguish the "other," to classify it, and possible to stand outside it, or to arrange and understand it. Yin unites, yang separates.

Now as we look at the four twos of the Minor Arcana, the following points attract our attention:

TWO OF WANDS
(Yang)

There is a measure of isolation here, due to the fact that, by systematization and organization, you have reached a high point and are faced by the duality of success and emptiness, of concrete fulfillment through action (Wands) and the opposite it evokes—a lack of fulfillment and stagnation, and therefore a lack of motivation. This card mirrors your activity: by living an active life you can obtain everything you desire, but will it make you happy? There are ambiguous feelings regarding the content of your life, and these need to be resolved.

TWO OF SWORDS
(Yang)

Through wanting to draw distinctions that are too sharp, you drive thinking to its opposite. The power of clear and rational discernment changes into destructive reasoning and idiosyncrasy. Whereas the Ace of Swords shows the ability to discriminate, this is reflected in the Two by its opposite. To what extent are you hiding yourself behind your ability to distinguish and classify? Are you genuinely involved in life? Do you see things as they really are? How far are you dichotomizing yourself with your dualistic thinking?

TWO OF PENTACLES
(Yin)

On the material plane, the potential expresses itself in rhythms—now enough, now not enough. The key is that the possibilities of matter rebound into the impossibilities—into the things you cannot obtain or attain, and which miscarry. But is what happens really a miscarriage, or is it the natural fluctuation of life? Are you concentrating on one pole (the pursuit of possessions) or the other (seeing yourself as a failure), or do you perceive the connection between your ups and downs? The question is this: are you prepared to enter into life and do you want to take steps to promote your inner growth regardless of the material consequences? The man on the cards is keeping hold of both poles (Pentacles), negative and positive, as if to assure you that the knowledge of this duality is something you can handle. The card expresses an ambivalent attitude toward your material prospects and your own activities in life.

TWO OF CUPS
(Yin)

Note the very friendly picture, but also the deeper duality, like all twos. The yin quality unites, and here we see two cups which unite (or at least bring into contact) two different emotional and experiential worlds. This is where the mirror lies in Cups—the mirroring of your own emotions in those of the other person. And that is sometimes quite frightening! But the Two of Cups shows the potential conflict more as an encounter than as a problem: this is always the way in which the pure yin seems to deal with the problem of the duality—through acceptance. So the question here is whether you are in the right frame of mind to come into the clear with your opposite number(s).

We see in the twos a decided difference between the yin and the yang outlook. In the yin cards, Pentacles and Cups, there is a degree of union and acceptance that is lacking in the Wands and Swords, where the emphasis is more on isolation and separation. Thus the two cosmic principles affect the theme two differently!

Three

THE TENSION IN TWO can try to resolve itself, either by dropping back to one, or by rising to three. It is important to remain aware of the possibility of moving backward! For example, by falling in love and marrying, you run the risk, on the plane of two-ness, of becoming embroiled in relationship problems (the duality and the negative tension of being the other), but an equally great danger is to be so wrapped up in the relationship that you lose all awareness of being a separate entity and relapse into a hazy feeling of one-ness. And oneness is a state of mind in which you cannot make headway! The tension of two can also seek resolution via creativity and the formation of something new. The traditional example of this is the relationship between a man and a woman that results in a child. (The number of children is immaterial; the essential point is that a child or children are a resolution of the tension inherent in two.) Thus there is always a movement away from two! It seems as if two cannot remain in existence.

Three is a sort of synthesis. But in dreams we never see three as a final state; mostly it marks a beginning. There still seems to be something of the tension of two in it, but this is outflanked by a new idea, a creative impulse. Three represents what is in process of formation, a force that is in operation; decisions have already been made, but the goal has not yet been reached. The form does not come into being until the following number: four. Von Franz emphasizes that within

Jungian psychology three constantly recurs as a dynamic process. We keep finding three where a stream of psychic energy is flowing (the impulse!), associated with time and destiny. Thus something is waiting to happen in the realms of time and space.

If we now take a look at the threes of the Minor Arcana, we can see the following significations.

THREE OF WANDS
(Yang)

The Three of Wands shows us a man gazing out over aureate water—turned gold by the setting sun. His ships are sailing into the distance. The man has achieved success in life and is consolidating it. He no longer needs to seize any and every opportunity. There is positive restfulness in this card. The Three of Wands is traditionally regarded as a success card, full of power and determination. The man's dealings and activities have led to a point of balance, but he has certainly not come to his end-point. That is not yet in sight, nor is it important. The Three of Wands depicts one who can reap the harvest of his transactions without yet being done with them, and without knowing whether they will lead to something new or not.

THREE OF SWORDS
(Yang)

This card displays a pierced heart. Three swords have been thrust through a red heart, and traditionally this indicates emotional suffering or love-sickness. But the traditional explanation in no way exhausts the meaning of the card. The situation is the consequence of energy in motion, and so is not a terminus. In the situations in

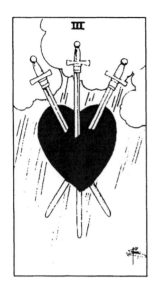

which you draw this card, you experience emotion, pain, and difficulties, but you are not sitting in a dark cell or anything like it. Nor do you feel that the situation is a definite stage; on the contrary, you are still on the way. You already have behind you some activity that is characterized by this movement; for example you have made one or more important decisions, have gone through several rough patches, or have had a difficult hand to play, etc. Perhaps you have been running through a certain project in your mind and are on the point of launching it with the determination to see it through in spite of problems and annoyances.

THREE OF PENTACLES
(Yin)

The flow of psychic energy is expressed here as a concrete process of realization: a monumental mason is at work. The fact that he is working in and on a church gives a spiritual dimension to his manipulation of matter, a spirituality that is also expressed by other symbols on the card. Here, too, there is no finishing point. Not only is the work still incomplete (and is apparently under discussion by a priest and an architect, the other men on the card), but this Three of Pentacles also suggests that when you sally forth into the concrete world with your skills (for example, your intellectual knowledge or technical training), you will slowly, but surely, achieve your goal. You are well on the way to reaching it, and this is reason enough to continue self-confidently and in a happy frame of mind.

THREE OF CUPS
(Yin)

The harvested fruit lies on the ground and three women are dancing happily with chalices raised—all signs that this card expresses felicity and joy. But things are not as simple as they appear. In practice, this card often shows up when you are experiencing an initial reward for your application, your activities, or your perseverance in a certain field. It does not promise promotion or remuneration, but indicates that you feel good, are aware that you are working well, and sense that people value you, and you want to share your delight in all this. Thus, generally speaking, we have been successfully doing whatever had to be done, and with this card we share with others our happiness over the course of events. However, our journey is by no means over, although the optimism can remain.

With three, the message on all the cards is actually, "Keep going, you are on the right road." Because three, as a creative impulse, is engaged in releasing the tension of two, all these cards feel good, even the Three of Swords, which is busy cutting knots in order to escape from an emotional straitjacket. The difference between the yin and yang cards is not so big here, possibly because all the cards depict a process, a coming into being, and not a static situation. The latter is more typical of four.

Four

IN DREAMS FOUR crops up in certain circumstances with the significance of an accentuated two, that is to say, with a more acute dualism which urgently demands attention. More often we see four as the expression of wholeness in the act of formation. Mandalas bring this out quite forcibly. Four is clear-cut but also contains some of the tension of two. The idea "divide and rule" usually applies, but can be interpreted less straightforwardly in the sense of "dividing and classifying as an aid to understanding and gaining a better grasp of external phenomena." But four, the number of form, can mean fossilization.

The number four plays an important part in human orientation: as in the four points of the compass, Jung's four primary functions of the mind, the four elements, and the four fundamental forces of nature known to physics. Even DNA and RNA are based on a quaternary structure. In Euclidean geometry, four points produce the first three-dimensional body, and von Franz points out that in mathematics the number four serves the function of a numerical boundary in many respects.

From three to four is a very big step: yet the world of formation is impelled to take this step into the world of form and reality with all its limitations. Three seldom stays as it is, but seems fated to become four.

Jung, moreover, says that the step from three to four is painful, because in the psyche it is associated with painful insights into ourselves. We see ourselves in concrete reality, even in those things we cannot do and in the things we overdo (think for a moment of the part played by our inferior, or fourth function), and so on. The necessary process of the becoming of four can, therefore, go hand in hand with denial and petrifaction, flight from confrontation, etc., while on the other hand the number four can, by the very fact of the confrontations, be a powerful step toward wholeness. Four, therefore, has a duality of its own, and not for nothing is it 2 + 2, and 2 x 2!

Now let us take a look at four on the cards of the Minor Arcana.

FOUR OF WANDS
(*Yang*)

This tarot card is always highly prized. You emerge dancing from the walled town, and an open and free atmosphere prevails. At first sight, there seems to be nothing of the twofold dualism that can belong to four. Yet bright and happy though this card may be, there is a snake hiding in the grass. Each four card warns us against getting set in our ways. The danger here lies in the wish to cling to this state of openness and mirth, which then becomes superficial and false. You can revel in conviviality and nearness, and think that if you just keep dancing all will be well. But, in practice, in spite of this danger lurking in the background, we see the wholeness aspect of four coming out: we are on the point of reaping the benefits of what we have done in the past, and these benefits can remain from now on—although this is not inevitable. Things have taken fixed form in a pleasant way (the harvest is in). And yet it is perfectly true to say that life still has many fresh opportunities to offer. Frequently I have seen this card associated with a rapid inner development or psychological growth.

FOUR OF SWORDS
(*Yang*)

An obvious corpse is lying in state in a church. Is greater stagnation conceivable? We are trapped in our dualistic thinking and are unable to escape from it. Rigid logic and hidebound theories cannot help us any further. We ought to get away from them, but in fact, we have already been swallowed by them. It looks as if whatever is alive and bubbly has disappeared. The form has become fixed, and there is scarcely a sign of motion— even of spiritual motion. This is a card that turns up quite frequently when we have to take a forced rest (due to illness,

for example) in order to recover our mental tone and physical vitality. And it is this very withdrawal on and into ourselves that can bring us the wholeness of four and remove our stagnation. However, we must no longer by stick-in-the-muds, but learn that life can produce new structures at unexpected moments.

FOUR OF PENTACLES
(Yin)

A man is sitting clutching his money and has other coins (Pentacles) under his feet and on his crown. He is up to his ears in matter that has become excessively stiff and unmoveable. The danger here is that, pleasant though it may be to have possessions, the desire for material security can stifle further growth. To safeguard our current holdings we avoid taking fresh initiatives, or confine ourselves to doing just what we think is necessary, regardless of whether this is what the psyche needs. There is an air of "staying put" about the Four of Pentacles, which admittedly suggests trustworthiness and stability but nothing vital or inspired.

FOUR OF CUPS
(Yin)

The man beneath the tree refuses to take the proffered cup (which is reminiscent of the one on the ace card). This portrays the danger of settling into an emotional pattern, or, worse still, of completely cutting oneself off emotionally from those around us. The man's arms are folded. His refusal to drink is not sensible, but is more like the behavior of a small child who is being given something new to eat and says, "Yuk!" In this situation there is often a failure to recognize the value of certain feelings of circumstances in life, or of the role of certain people in one's life, or of one's own qualities. You are passing up choice dainties that are there for the taking. Owing to this mood of refusal, you are not prepared to mingle with the world or

with those around you. It is not surprising, therefore, that this card is often a
warning of boredom or imaginary wor-
ries. While there is the opportunity of
making a great leap forward in terms of
emotional growth, there is also the risk
of settling down in your own unreal
world, and perhaps of nursing some
unjustified grudge.

If we compare the four different cards in
the Rider-Waite deck, the design of the
Wands appears to deviate somewhat from
that of the others. The Pentacles, Swords,
and Cups clearly show the petrifaction,
but this is less noticeable in the Wands.
    Now Wands are very much
involved in transactions and activities, so that these cards always
depict movement of some sort. But even movement can become
stereotyped if you move simply for the sake of moving!

Five

FIVE HAS A REMARKABLE relationship with humanity and life, and a
deep association with eros. When dreaming, we often see the number five in connection with the search for genuine involvement in life,
whether or not this is expressed sexually. In drawings (especially in
cartoons!) sexy maidens often flaunt five ringlets (or display the number five in some other fashion) while characters with no particular sex
appeal have many more curls.
    One way or another, we know unconsciously that there is a cer-
tain amount of "oomph" in the number five. It has an attractive
vibrancy, but to benefit by it we have to enter into the spirit of its get-
up-and-go! First and foremost, *eros* is union, and the willingness to
form a genuine relationship. Sexuality can play a role in it, but *eros* is
much more than that.

The number five is the sacred number of the goddess Ishtar (Astarte). This goddess embodies the mother-hetaira antithesis. She is the goddess of love and sexuality, of fruitfulness, but also of war—a paradox to us Westerners.

We encounter something of that paradox in the number five, itself. It is a confrontational number in this respect: the arithmetical series 1-2-3 is a picture of father-mother-child, and four represents the confines of matter—hearth and home. Thus three stands for the natural family and four stands for the social family.

But when we come to five, a new dimension makes its appearance. According to some, the world of Eve is fenced off by the number four, and the number five introduces Lilith—the deeper, mystical, uniting feminine facets and energies—which are also darker and, as far as our conscious is concerned, more alarming. The Lilith in us drags us out of our security and gets us on the move. As human beings, we have to grow through confrontation; if we stand still we shall get rigid.

Interestingly enough, the number five does not occur in the classification of natural crystal systems: thus there is no hardening of form at the basis of five. Five loosens, and in a sense it also has something revolutionary in it. What is more, five is characteristic of humans: we have five senses, five fingers on each hand, and five toes on each foot, and if we stand with head erect and arms and legs spread out, we find that these five extremities form the points of a pentagram.

On looking at fives in the Minor Arcana, we see how much difficulty we have in allowing this revolutionary influence into our lives, how much difficulty we have in our society with the role of union and Lilith. The fives of the Minor Arcana each represent problems that have to do with a lack of *eros*, and with the trouble we find in being part of life. In Wands and Swords, the yang cards, this is expressed in the form of conflict and strife (more strongly in Swords than in Wands), and in the yin cards, Pentacles and Cups, it is expressed in the form of privation.

FIVE OF WANDS
(Yang)

There is no stable pattern of activities here, but great unrest. This easily leads to new things, but just as easily to altercation. The urge for revolution expresses itself in squaring up to others. The pugnacity is often playful, but there is a danger that it will lead to serious strife. The card alerts you to the potential for trouble. By paying heed to it, you can handle confrontations in a controlled and alert manner, which can lead to renewal and to gratifying progress in your activities.

FIVE OF SWORDS
(Yang)

This card is thought of as totally negative; and in fact it depicts the contrary of what five ought to be. There is not a sign of connection with others or with life. Opponents are defeated by means of mental stratagems. The vanquished feel devalued and worthless, and even less able to cope with life. You often see this degenerating into a "hangdog" attitude which can lead to further rejection and defeat! In short, there is no *eros*, no renewal, no positive revolution. And yet these forces are at work in the background of this card. Naturally, this internal restlessness and dissatisfaction has put the conscious under pressure. If this is misapprehended, anxiety easily arises, with the result that the individual goes all out to return to the condition of four—stability and the status quo—even if that is no longer appropriate. And the insecurity can increase the need to prove oneself. By adopting an acerbic and uncompromising attitude, one almost digs one's own grave, so that in the end, when one has completely isolated oneself, one is compelled to realize that there is something more to life: other people, love, attachment, etc. In the Five of Swords we see Ishtar as the goddess of war. It is important to understand that wanting to get the better of others, however negative it may be, does represent a connection with others: it evokes emotions in us that have an inner significance. We need to work on this.

FIVE OF PENTACLES
(Yin)

Due to paying no attention in the past to signposts pointing to the need for change, we are now altogether on the wrong track, and this can express itself concretely in the form of financial reverses or illness, for example. The Five of Pentacles goes with the feeling of being left in the lurch, of being misused, and the like. Here also there is little evidence of the uniting and renewing aspect of five; indeed the reverse is true. As with the Five of Swords, we seem to be set in our ways. Nevertheless, the church-window forms a deeper setting of hope: we shall find a new form of security if we make the attempt to unite with our inner spirituality and learn to experience a new dimension in the concrete material world, i.e., the connection between ourselves and the world, between inner and outer. The danger of the Five of Pentacles is that of continuing to run in the same old way for fear of losing the little bit of security left to us. There is also the danger of being satisfied with little or nothing, and of no longer being prepared to hold our own. The problem will continue, if we fail to take control of ourselves, until we reach rock-bottom and simply must do something to help ourselves. But with this card we can take action before matters have come to such a pass: we can stand up ourselves!

FIVE OF CUPS
(Yin)

Sorrow: the overturned and empty beakers symbolize problems of an emotional nature which have arisen through one's own meddling or negligence. The result is isolation and loneliness. In this card, too, we see the contrariness of five: while clinging to certain emotional and egocentric values, even though they have served their purpose, we have kicked down many walls that would have been beneficial to us and now we are left with the pieces. As a rule, this has not been done deliberately, but as a result of fear of the new. However, there is still hope: two of the beakers have been left standing! We must begin to reorient ourselves emotionally (Cups represent the emotions): the person in black must turn around in order to see the upright beakers. Then five, as a new movement, can bring us into union (*eros*) with dormant vital emotional values, and we can set a new course. If we experience a refusal of any sort with this card, we should consider whether it would not be good to adopt a new stance, to change our attitude and our mode of relating to people. Painful emotional experiences can lead to a turn of the tide here.

IN ALL THE FIVES of the Rider-Waite deck, it looks as if the card of action (Wands) is beset by the least problems, while the others can display the true meaning of five only after a crisis. Possibly this judgment is based on the fact that five, itself, is full of activity. But just as with the Four of Wands, so here there is a danger of activity for activity's sake, which can create tensions and certainly not the kind of union that five is trying to express.

The three other cards illustrate how much the necessary processes can be made to stagnate if we cling to the old. In these days, thought (Swords) is very largely concentrated on the problem of "sink or swim." The fear of losing a job or becoming financially embarrassed in some other way makes many people choose careers they would otherwise have avoided (Pentacles), seeing they are not cut out for them. Or they give way to the temptation of greed (aroused by advertising) and land themselves in acute financial problems.

Involvement on the emotional level is also not something that is stimulated by the callous world (Cups). Therefore, as a warning, the card in the Rider-Waite deck presents us with a symbolic picture of emotional regression.

We must not forget that Five can transmute into a very cheerful dynamism. Perhaps in future centuries these cards will be able to carry a new pictorial image? *Eros*, or true union, and Lilith, the attributes of the night and of irrationality, are still big problems in our own century. But energies are already astir within us that can gradually change the way in which the fives now express themselves in us.

Six

SIX IS OFTEN TREATED as 2 x 3, but has several remarkable characteristics of its own. If you add the divisors of six (1, 2, and 3) you get six again. There is hardly another number where that happens; in nearly all other cases the addition of the divisors of a number is smaller than the number, itself.

Thus six juts out, and is regarded as the most important of the few numbers with which it shares this feature. (The numbers which added together make six are also prime numbers: numbers that are divisible only by themselves and one.)

Not only does the addition of the divisors of six yield six, their multiplication does too: 1 x 2 x 3 = 6. And so, whichever way we treat them, the divisors of six produce six! Six is the pivot of its divisors $(1 + 2 + 3 = 6 = 1 \times 2 \times 3)$, and also the pivot or center of the first five even numbers: 2, 4, 6, 8, 10. If we link this with the fact that we encounter three two times in six, and three is connected with the ingress of psychic energy into the realm of time and space, then it seems that six with its pivotal action has a cyclic function.

Cycles bring us back to points where we have been before, but where we can make a fresh start with new trends and new cycles. In the meantime something old, the previous round, is completed. Historically, the ancient Greeks called six an *arithmos teleios*, or perfect number. Cognate with *teleios* is the Greek verb *tetelestai*, which in the old mystery plays meant, "It is finished."

Thus in six something has been completed (6), but at the same time there is movement due to a duality or stress-field (2×3). Here is a remarkable association of rest and tension, in which the completion of a cycle preponderates, but the impulse to enter a new stage is also present. Whereas in the number three we saw a process still going on, in six we see a finish and the urge to start a new process.

The sixes in the Minor Arcana work out as follows.

SIX OF WANDS
(Yang)

The knight on the horse has gained a victory for which he has been honored (the laurel wreath). He is not resting on his laurels, but is on his way to face a new challenge or to undertake another quest. Among other things, Wands represent executive power and the love of action, and here one cycle has clearly come to a close. This card is often turned up when you have already achieved results (in one form or another), but something is still gnawing away at you, not in the form of a problem, but because you simply cannot sit back and do nothing. Therefore positive changes are often signified by this card.

SIX OF SWORDS
(Yang)

Crossing the water shows that the old is being left behind. The new is still unknown. The rather miserable attitude of the people sitting in the boat reveals that the crossing is not easy for them. The swords are being taken along, too: old thought patterns will still be deployed in the new situation. Even though we may imagine we have washed our hands of the past or of a certain matter, this does not mean that we are rid of it; we must take it with us until we have confronted it. So although this is a new cycle, we are still burdened by unquiet thoughts from the previous cycle, in addition, perhaps, to some anxiety over the unknown future. This card cautions us against going back. On the far shore glimmer hope and opportunities. Our greatest liability is our own ballast: the swords in the boat.

SIX OF PENTACLES
(Yin)

The merchant has finished making his fortune and can let others share in his riches. Life has remunerated him with this position and he realizes that he must do something new with it. The old cycle of trying to become a success is over, and in the new cycle he has to learn to use his wealth ethically and spiritually. This is expressed by the alms-giving and the weighing out of money. The card is normally regarded as lucky: things are turning out well for us.

SIX OF CUPS
(Yin)

The two individuals on this card are children; the card refers to our youth. This lies in the past, this cycle in our life is over. Childhood problems can persist into current situations; but, as we try to apply to them the purity of the inner child, we can step into a new cycle. The Cups mainly refer to all those circumstances in life in which feelings and emotions play a part, which they usually do in interhuman contacts and relationships. Emotionally, we are entering a fresh cycle, yet can still be dogged by various reminders of the past, as we run into people who once meant a great deal to us, or experience a rearousal of youthful desires.

The card conveys a delicate warning not to romanticize the past at the expense of the future. We are now in another cycle and are no longer children.

Seven

WHETHER YOU EXAMINE the way in which the number seven occurs in the context of dreams, or you study the role it plays in religions and cultures, you will find something paradoxical about it. Therefore it is not an easy number to interpret, and perhaps it actually symbolizes paradox. In dreams, the number seven is often associated with a state of unrest because it is obvious that something cannot be solved in the usual way.

Here is a certain field of tension or point of departure which seems to stay as it is. Naturally nothing remains the same in the course of years, but within the context of dream, fantasy, or spontaneous drawings, it seems that whatever is associated with the number seven is not in motion; yet it is a cause of motion or has motion going on around it.

In this sense, the number seven could have to do with a character trait or form of behavior that produces the required reaction in the outside world, while the individual may (still) not absorb the consequences of what he or she is doing.

The number seven is composed of the number three, which is in motion, which is still part of a process, and the number four, which is expressive of external form and rather runs the risk of petrifaction.

The strange ambiguity of seven is seen in antiquity. In ancient Babylonia, this number was an utterly unlucky number, and nothing was to be undertaken on the 7th, 14th, 21st, and 28th days of the month, or on the 19th of the following month. 19 + 30 = 49, and that is 7 x 7, or bad luck squared!

Since, back in history, the Jewish people had close contact with Babylonia, and they, in their turn, have exercised a big influence on Christendom, some people think that this significance of the number ties in with what we are told about Jehovah resting on the seventh day. To add to the paradoxical image of seven, we find that it was slowly converted from an unlucky number into a sacred one.

Thus, in ancient Babylonia, we see that the number seven is already involved in paradoxes: the number seven represented not only sin but the preparation for atonement and redemption. In the Old Testament, too, we see this theme concerning the number seven: God cursed Cain after the latter had murdered his own brother, but at the same time, he protected Cain by decreeing that "whosoever slayeth Cain, vengeance shall be taken on him sevenfold."

St. Augustine, too, refers to the connection between good and evil in the number seven: he called seven the number of the Sabbath and redemption, but at the same time the number of sin. And Albertus Magnus mentions the seven words of Christ on the cross, the seven deadly sins, and the seven petitions in the Lord's Prayer. The number also plays a big role in the Book of Revelation, and not always a cheerful one. Sin and forgiveness, drama and redemption, unlucky number and sacred number, these form the paradox of seven.

Now it is time to look at seven in the cards of the Minor Arcana.

SEVEN OF WANDS
(Yang)

The paradoxical nature of seven is immediately obvious in the illustration on this card. The interpretation often has two sides: the card may be said to encourage you to fight for what you believe in, but equally it suggests that you are in a sort of war of attrition through what you have stirred up with all your initiatives. On the one hand, there is the thrill of the challenge, and, on the other hand, you have no control over the direction in which matters are going. The paradox of seven, good and evil, is linked here with your own actions (Wands): you have made some decisions and are pursuing a certain course. But look ahead and be on your guard. Although you think that everything is going swimmingly and people are still good-humored, changes easily occur with this car and bring some fairly furious fighting.

SEVEN OF SWORDS
(Yang)

A man is making off with swords stolen from an army camp; a rather dubious picture—stealing is a crime, but when it is an enemy's swords that are taken, the theft is praised. The unobserved removal of such a quantity requires a crafty or furtive approach, possibly trickery, and of course a degree of courage. But usually there is no heroism in the Seven of Swords; there is too much falsity, too much underhandedness, in the card. The cunning presupposes planning ahead, which brings the mental side of Swords to the fore. But at the same time the Seven of Swords warns against underestimating the result of your actions, and here, once more, there is a paradox: a well-considered, consummate plan, but no thought for the consequences! The Seven of Swords always warns us to watch out for the intrigues or machinations of others where we are the intended victim, but equally warns us that if we resort to similar behavior, we shall almost certainly end up losing.

SEVEN OF PENTACLES
(Yin)

A man is leaning on his staff in a state of quiet watchfulness and sees the pentacles growing like fruit. Past dealings or ideas are coming to fruition; but there is nothing more you can do about them and you just have to wait and see. The trouble with this seven card is that developments are taking place that are important to you, but there is no pressure you can bring to bear on them or guidance you can give them. Any help or interference on your part will only delay matters. Remuneration and frustration, growth and waiting, especially in the tangible side of life and in the materialization of plans, all lie in the Seven of Pentacles.

SEVEN OF CUPS
(Yin)

Our emotional world is wide open to a host of fantasies and dreams, which can develop in a positive manner, but (as might be expected of paradoxical seven) can just as easily draw us away from reality. Without clearly realizing it, we are standing facing two rows of cups, all of which look like beautiful gifts from cloudland. But the lower row can lure us into powerplay, greed, ambition, or aggression, before we are aware of it, while the upper row can lead us to improved contact with our unconscious, to the unobstructed flow of psychic energy, and ultimately to fusion with our inner center, our true being, which is now still under a veil. This is a card with two aspects: it warns against wrong desires and against the development of disagreeable character traits of which we are unaware, and on the other hand it reveals a potential for tremendous spiritual and psychological growth and for becoming ourselves.

If we look at the difference between yin and yang, we see that in the yin cards we play a passive role: in the Pentacles we are forced to wait and must not intervene, in the Cups we are apt to allow ourselves to be influenced by highly charged atmospheres, and our own desires and to be lost in dreams. Conversely, in the yang cards we see more strife (Wands) or the danger of strife. However, the paradox of seven is present in all four suits, and all four urge us to exercise great caution.

Eight

FOUR IS A PRINCIPLE of order, and we also see this in 2 x 4 = 8. When the number eight occurs in dreams and drawings, in fantasies or in fairy tales, interpretations of two sorts are possible. One form in which eight manifests itself is a firm anchoring, a powerful regulation and control, but at the same time the danger of coming to a standstill. As if eight as 4 + 4 strengthens the risk of stagnation inherent in four. (In astrology, the number eight is ascribed to Saturn!)

But there is also a kind of movement in this eight, one that tends to take place more below the surface. In a positive sense (certainly when it appears in mandala-form in a dream, for example) eight is involved in "getting the psyche back into shape." After turbulent times, with much inner unrest, the occurrence of the number eight in dreams can indicate that one will shortly have a better perspective and grip on life and will not be so unsettled. So eight can become a starting point for putting our further development on a secure basis. As 2 x 4, eight also displays a twofold patterning which creates a stress-field that can lead to movement. Thus in various old cultures we encounter eight as an orderly pattern that lies at the basis of all the phenomena of life. For example, the eight immortals in traditional Chinese symbolism; or ancient Egyptian cosmology with its "City of Eight" (Hermopolis) housing eight gods grouped as 2 x 4, who ultimately underpin existence—Nun and Nunet as the Primeval Waters in male and female form, Hu and Huhet as endless space, Kuk and Kuket as darkness, Amun and Amunet as the void.

Note the male-female polarization, or yang-yin, in this symbolism; and eight as the third power of two is a particularly apt symbol of primeval polarity. Therefore, there is considerable tension in eight that calls for release, and at the same time, something creative and renewing in it. Bindel remarks that over the centuries eight has constantly been associated with creation, construction, and healing.[5]

Thus there is an element here of rounding off and making a fresh start, but not in the same way as with six. Six is cyclic, but eight, per se, is not. To realize that this is so, one has only to think of the octave, of which the eighth and last note is also the first note of the next octave in the same key.

Now we are ready to see how eight works out on the cards of the Minor Arcana.

---

5. Ernst Bindel, *Die Geistigen Grundlagen der Zahlen* (Stuttgart: Freies Geistesleben, 1975), p. 254.

EIGHT OF WANDS
(Yang)

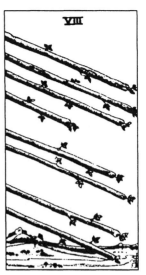

The Wands (which are here in bud) hurtle like darts through the air, and quickly strike their target. One phase is almost at an end, but the restlessness of Wands (which represent activity and motion!) is surging ahead to a new beginning. The imagery of this card shows that we can look forward to a rapid completion of what we are doing, but that we shall soon be occupied with something else. The action largely takes place outside ourselves (there are no people in this card!), although we may initiate it. All we need to worry about is doing the right thing at the right time. A new day is dawning, but we have to see the old out first. In this context, eight means seeing that matters are properly ended, as well as the possibility of further movement.

EIGHT OF SWORDS
(Yang)

The rigidity of eight comes out strongly in this card. As far as mental constructs and theories are concerned, we are completely nailed down. All flexibility has disappeared and the Eight of Swords represents hindrance and blockage on all fronts. Swords represent hindrance and blockage on all fronts, whether in work or in relationships (depending on the query). We have lost sight of our own situation, but our legs (as in the picture) are still free, so we can get away and seek help. This is where the little bit of movement in eight comes in. The card carries a warning that we are in danger of getting stuck in old convictions and ideas, in self-denial and all sorts of oppressive rules which will gradually paralyze our inner development. A confrontation with these things is unavoidable if we are to escape from this inhibiting situation. But, as already mentioned, it is open to us to go in search of help from others.

EIGHT OF PENTACLES
(*Yin*)

You are working away, and what you are doing is nearly finished. Pentacles always have to do with the world of matter and concrete forms. However, with the Eight of Pentacles, finishing a piece of work does not mean coming to a standstill: the involvement of the man in his work reflects another side of this card—the desire to express oneself in life, to be able to experiment with matter so as to acquire new ideas and skills, even though one is ending a given activity. Therefore this card indicates both motivated work and inspired experimentation in the circumstances in which one finds oneself. It indicates taking concrete measures to work toward a goal, and acquiring a knowledge of new things in the process.

EIGHT OF CUPS
(*Yin*)

A man is walking away from eight full beakers. These upright beakers symbolize an existing situation in the emotional field. This can be a relationship, but equally feelings concerning oneself or concerning one's work. Although the beakers stand for a concrete situation, the man has turned his back on them and is striding away. Here eight is exhibited as a fixed and possibly even a fossilized form, which has already provoked a response. But there is certainly no new situation. That would not come within the purview of eight; at most, eight leads to completion, and the choice of a starting point for something new. In the Eight of Cups, an old emotional situation is left behind: therefore the card often has to do with saying goodbye (for example, on retirement). The new is still unknown; so the Eight of Cups also often speaks to us of emotional insecurity, or of the feeling that we do not know exactly what we want. We should be careful not to ignore our feelings.

Nine

JUST AS THE ANCIENT Egyptians had four pairs of gods and goddesses, a set of eight divinities, so the number nine figured in their divine world. For example, there was a god who stood at the head of eight other gods, again divided into pairs of four, each with its own meaning as a variation on the theme of yin or yang.

Now, in the East, five is often seen as the number of an element additional to the four elements known in the West, and space, too, is expressed by the number five, because the four points of the compass surround a center. In the same way nine is regarded in the East as eight plus the center (for instance, the eight approach roads and the heart of Beijing). Thus nine is eight with a center, but at the same time it has its own meaning as 3 x 3.

Whereas three indicates a process that strives to become realized in matter, the realization is not so apparent in nine. It seems that the process, itself, is more strongly emphasized in nine; which is why Bindel describes it as the number of ups and downs, of depths and heights.[6] He links it with the concept that expulsion from paradise is a fall into the depths, out of which we have to emerge by our own efforts. Nine represents both the fall and the scrambling up.

In the Middle Ages, nine used to be known as the number of the Holy Spirit. On examining symbolic expressions in individual dreams, doodles, and fantasies, our attention is attracted by several features. Sometimes the number nine seems to point in the direction of a synthesis: our situation is gotten into perspective, we are able to call a halt for a moment and then to start doing something productive. So there is a certain stability here but movement, too (nine as 4 + 5?). This looks very like eight directions plus their center.

In dreams, nine seems to be more connected with a movement that is pursued very strongly in one direction, yet without a goal: is this nine as 3 x 3? Here the movement of nine to the depths or the heights seems to be prominent, also the turning point from low to high and vice versa. Thus nine appears to be open to various interpretations.

NINE OF WANDS
(*Yang*)

The card shows a wary man with a belligerent attitude, which has already earned him a broken head. Nine emerges here as a movement that is too much in one direction: that of springing into action and starting a fight without considering that other responses may be possible. The card can refer to past setbacks that have increased our distrust. This card alerts us to the danger of continuing to react too one-sidedly, and so to invite problems. The turning point comes with the cultivation of an open mind and a willingness to let the past rest.

---

6. Ernst Bindel, *Die Geistigen Grundlagen der Zahlen*, p. 242.

NINE OF SWORDS
(Yang)

Once again nine seems to be carrying us too far in one direction. Now thinking and the intellect are involved—which results in a state of depression. Fears and negative thoughts are constantly lurking in the background, and symbolize a depth that seems fathomless. The fear can cause you to clutch at any small piece of security, even if this is negative. The worst is over when you are prepared to be open to life once more, and to permit obsessive thoughts to flow away, instead of being swayed by them. It is essential to refashion your thoughts in order to be able to ascend the way of return, which is something else the number nine represents.

NINE OF PENTACLES
(Yin)

Here we have enjoyment in plenty. Nine is clearly at a high point; the individual depicted is in harmony with nature, is self-satisfied, and is successful in Pentacle affairs, yet has both feet on the ground. A meaning of nine in which the center function comes to the fore. The picture shows us the Pentacles in a group of six—a cycle has been completed, and a group of three—movement. There is rest and movement; there is wholeness without stagnation. No wonder this card is always highly prized.

NINE OF CUPS
(Yin)

In this nine card, too, enjoyment is prominent. But the situation is less serene and unassuming than in the Pentacles. In the Nine of Pentacles, there is a natural connection with the Earth and with all that lives, whereas the Nine of Cups personage is sitting luxuriously in a garment of animal skin. This is also a nine at its high point, but with the danger of easily becoming rather superficial and interested only in pleasure-seeking. Emotional fulfillment is also very compatible with the Nine of Cups: not for nothing has it been called the "nine months card"!

It is striking that the yang cards chiefly show nine at its low point, Swords more deeply than Wands, and the yin cards chiefly show nine at its high point, Pentacles more so than Cups. So the two polarities are associated with the number in very different ways.

Ten

NUMEROLOGICALLY, TEN is 1 and 0, and the 1 is often treated as male and the 0 as female. Therefore, it is not surprising that ten, even in dreams, is liable to appear in connection with marriage and/or cohabitation. Paneth refers to ten as 2 x 5, and to its significance as an erotic relationship (five) that has resulted in a fixed union. This creates a new tension field, two being a number indicating polarity, which is why some writers ascribe to ten not only marriage, but also a form of disillusionment, as far as romance is concerned.

Ten is also regarded as a heightened or accentuated one. I have observed on more than one occasion that, in dreams, a number appears to carry greater weight when it has one or more zeros behind it. Thus 1000 may very well say we have a number-one type situation here which is very, very important.

One is a number without which no other number can exist. Ten, on the other hand, does not have this quality. It stands for the "ten in the one" or the integration of qualities.

But ten conveys something additional. One is a single great potential force, but this force can unfold only by developing via other numbers. Thus ten consists of a one that has been able to contact its power. That is why the tens in the Minor Arcana are free to exhibit the full meanings of the given suits.

The idea of ten forming a single whole is seen, for example, in the ten Sephiroth of the Kabbalah, the Ten Commandments in the Bible, and our own ten fingers and ten toes. Looking now at ten on the cards of the Minor Arcana we see the following.

TEN OF WANDS
(Yang)

This card depicts a man who is carrying ten heavy poles (in a way that will surely cause him back problems). In this ten card, the Wands, representing actions and transactions, remind us that if we try to do everything in a rush, we shall have to suffer the consequences. Acting on the spur of the moment is the fun side of Wands; but in the end, the little matter of perseverance always raises its head. The Ten of Wands asks us to stop and examine our dealings and activities, and to reorganize them in the interests of greater efficiency. We need to discover how much we can cope with. We are at the stage where everything is starting to get out of control; it is a time for revision. We see here that the power of action in Wands, insofar as it is potentially present, has completely embodied itself in form in the ten: it confronts us with all our actions. The purpose in the Rider-Waite deck seems to be to represent the positive side as a by-product: results and proficiency will not be obtained until there has been some reorganization. The "marriage aspect" of ten can appear in the connection between ourselves and our activities: there is our involvement in them but also a certain disenchantment due to the confrontation with the attendant responsibilities.

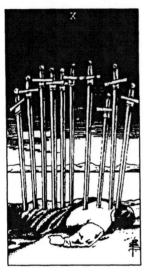

TEN OF SWORDS
(*Yang*)

The Ten of Swords shows the irrevocable end of something. It is stern and inexorable. That is why this card is associated with very hard experiences. Here the highly intellectual and mentally-oriented Swords can carry the risk that all emotion and all humanity will disappear, with life being channeled into logic, statistics, rationality, and the like. Ten swords sticking out of a dead body illustrate this form of behavior run to excess. Thus, in the Ten of Swords, we have the culmination of our reasoning powers but, at the same time, such a rigorous application of them that we really must change. On the card, day is already breaking. Nevertheless, the Ten of Swords warns us not to cut off all situations too sharply, too uncompromisingly, or too violently, for the card is saying that we are overlooking promising things, or that we are being so cold and suspicious that we have already shown the door to what might have benefited us. Ten as a form of union is encountered indirectly here in the need to reach out to the life outside us again. In Swords, the culmination of ten is very negative.

TEN OF PENTACLES
(*Yin*)

From the way in which it has been designed for the Rider-Waite deck, the Ten of Pentacles stands out as an important card in many respects. Here we see ten as the total culmination of all the good of Pentacles, but equally, there is a spiritual dimension in it: the

Pentacles are grouped in accordance with the Kabbalistic Tree of Life. You can be yourself in an uncomplicated way, and can enjoy life as it is, genuine and unadorned. Earthly pleasures can be tasted and enjoyed, and union with the All is part of the delight. Matter (Pentacles) and spirituality are walking hand in hand. Ten as marriage expresses itself here as an association between humanity and matter, not in a slavish hedonistic or covetous way, but freely. The Ten of Pentacles allows us to enjoy life to the full.

TEN OF CUPS
(Yin)

This card represents great emotional peace and security, the fulfillment, so it would appear, of our bond with life. The ten beakers in the rainbow impart a spiritual dimension to this card: they depict fulfillment without great egotistical desires or impulses. You accept yourself and others for what you are. However difficult your circumstances may be, the card indicates that everything is going to be fine emotionally (Cups!) and that your experience of life is developing very positively on all fronts.

THERE IS A GREAT difference in interpretation between the yang tens and the yin tens. It is obvious that the Rider-Waite deck treats the yang pole as a problem area, while the yin pole is almost euphoric. In the yin tens, the chance of disillusionment inherent in ten is altogether missing, whereas in the yang tens, we literally bend under its weight.

Although this deck came out in 1910, at a time when society took the view that hard work combined with ongoing developments in the (so-called rational) sciences would eventually solve all the world's problems, the Rider-Waite deck was already giving the lie to this belief.

Perhaps the heavy emphasis on the yin cards, the cards that invite us to get stuck into life, to enjoy ourselves, to express our feelings, and to give the irrational a place, was a reaction—conscious or otherwise—of the Rider-Waite deck to the current trend. For if we run through the whole series, we see that the higher we rise in the yang cards, the bigger is the helping served up of their problematical side, but this is less true of the yin cards.

Now, for centuries, the intuitive, the idea of "going with the flow," of "just being," has been forgotten or consigned to the background. In his deck, Waite showed how important these qualities are for us if our balance is to be restored.

In this respect, the Rider-Waite deck is the tarot for today. Maybe, in centuries to come, a number of cards of the Minor Arcana will have to be given some small symbolic additions. However, for our own day and age they are very applicable. Doing, willing, intervening, and reasoning are activities that are often dreadfully overdone in our society, and we seem to be pitifully ignorant of it.

Frequently we are incapable of seeing that a problem can be solved by approaching it in a different spirit, or by simply doing nothing—called by the Chinese *wu wei* (doing by not doing). That is the value of yin, and Waite was very much aware of it.

Therefore the higher yang cards can imply positive developments provided we are conscious of the fact that the society in which our lot is cast can so stimulate and incite us that we are inclined to overdo the yang side of things.

Chapter Six

THE COURT CARDS OF THE MINOR ARCANA

THE ORDINARY DECK of playing cards has three court cards—the King, Queen, and Knave (or Jack). The Minor Arcana has four: the Page, Knight, Queen, and King. Each of these picture cards has its own meaning, which adds to the significance of the suits of the Minor Arcana. We shall look first at the court cards, themselves, and then at what they mean in Wands, Swords, Pentacles, and Cups.

The four court cards may be regarded as a series that increases in importance. The Page, or shield-bearer, is the youngest and least significant member of the court; the Knight is a warrior, with a sense of honor and a need to prove himself; the Queen is the wife of the most powerful man in the court and creates its warmth and social atmosphere; and the King is the final power and authority.

Seen in this light, the Page might be expected to impart the most animated and playful mood to the four suits, and the King the most responsible and severe. And, in fact, this is borne out in practice to some extent. But there is another light in which the picture cards can be seen. Therefore, in what follows, we shall split them up in a way that really amounts to the polarity of yin and yang.

In the case of the court cards, yin indicates liveliness and acceptance. Not proving oneself and fighting—spasmodically or otherwise—but assimilating, approving, going along with, and welcoming the new, and integrating it. Yin moves and bends with whatever comes on its path, but without losing itself. In a positive sense, yin displays directness and involvement. It stands in a relationship with others or with a partner. In a negative sense, superficiality and sheer lack of involvement come into play, and there is no fixed goal.

Yang sets is sights on things, and will fight and take action. It does not let matters rest, but will organize and, preferably, manage them. Yang will not tag along behind others, but wants to be the prime mover, or to make others do the bending. In a positive sense, yang can achieve much and can kick things into shape. In a negative sense, it causes an unnecessary stir and spoils the atmosphere because it has no feeling for it.

The two court cards that are receptive to the world are the Page and the Queen. We shall not go far wrong if we call these yin. The court cards that tend to be controlling and active, which we can call yang, are the Knight and the King.

Page and Queen as Yin

THE PAGE IS STILL too young and too inexperienced to be able to govern or even to wish to do so. He is often seen as a child, with both the positive and negative sides of childhood. A child can unrestrainedly enter into whatever it encounters; which is why Page cards traditionally have to do with fresh opportunities, and then mainly with the readiness or need to be open to them. Just as a child, absorbed in play, does not observe the tensions and problems around it, so the Page, due to an unconscious involvement in pleasant things that arises from being fun-loving and full of childish curiosity, is still capable of uninhibited enjoyment, and is frequently not even aware that there are any obligations.

Of these two yin court cards, the Queen displays the adult and more experienced side. It is she who expresses a given suit of the Minor Arcana in a concerned and warm way, for she shows love for the theme of the suit in her environment. She takes responsibility for it in a yin manner: she creates a good atmosphere and positive conditions, she provides for participation and gives incentives, and yet remains in all these circumstances wholly herself. And she can be playful when she wants to be, because that facet is a part of yin.

Knight and King as Yang

JUST AS THE PAGE is the youngest representative of the court cards, so the Knight is of the yang cards. In comparison with the King he is still inexperienced and insecure, and therefore unstable. This gives a noteworthy combination of a love of action, pugnacity, and some bravery, but at the same time a measure of self-doubt which has to be hidden behind a mask of apparent self-assurance. Therefore the Knights can sometimes be harder than necessary, in order to look valiant and to keep control of themselves and of the things around them. They can do much good with their forcefulness, energy, and dedication, but their activities easily get out of hand. So the Knight cards warn us to take care.

The King, in contrast, has a maturity that makes him calm and controlled. He defends social values, and is able to keep order by his level-headedness and judgment, by his government and legislation. He bears very substantial responsibility and has the power to go with it. His authority and ability confer respect on him, so he does not have to fight so hard for attention or esteem. However, he runs the risk of becoming used to his high position. The King has the most composure of the four court cards, and therefore the least spontaneity.

Thus, in both yin and yang, one sees a division into not-fully-grown and adult, into youthful rashness and maturity. The immaturity of the Pages is shown in their lack of concern (yin), that of the Knights in their quick temper and hasty action (yang). The maturity of the Queens lies in the knowledge that things have to be relinquished and let go in love, that of the Kings lies in the knowledge that things have to be led, directed, and regulated harmoniously.

In interpretation, court cards can stand for actual people, in which case, they describe the characters of these individuals as well as the atmosphere or circumstances for which they are responsible in the context of the query. On top of that, these cards often represent a certain facet or striking piece of behavior of ours, or behavior that is necessary in a given context. How one reads it is extremely dependent on the position of the card in the layout.

The Pages

PAGE OF WANDS
(*Yang*)

The Page of Wands is the childish innocence that seizes opportunities with both
hands. As an action card, Wands produces plenty of movement, but the Page
of Wands is inclined to try anything anyway. This card often has to do with fresh
initiatives, which can arise both internally and externally. There is also a very
uncomplicated and pleasant tone about
it. Enjoying being busy and the impression of still having plenty of scope is a
Page of Wands feeling. Initiatives are
taken with a childlike joy, straightforwardly, and with no ulterior motives.
The card can also represent young or old people whose behavior is
of this type. Due to the activity natural to Wands, one often sees
much chopping and changing in people represented by this card.

PAGE OF SWORDS
(*Yang*)

The Page of Swords is brandishing a
sword that he has not yet learned how to
use properly. What the card is warning
against is mistakes caused by rashness
and jumping to conclusions, when
impulsive thinking leads us to react very
clumsily and abruptly. Although this
Page is presented with new options and
chances, he is cutting them down by
carelessly swinging his sword (in other
words, by impetuosity and obtuseness).
Therefore, he will soon be on his own,
and this will throw him back on his own
mental resources, and create problems in
the formation and maintenance of gen-

uine contacts and attachments. Take care that your mental restlessness does not lead to suspicion and mistrust! The Page of Swords is the only Page who is not looking at his suit symbol. His gaze is averted from the sword, and this is meant to caution us against being remote and defensive.

THE PAGE OF PENTACLES
(Yin)

PAGE of PENTACLES

The Page of Pentacles card possesses a measure of duality. The cheerful and naive impressionability of the Page is not wholly in keeping with the more materialistic Pentacle. The Page of Pentacles symbolizes fresh opportunities on the material plane, usually in the form of a task, activity, or job involving some responsibility. Just dive into it, if only for the thrill of having something to do, and do not worry about the end result. You will find that everything runs like clockwork. Be like a child at play—eager and absorbed. Receive what comes on your path and relate to it—the yin attitude!

THE PAGE OF CUPS
(Yin)

PAGE of CUPS.

The Page of Cups is still living, to some extent, in the world of inner images, dreams, and fantasy. Many creative ideas can spring from these, but because of his youthfulness, the Page of Cups is still not always aware that he can, or even must, do something with them. The problem of the Page of Cups lies in the area of self-realization; but, at the same time, there are unsuspected possibilities in the very same area. Through his sensitivity to the world of the unconscious, paranormal gifts of one sort or another can reveal themselves. The Page of Cups is still open to the world of the intuitive. New opportunities in the domain of the feelings, and of unconscious manifestation, are all part of this card.

The Knights

KNIGHT of WANDS.

THE KNIGHT OF WANDS
(Yang)

The Knight of Wands wants to blurt out whatever enters his head. He is characterized by impatience and a love of action, with the danger of "act first and think later." His impatience leads to aggressive insistence in the face of any protests or criticisms, or to a cross-grained redoubling of his efforts to have his own way. The Knight of Wands can achieve much and can break out of many stagnant situations, but runs the risk of needlessly losing a great deal of energy by rushing matters, by being a bad listener, or by failing to think things through. This is a card of energetic movement, which can convey warmth, but it can easily go too far.

THE KNIGHT OF SWORDS
(Yang)

Of the four knights, the Knight of Swords is the most fierce, most aggressive, and the most militant. Through the association of Swords with the mental world, this card is associated with hard words, quarrels, jeering, disparaging remarks, and all the other verbal expressions that cause bad blood between people and evince aloofness, incompatibility, mistrust, etc. This card also warns against hot-headedness, sudden fits of anger, and a readiness to take offense without considering whether there is any justification for doing so. Traditionally, the Knight of Swords signifies conflict. With favorable cards around it, it can represent the quarrel that brings relief, but be careful. In commercial life, it represents the hard-boiled approach that undermines one's competitors. Statistics and balance sheets are the sole criteria; humanity in any shape or form does not enter the picture. With the Knight of Swords, we run the risk that "setting things right" will be handled one-sidedly and insensitively.

KNIGHT of SWORDS.

THE KNIGHT OF PENTACLES
(Yin)

Of all the knights, the Knight of Pentacles is the only one sitting still on his horse. Every so often, Pentacles are in no hurry; but the Knight cards are typically reckless and boisterous, so there is a certain amount of tension in this card. In any case, it is not easy to ride with this large coin or pentacle in one's hand, which is why the Knight of Pentacles has acquired the significance of caution. What is more, the yin theme does not go well with the concept of knighthood, so belligerence and violence are not conspicuous in the Knight of

KNIGHT of PENTACLES

Pentacles. He does have the excess of energy of the knights, and can deploy it and translate it into hard work at a moment's notice. He is also capable of perseverance. But the reining in of the horse and the natural reserve of the Pentacles turns him into a conservative knight, with little vision for the future. Thus, the yin theme is converted into a measure of passivity.

KNIGHT of CUPS.

THE KNIGHT OF CUPS
(Yin)

The Knight of Cups is riding a less spirited horse than those on the yang cards (the Knight of Wands and the Knight of Swords), but his mount is more animated that the one belonging to the Knight of Pentacles. With the chalice in his hand, he is fighting for an ideal or sentiment, or is proclaiming it. Yet it is uncertain or unrealistic, because the knight cards often lack composure, and fail to take an overall view. Perhaps, with a certain amount of awkwardness, this knight can convey feelings, help to create a pleasant atmosphere, and possibly go on a quest. Apart from their connection with the emotions, Cups frequently have to do with the world of the irrational. The armor and the link with the irrational seem to be in conflict. So there is tension in this card. However, whenever the conditions are right, this knight can actively help to reach greater depths in the psyche.

The Queens

THE QUEEN OF WANDS
(Yang)

The Queen of Wands combines receptivity (yin) with independence and activity (Wands); so it is not very easy to interpret. In a positive sense, she knows what she wants, and she translates it into deeds in which sincerity and involvement are her great qualities. Wands also stand for the need to be someone, and the Queen of Wands is no stranger to the desire for attention. Her penchant for getting involved, and her natural activity, often result in fiery enthusiasm, which she is mature enough to keep within bounds, however. Thus the Queen of Wands provides a powerful stimulus to action.

THE QUEEN OF SWORDS
(Yang)

The Queen of Swords is a card that combines receptivity (yin) and determination, as a consequence of comprehension and insight (Swords). Because of her power of discrimination, the Queen of Swords has an outstanding ability to pass judgment, and although she may seem somewhat aloof, she is closely involved in the things that occupy her mind. Her analytical powers are not employed on dead statistics, but are occupied with life and humanity. The maturity of the Queen of Swords involves recognition of the necessity of learning through slips and recoveries: in this card, unavoidable difficulties have been passed through and independence has become an ally of wisdom.

QUEEN☆PENTACLES

THE QUEEN OF PENTACLES
(Yin)

The Queen of Pentacles represents complete absorption in the good things of the earth and the ability to enjoy them with restraint. Here there is no luxurious indulgence, but an honest heart in tune with nature and life, and the taking of what may be enjoyed without harming others. Indeed the Queen of Pentacles is in a very good position to share her riches with others. She is a warm and involved stimulus to everyone, and helps us bring out our creativity and use it in a positive manner. The material aspect of Pentacles, plus the mature involvement of the Queen, automatically creates an image of daring to be oneself without harming others, of enjoying life in all its facets, and of respect for nature. Pentacles, as a yin theme have a modest side, which is why the Queen of Pentacles can display great cheerfulness, but is certainly not excessively exuberant. She also has a serious and introverted side.

THE QUEEN OF CUPS
(Yin)

The Queen of Cups enjoys a mature relationship with the depths of her soul, her feelings, her intuition, and her irrational side, without expressing this in unpredictability and caprice. Her strong point lies in being immersed in life (as Queen) while remaining open to the forces of the unconscious (the Cup). She knows what she wants because she understands these unconscious forces, and therefore reacts with great emotional sensitivity and harmony to herself and the outer world. The emotional side gives her the capacity to care for others, or to see that they are doing well. The quiet side of Cups, and the fact that the queens belong to the yin pole, gives the Queen of Cups a rather introverted, calm, abstracted quality, which sometimes seems rather passive, but is intended to give her space without losing herself. Because she is in touch with her feelings, she can, as queen, sense what her subjects need, and can therefore be a unifying, stimulating, and even spiritual factor.

QUEEN of CUPS.

The Kings

THE KING OF WANDS
(Yang)

The King of Wands is a card that expresses deliberate action. The turbulent Wands, which want to do everything, are held in check here without losing their élan. Therefore a calm but deep enthusiasm can emanate from the King of Wands that is very stimulating. The king does have to keep a grip on the process because Wands are inclined to shy away from pressure or control: they need space for deployment. The king provides more than enough of this, but he understands that there has to be a certain amount of structure, order, and responsibility. The state of tension between the two things is no problem, as long as

KING of WANDS

there is enthusiasm. However, organization and enthusiasm have the drawback that one can thunder at others without realizing what one is doing. Thus the King of Wands, who has the power in his hands, can unintentionally be too interfering and can become self-willed. The yang side tends to become obtrusive when combined with the active Wands.

KING of SWORDS.

THE KING OF SWORDS
(*Yang*)

The King of Swords combines a mature mental and intellectual capacity with the urge (yang) to do something with it in the outside world. Owing to his authority and his elevated station, a mental power struggle, or war of words, can easily break out. Lucid but also cold (often out of a fear of emotionalism), he can revel in ideas and insights, make plans and elaborate proposals, some of which are tinged with self-interest; but, because of his regal maturity, his ideas are often well-founded and very worthwhile. He is an outstanding researcher, who effortlessly locates and corrects faults, and who knows how to put each fact in place, but he runs the risk of grossly underrating psychic (of the psyche) facts in the realm of feelings and intuition, so his intellectual approach gives the impression of being sterile or frozen.

THE KING OF PENTACLES
(*Yin*)

The King of Pentacles has an outstanding ability to perpetuate or improve an existing situation. He has a sharp eye for what is necessary in substance (Pentacles is realistic) and can give a wise and experienced lead. He is in a position to carry out his policy in a powerful (yang), yet conservative and prudent way (Pentacles), and to take pleasure in it. Pentacles is very much connected with the capacity for enjoying what the earth and life have to offer, and the King of Pentacles does make sure of his opportunities on this plane. At the same time, he is wise enough not to do so at the expense of others: the more yin-oriented Pentacles are responsive to others. Therefore the King of Pentacles is a card that is valued for a good and appropriate use of skill without a loss of humanity, and for giving guidance without going on a power-trip.

THE KING OF CUPS
(Yin)

The King of Cups presents us with a paradox. A mature and wise king is sitting on his throne, and others are looking to him for energetic leadership. Yet, this same king is very much involved in the world of feelings and is receptive to what is unnameable and inexpressible. In the eyes of "doers" he is rather impotent, and the King of Cups is actually the least organized and least structured of all the kings. But he is also the most intuitive, and is prepared to act on the basis of inner norms and deeply rooted feelings, which means that every once in a while

he is not always business-like! He is involved in life, has a spiritual dimension, and is not quite sure what to do with his authority. His intuitive ability can be serviceable to his subjects, because he realizes the direction in which society, the nation, and life are developing. He perceives hidden trends and is able to come to terms with them.

WE HAVE SEEN ABOVE how the yang-yin tension works in the cards. If a card naturally has a yin coloration, as do Pentacles and Cups, this involves the yang characters in some difficulty. The knights and queens do not get on so well in the yang cards, Wands and Swords, as their counterparts do. Conversely, a certain paradox is produced when the yin characters (pages and queens) have to express themselves against a yang background. When making interpretations in practice, one should be aware of this underlying tension-field, for it can explain a great deal about what is currently going on in your circumstances or your personality.

Chapter Seven

INTERPRETING THE
MAJOR ARCANA

A S WE HAVE ALREADY seen in chapter 4, the Major Arcana represent the Way of the Hero in each of us. Each card stands for a
specific psychological drive, with its attendant possibilities and external circumstances. In themselves, these drives are neutral. They perform an important function in our personal development, but it is our
ego or "I" that has to take up each drive and understand and shape it
within the limits of the given circumstances and demands of the time
in which that ego finds itself. These factors are not always self-evident.

When, for example, there is an inner impulse to conclude a certain phase of life because one's psyche is taking a new direction, this
may well express itself in an increasing disinclination for work, or for
other things that have so far been regarded as important. This
becomes a problem when the impulse occurs at the moment when
promotion is in the offing, a promotion that will entail greater
responsibility and more commitment to the workaday routine than
one's deepest psyche thinks is good. So there are choices to be made,
and sometimes it seems as if inner needs and drives are at odds with
one's role in society and the outside world.

When a drive makes itself felt like this, the time has come to aim
at fresh targets that are well within reach. Even if these are ignored,
the drives themselves cannot be entirely repressed or suppressed.
They burrow away in the unconscious until The Fool seizes them
and brings them back to the surface. A drive is by way of being a
comrade, a helper dispatched by the unconscious to bring the conscious into line with (or to keep it in line with) the total psyche. It is

sensible to walk side by side with this companion to learn what it can teach and where it points.

However, the cards themselves do not hold the secret of how we will respond to these drives. The cards do no more than convey the broad potential.

Each card of the Major Arcana has creative and destructive sides. We can become locked, so to speak, into a drive, so that what is initially creative stagnates, and turns into a force that opposes the original aim.

Take Temperance, for example: if you have regained your inner composure after a crisis that essentially changed you, you will experience this as decidedly pleasant. The trouble is now in the past, and you feel that you are in control again. You observe that you are less uptight than before, and find it easier to adopt a relaxed attitude toward yourself and others. This is a marvelous situation in which to recruit the forces needed for an advance. You are not dissipating your energies in big frustrations, or in too many activities. But this phase is short. It is an intermediate phase on the way to the next development.

The next development, however, can be held up if you allow your state of rest and tranquillity to persuade you that you have arrived. You may affect a friendly, all-knowing attitude, which is really a flight from emotional involvement in life. Temperance should be a help in rearranging one's life, but in its destructive aspect it encourages us to keep taking things easy. If the stagnation deepens, the consequences for yourself and others can be very unpleasant.

Taken together, the cards of the Major Arcana form a grand cycle. We go through this cycle several times in our lives. Although the sequence of the Major Arcana presents a clear pattern of inner development, we see that in the course of our continuing development, cards or psychic conditions can "miss a step" and can also jump backward and forward through the deck. This has absolutely nothing to do with progress or decline; quite the reverse. We must realize that although the order of the cards in the Major Arcana is archetypal, developments and events unfold in a unique manner, and also in their own order in each individual. The usual order remains the fundamental pattern and continues to be active in the background.

Thus you cannot say that you are "ready" even with the last card, The World. New dynamics are activated by your new attitude to life, and various drives (depicted by the cards) will re-enter and

become part of your new attitude, so that there is a further development of their theme.

In the following description of the cards of the Major Arcana,
the main emphasis will be placed on the psychological dynamics. We
shall be asking: what drive is represented by a card? What is the best
attitude to adopt? How should we handle these dynamics, and what
are the dangers when it becomes routine?

THE FOOL—CARD 0

The Fool stands for our deep-seated
urge to become a fully-fledged individual
and to cultivate our gifts and talents, an
urge that causes us to make radical decisions and prompts us to develop. The
Fool is best regarded as a sort of life-
force, buried deep inside us, which continually encourages us to undertake self-
development. The Fool is not concerned
with the question of whether or not this
development fits in with our culture or
society: he is the life-force that tries to
make things work out in a way that will
benefit our psychic development and
produce a feeling of wholeness.

In Jungian terms we can say that The Fool is restricted to being
a motor behind the individuation process. The Fool is the absolute
beginning of everything, even before there is anything palpable. The
Fool seems to be drowsing inside us, but is definitely not asleep.
Whenever we are in danger of becoming too one-sided, or when
inwardly we are accepting fresh challenges (not "for kicks," but in
the service of our psychic growth), The Fool intervenes. He has prepared our feelings of unrest and has slowly made us ready for change;
unobserved, he has already been hard at work. If you are in the habit
of paying attention to signals from your unconscious, such as dreams,
fantasies, doodles, emotions, etc., you may have already realized that
something has been going on. You have found new interests, are
unsettled and looking for something, without perhaps being able to

put your finger on what is unsatisfactory in your daily life. You experience frequent spells of vague unrest, uncertainty, or unease.

It is The Fool that provides the stimulus, but then he disappears, leaving you to proceed with other instruments at your disposal. One of the most important demands of The Fool is that you live life. That is to say, you do not rely on book knowledge, but acquire knowledge through experience of all sorts, both agreeable and disagreeable. Thus The Fool is purely impulsive and does not pass judgment. This can mean that The Fool in you maneuvers you into the most complicated situations, or into emotional circumstances that are hard to assess.

Our conscious mind can pass judgment and say, "That is no good." The Fool simply says, "Be content to experience it and to profit by it! Live it and feel it. Nothing is bad, and everything I bring is usable." For The Fool is a factor that does not pass verdicts and, above all, has no guilt feelings. This traveler takes us onto unfamiliar ground and asks us to use our creativity directly, without recourse to finesse.

When The Fool turns up in a spread, he invites us to have an open and fresh outlook on life: not stopping to calculate the profit, not asking if we stand a good chance of success, not being afraid of loss. And that is often more difficult than we think. As a matter of fact, The Fool is chaos, in which the germ of form is present, but unseen, all along. He is like a wet bar of soap, which so easily slips out of our hands. You cannot hold onto him; he is entirely dynamic.

But when you turn up The Fool in practice, it is best to alter or adjust your attitude and behavior in such a way that you cheerfully and confidently welcome further developments, allow scope for your original ideas, and do not suppress your spontaneity. Openness to life is very important to The Fool. With The Fool's attitude, it is not to be expected that everything will run like clockwork. Naturally, what happens will be good, but what the uncritical Fool regards as "good" is not necessarily our own idea of "good." The Fool may think it advisable to send you on some escapade that lands you in trouble; but, through this experience, you reach the point of departure for further progress.

The Fool often signifies a hard way, with risks and paradoxical situations. Do not let that worry you; it is all part of your own internal dynamics, which is aiming at nothing else than the development of your potential. However, if you remain at this stage too long, you run the risk of reacting like a maladjusted eccentric, or like a child who will not (or cannot) take any responsibility. Then you will seek controversy for controversy's sake, will go along impulsively with the silliest things under the false impression that everything you encounter is "meant," and will be thoroughly rash and unthinking. You will no longer be aware of the fact that it is the "I" that is supposed to make our decisions, and that it is free to say yes or no to whatever happens to be on offer.

By acting rashly, you can harm others, and childishness can often make you quite unintentionally very demanding, or very determined to get your own way. Everyone has to dance to your whimsical tune, stay on their toes, and keep an eye open for your heedless and capricious reactions, which are no longer an expression of creativity, but of impropriety and a lack of readiness to go through genuine experiences.

Whereas the creative Fool wants to taste and feel life in order to make further progress, the silly Fool clowns around, skipping here and there to avoid involvement. Sooner or later the "real" Fool will cut the ground from under all this side-stepping, but that often makes one feel that one is falling into the abyss.

When The Fool occurs in a layout, its position shows where far-reaching developments can occur; sometimes it means the imminent start of a whole new life.

THE MAGICIAN—CARD 1

THE MAGICIAN.

When the impulse of The Fool makes itself felt, there is a desire to do something about it and to give it a direction. You feel that you must take action; often you long to tackle all sorts of things. You set your goals according to what is welling out of you, and may have found new interests. You set to work.

Thus The Magician indicates making an active start and doing something. However this start is still so embryonic that all possible activities fall within its ambit. It will not necessarily be visible to the outside world. Thus The Magician can be silently ferreting things out and laying plans. His brain is working at top speed, but others do not (yet) see anything to show for it. In general, he can also engage in research purely for its own sake. He is inquisitive and wants to understand the world and life—if evidence is needed for this statement, one has only to look at his table!

But The Magician can also visibly step into the world in order to lay his plans before others, before civil authorities and the like, and to take the first steps on the path of realization. Apart from that, The Magician, himself, is not really interested in the outside world, which takes second place to his impulse to work at what he feels is important.

Inherently, The Magician represents making a tangible start, and although there is much that is chaotic left over from The Fool, The Magician in us no longer experiences everything as disorganized. On the contrary, he forms the direction in which further development will take place. The pure active principle certainly possesses resolve, but this is not necessarily the same as perseverance. It is simply an expression of involvement, enthusiasm, and a love of activity. The Magician does have an objective, but not a clear-cut goal to be achieved by meticulous planning. He has a vision or ideal to which he is devoted, and on which he expends his energies.

Hence The Magician possesses both flexibility and courage, and his vitality makes him want to do something worthwhile. He is not put out by reverses: they motivate him to try another approach. His courage is not a matter of being ready to take big risks, but of daring to stand up for what he feels is important. This combination of involvement, application, activity, and the urge to keep busy is often a good augur of success. Therefore this card is generally seen as promising victory.

If you dwell too long at the stage of The Magician, the danger is that you will become too active, and engage in activity for activity's sake. Your aims and inner motivation gradually disappear, and what remains is an individual who is in a constant mad rush and who behaves toward others like a slave-driver. His motivating power degenerates into harrying and restlessness, his enthusiasm becomes coercive behavior. The natural freshness and cheerfulness of this card are gone, and what is left is a nagger. As long as this state of affairs lasts, set-backs are bound to happen, and you will blame others and waste a lot of energy disparaging them, working against them and mistreating them. Whereas the true Magician has an aim or ideal with which he can whole-heartedly identify, the false Magician makes a goal out of himself and manipulates others or forces them to identify with him. The consequence is a negative egocentric attitude, which others can find intimidating. For what remains is the strong yang function: action! Sometimes the negative Magician overdoes things because he doubts his own sense of purpose. In other words, he overcompensates in order to hide his blockages and aimlessness from himself. He gives the impression of being very frantic, whereas the true Magician seems bubbly and flexible. The latter lives in the optimistic belief that everything is going according to plan and that he is able to take an active part in it. At the same time, The Magician belongs to the world of pure deed and pure action: the undiluted yang principle.

THE HIGH PRIESTESS—CARD II

The enormous vitality, love of action, and animation of The Magician find their necessary counterpart in The High Priestess. Just as our heartbeat alternates between movement and rest, so The Magician's love of activity can forfeit the right to exist or to be at variance with itself, when there is no room left for this phase of The High Priestess. She represents our need for complete internalization: an inward-looking that is not based on logic.

The High Priestess withdraws from the outside world and is subdued and passive, receptive and meditative. She is not engaged in any activity and she shows no animation. But she does have a mysterious power of attraction. We feel in her the fathomless depths of our soul, but without being able to put into words what we feel. We also feel in her a remarkable combination of being oneself and of total quiescence, without wanting to get involved. She is apparently will-less and yet possesses a will; apparently lifeless, yet fully dedicated to life.

But the life of The High Priestess exists in the depths, in our unconscious. It is this energy that puts us in touch with a deeper knowledge, intuitive and sometimes paranormal. For The High Priestess herself, this is generally a natural component of her being: in her eyes, the paranormal is nothing special. She represents a deep rest, a great calm, such as may be experienced in sincere prayer or in meditation. By virtue of this stilling of the mind, we can gain a new perspective on ourselves, our lives, and the problems with which we wrestle, and can find solutions—not in the form of cut and dried answers (that is not how The High Priestess works)—but in the form of a fresh, more intuitive, look at things.

We also surrender ourselves to what comes on our path. In social matters, we do not seem to be so useful in The High Priestess phase. We appear to be standing still, to have no burning desire, and to hesitate over something or to be unwilling to do it. Yet underneath all this lies the great strength of The High Priestess: various gifts and talents are maturing in the quietness, and they will come to the surface when another stage arrives (with another card of the Major Arcana).

Much growth and development is occurring, the major part of which is unseen. Often we ourselves are not aware of it. I have observed that many people who have drawn this card have complained of fatigue, and have said that they just felt like sleeping. That is one form of expression, but the tiredness springs not so much from physical problems or from illness as from a "reorganization" of psychic energy in the unconscious to enable them to cope better in the future. If we do not inwardly permit this stage, we shall discover at a later date that we are lacking in power and motivation just when we need them most.

Therefore The High Priestess is a very important yin card, which, sad to say, indicates a process that is pushed aside all too easily in a culture or society oriented toward hurry and achievement. When children draw this card, you often see them going through a period when they very much need to be alone (within the framework of their personality as a whole, of course). They fantasize and daydream a lot, while school work takes second place to their inner world. Adults who draw the card often need to slow down or to have some time off work.

When you definitely enter your inner world and withdraw a little from daily cares (which you will find less important in the phase of The High Priestess), you will be able to experience the feeling of happiness that belongs to this cultivation of calm. You, so to speak, "tank up" on it.

But if the effect is negative, it can mean that you withdraw altogether from a daily life, suspend your activities, go and live in an ivory tower, or isolate yourself in some other way. Those around you no longer understand you, and you understand yourself less and less. The feelings and images you get are no longer the result of a deep union with the pulse of life, but emerge from an extremely subjective experience having little to do with reality.

Whereas in a positive sense The High Priestess, with her closeness to the stream of life, can use the irrational and emotional as instruments to tune into people and situations, in her negative phase she uses her energy to control others through the emotions. She herself no longer does any work, but compels them to do it for her, and thrives on their energy.

At her worst, she is an emotional parasite who manipulates people while she, herself, remains impassive, or else she is an almost hysterical and emotionally unbalanced individual who, at every turn, sows discord in her environment. The mysterious and unfathomable depths of The High Priestess display here a malign magical allure produced by her capriciousness and sympathy-seeking. The above applies to men as well as to women.

In herself, however, The High Priestess tends to unlock for us our rich inner life, our hidden gifts and talents, and the knowledge flowing from our divine source. Through internalization, she indicates how we can draw from this wealthy source without being drowned in it. When this card turns up, try to relax in this field for once; try to be at ease and to occupy yourself with things belonging to the riches of the unconscious.

However, there is no need to remain passive; for each impulse can lead to something being done, even in a refrigerator. Take an interest in expressions of the unconscious, take a nature walk, draw or work with symbols. It makes no difference what you do as long as it is inwardly calming and has no connection with the world of hurry, scurry, and achievement.

THE EMPRESS.

THE EMPRESS—CARD III

When the activity and love of action of The Magician can go hand in hand with the internalization of The High Priestess, and both are free to be themselves, we see that creative capacities, in the form of gifts and talents, are born. They force themselves on our attention and ask to be developed for their own sakes and for the wholeness of the psyche, but not for the sake of respect or money. This upsurge of creativity is depicted by The Empress. Her card indicates that you may surrender completely to the life that streams through you, and that it is important to provide your creativity with an outlet.

The Empress is a very creative card, which is often drawn when the question is not about fame or wealth, but about the practical application of one's abilities. Develop them, occupy yourself with them, dive into them, study them, and above all enjoy using them, enjoy life and do not put yourself under pressure. What is more, The Empress is receptive, just like The High Priestess. She listens to her intuition, her emotions, and to the world of the irrational. But she is not passive—far from it.

The Empress loves life and can become fully absorbed in whatever she is doing; but she can equally take time off to lean back and have a relaxed look around her, in order to draw fresh inspiration during what might seem to be moments of idleness. The Empress is the phase in which our creativity really makes itself felt, sometimes in such a way that it rules our lives and absorbs our time, so that all other activities are put on a back burner, or only the most essential are carried out. However, this creativity is still rather unstructured, although this is not a problem. The happiness felt when you are occupied with the things that really suit you provides sufficient motivation to do more structuring at a later stage. Now it's time to relate to the ideas that bubble up, to the inspirations that rise to the surface. The Empress enters into them with heart and soul, without asking herself where they are leading or, to put it more bluntly, if they are actually leading anywhere.

The Empress, like The High Priestess, is a yin card, and therefore expresses the feminine energy of the cosmos. However it is a big mistake to see yin as nothing but passivity—that is only one aspect of yin. Yin and yang invariably stand in relative association to one another. In contrast to the purposefulness and directness of the activity of yang, yin is more passive and more receptive. But yin is active in her own fashion. She is not directed, but inspired; she does not aim at perfection, but at wholeness. She is not interested in achievement, but in enjoyment and in the feeling of being able to be. All these yin facets are portrayed by The Empress.

When we draw The Empress, the time has come for change and renewal in the sense that it is the right moment to dare to come out with our ideas, plans, and insights. Certainly, our involvement with them and our enthusiasm for them will be quite contagious. The Empress often signals a period of emotional fulfillment, a time when we can enjoy life. The obligations and burdens of everyday life fade in the light of the pleasure given us by our creativity.

If you don't change at this stage, and the energy turns against itself, the danger arises that all you will want to do is to enjoy yourself, and you will not have that feeling of fulfillment that accompanies working at what suits you best. You will lose sight of those things that come from within. The pursuit of pleasure and fun in the restless search for fulfillment can result in losing oneself in greed, sexual excess, and the like. In this way real joy will recede further and further and life will grow hard.

In other cases, I have seen the opposite occur when The Empress becomes stagnant, namely an attitude in which all pleasure and enjoyment is rejected, and the joy of living is regarded as sinful or, because of false guilt feelings, is not permitted. If this attitude becomes more extreme, inner creativity cannot flow freely, and the energy builds up in the unconscious. Like any other drive, it cannot be repressed indefinitely, even though it can be held back for a short time. Now such repressed factors can gradually become destructive.

Thus the negative Empress can hinder others from giving full rein to their creativity. All joy in life is extinguished, and we get crabbiness and complaining instead of a cheerful acceptance of life.

In the least serious cases, I have seen people who have drawn The Empress leave the course for a short time. So much came to the surface that conflicting interests appeared. It was not possible to identify with all of them, and in The Empress the need for emotional involvement is largely unstructured. This quickly led to an overdose of impulses, which were not satisfied, because at every turn these people identified with something for a short while only. In any case, completion is not the aim of The Empress; she lives by her inner impulses and strives for wholeness by developing her talents in a playful way. For her, plunging into the use of these talents is an involuntary and often unconscious goal.

THE EMPEROR.

THE EMPEROR—CARD IV

Active government and intervention with a view to reducing chaos to order, and bringing all sorts of undisciplined impulses into line, is the work of The Emperor. Regularity and arrangement, lucidity and the efficient use of power and energy is his objective. How different this is from The Empress! It is The Emperor who imparts stability to what occupies The Empress, and at the same time he forms her direct opposite. He will have none of the world of the irrational, which is impossible to organize or control! Above all else, he seeks clarity, and this is best obtained from those things that can be categorized in an understandable way. Defining and delimiting for the sake of accuracy, making rules and regulations for oneself and others, giving things structure, drawing up plans, and, in short, every endeavor by which order and precision are created and authority is exercised, belong to the realm of The Emperor.

The Emperor is the yang that introduces a controlling activity into the world, and he is not interested in any form of play.

Whenever you draw The Emperor, you are often in a phase when you have to keep hard at work, must carry out concrete proposals, and have to forego the lighter side of life. Thus The Emperor is not always an easy card—there are no free gifts. You have to work for what you get. Gambling does not pay when The Emperor is around—it falls outside ordinary control and seems not to be usable by this energy. The things that are effective are the accepted instruments for arranging order—research, analysis, and statistics.

In a positive sense, The Emperor is the energy in us that helps give the uncontrolled impulses of The Empress an aim and function. Thanks to The Emperor, her creativity can be employed in a useful way for ourselves and others. As a matter of fact, The Emperor also sorts out the things represented by the other cards. He is down to earth and certainly not spontaneous, so that you cannot approach him with levity, something he will not tolerate.

If you draw this card on behalf of a certain project, you will have to work hard, and need to make sure that you have a well-formulated plan; you should not make a decision until you have carefully weighed the pros and cons. In this way, The Emperor can make situations that are out of hand manageable again, but there are attendant dangers. The greatest danger is that he is inclined to act in a way that dampens or destroys all creativity, all spontaneity and joy.

When this, socially very useful, Emperor turns against himself, he becomes a dry, almost cynical energy that does nothing but obstruct and criticize, with a striking lack of cheerfulness or humor. In his negative form, The Emperor hounds you to achieve a stifling perfection that makes no one happy. He then goes through life being hard on and strict with himself and others; he is very demanding and without any animal spirits or strong attachments, and he judges every person and situation from a stiff and limited outlook. Very little is any good, and nothing is good enough: which means that in his negative form, The Emperor spreads a soured atmosphere around him.

Another negative expression of The Emperor is constant analyzing. New facts crop up on our path at every turn, and these have to be fitted into our conceptual model, which is therefore never clear.

And so The Emperor runs the risk of confining himself to weighing things up without reaching any definite conclusion. Due to his urge to play an active part in controlling and arranging matters, the need for continual reassessment can so frustrate him that all at once he makes a rash decision and creates mayhem.

Whereas originally he is a powerful resource in us for tackling chaos, in his reverse role, he can strengthen this very chaos without even being aware that this is what he is doing. The Emperor does not take kindly to being lectured, so letting him know where he is going wrong is a rather thankless task!

THE HIEROPHANT

THE HIEROPHANT—CARD V

In everyday life we observe a continual alternation between conflicting needs and drives, energies and situations, which create inner turmoil. Choosing is not always easy, but there is an inner energy which can come to our aid. Jung called it our religious function. In old cultures we encounter this function in widespread systems of taboos and religious customs which had to be strictly observed. Any breach of these customs and taboos was punished very severely. In such cases, the community was convinced that the gods or spirits would wreak vengeance on everybody if they did not deal with the offender. But in essence these customs and taboos perform a very important function, by channeling the opposing forces within a group or nation, and forestalling any outright and injurious clash of these. Although the taboos sometimes strike the Westerner as odd, they seem, on closer analysis, not only to play an important role in the group that observes them, but also to give meaning to the existence of the group.

In a certain sense, the Church, and similar institutions in other religions, makes the same provision: a set of rules on a religious basis to govern our actions; actions which, if left to themselves, would be decided by various conflicting impulses and would disrupt the smooth functioning of society. The observance of such rules is the external side of The Hierophant, but strictly speaking this card refers to our inner desire to give meaning to things and to lift our conflicting needs to a higher plane.

As long as, in our own psyche, there is not enough appreciation of, or feeling for, creation, and no sense of oneness with it, this urge easily falls into the precepts of some religious organization. But the ideal is that, out of our inner union, our inner religious sentiment, we adopt a way of life that wrongs no one and shows respect for life in everything we do.

Thus The Hierophant is our desire to experience an extra dimension of life, the feeling that there is something more than just the mundane. This feeling can find expression either within some existing religious community, or in an individual manner. The Hierophant also boosts our morale and our confidence in life.

When you draw this card, you are ready to look at life in a different way. You need to take action that you regard as significant or that gives you moral satisfaction. Often this is because you are now more open to your less attractive sides. The Hierophant is not saying that you are actually coming to terms with your less attractive sides, but with this card you can do penance in the way your religion prescribes in order to ask for forgiveness of your sins, and so on. There are other cards that indicate the fight with your Shadow. With The Hierophant you can certainly become conscious of these aspects and can feel the need to do something with or about them. If you take that initiative when this cards turns up, there is usually a blessing in it.

Entering the haven of some greater and spiritual Whole, such as a religion, can give you the peace of mind from which to make further progress. The security and safety immediately on offer can help you to have faith in life, so you can go on and take responsibility for your deeds and transactions.

However you can also get bogged down in this security, in which case your religion, or religious convictions, become a kind of substitute father or mother for you, a substitute structure of rules by which you abide (the father-image) or the substitute lap to which you can keep returning and which takes pity on you (the mother-image). But you do not assume responsibility for your own activities—what you are taught decides everything. The energy of The Hierophant can then change into a lack of oneness with life, which in turn lacks meaning. It expresses itself in a moralistic attitude, which usually goes hand in hand with hypocrisy. In the worst cases, we see a form of pride that has its source in the conviction that you are holding cosmic, moral, or ethical truth by the right end of the stick and that "therefore" others must be wrong. In this way, all kinds of "isms" are spawned, which are propagated fanatically, becoming very inward-looking and un-cosmic, and eventually are then no more.

Whenever The Hierophant is in action, the time is ripe to make up your own mind about the values you have adopted from your upbringing and from your society, and to develop an outlook based on a sense of oneness with the Earth and her inhabitants—the other living organisms and humanity. Perhaps this is why a number of tarot deck, including some of the older ones, portray The Hierophant (who looks epicene, but can easily pass for a man) as a lady pope—in France, La Papesse—a female religious.

This yin manner of spiritual experience is the feeling that you are at one with the Whole. It also symbolizes the knowledge that when you injure another part of that Whole, you invariably injure yourself.

We can reconstruct the cosmologies from the remains of Paleolithic times, and also from the original ideas of the Maoris and the Native Americans, to mention but a few examples, for they represent the yin way of religion.

In an age such as ours, when the Earth has been so misused, it is extremely important to get back to their approach. What we see mainly in The Hierophant is the need to make sense of things within a religious framework, regardless of the pattern involved. And, as already mentioned, often this comes to us in the first instance in the form of traditions laid down by our own religious community. However, what matters is to understand the traditions through personal development, to weigh them, and internalize them. This happens with other tarot cards, such as Judgement and The World. There is no longer a question of choosing between the yang way and the yin way; a balance is struck between the two, and both have a place. The Hierophant is the innate desire to achieve this balance, and the incentive to attain ultimate union.

THE LOVERS—CARD VI

THE LOVERS.

The inescapable confrontation with everything that is different from ourselves compels us to make choices in everyday life. The urge to make choices that unite opposites and relieve tensions is embodied in The Lovers. What we do not realize at first is that all those things involving our emotions in the outside world have to do with factors in our unconscious, regardless of whether the latter are connected with repressions or with hidden gifts and talents. We can place people on a pedestal when they exhibit qualities that lie dormant in us in some form, and we are annoyed by those who show traits that we have repressed in ourselves, have not encouraged, or do not want to know. It is a recognized fact in Jungian psychology that the more emotionally you react to the things you see or experience, the bigger the complex in you that is being mirrored in these external circumstances. Thus, if you have taken a great dislike to someone, this individual is, so to speak, a symbol of an unconscious part of yourself that you can come to know by projecting it on him or her.

It is this mechanism that makes its entrance in the card of The Lovers. We take the first step outside and come into relationship with people and things in the world. The Lovers card represents the desire to enter this relationship in a genuine way, and that often has nothing to do with any love affair! What is significant here is involvement with the "other," with that which we find outside ourselves. In our encounter with "the other" we have confrontations that force us to make choices. But what we need to learn is that, in a deeper sense, these choices and confrontations have to do with ourselves, and with what is in our unconscious. By clearly perceiving and comprehending this, we can find our inner other half. Conscious and unconscious can have a mutual understanding and cooperation, and this process can assist the growth of the personality.

However, in the phase of The Lovers we are still not entirely aware of this. This phase symbolizes the beginning of the process by which we gain self-knowledge through "mirroring" in the outside world and through uniting inwardly with that unknown other side of ourselves. We learn this by striking up relationships in the outside world. Normally, The Lovers will then enable us not to lean on others, but to discover self-reliance, to make independent choices, and to accept responsibility for these choices.

This is why the card often plays a role when young people leave the parental home and become independent. They leave their secure environment to become fully responsible for the choices they make.

The theme of choosing between some form of safety, on the one hand, and personal independence and taking responsibility for whatever is necessary for our growth on the other, is a prominent part of The Lovers. It is an important mechanism for getting to know ourselves better and for developing our ego.

If we stagnate in the stage of The Lovers, we present a picture of someone who carefully weighs the pros and cons, but does not take any important steps or, at any rate, no steps demanding any great dedication or involvement. Instead of a significant move being made into the outside world with the shouldering of personal responsibility, there is a flight from an existing relatively safe situation into another safe situation, so that a real choice is avoided.

We then run the risk of walking straight into the predicament we were trying to avoid, and falling into the arms of someone who will take us and break us in for the task of pulling their little cart before we know where we are. All sorts of problems and entanglements are the result. The fear of involvement with the outside world can also mean that decision-taking becomes difficult. There is no feeling for the other person, and no ability to take into account the total situation in which others are involved. All that is left is the aim of establishing oneself.

At the back of that lies the fear of ever abandoning one's own security, and especially of leaving ease and comfort and safety in order to step into life. When The Lovers card works negatively, you keep lingering at the threshold, cautiously poking one foot outside the door and pulling it back in again as quickly as possible, or you first build a new safe shelter into which you can step immediately— only to encounter the same old problems once more.

The main problem is a lack of balance in relationships, but this is not the same as adopting the role of victim. For instance, consider someone who, within a marriage, plays the part of the great protector or protectress, and subtly, but clearly, informs the partner that she or he must stay small and dependent. This person finds safety in playing this part, and if he or she cannot be the protector or protectress, feels very insecure.

Thus it doesn't matter what side you stand on, but how much courage you have to swap safety for experiences and confrontations that lead to greater awareness.

THE CHARIOT—CARD VII

THE CHARIOT.

Through the choices we are obliged to make, and the dangers we have to brave, we are able to develop our ego. The Chariot depicts the need and the desire to function more powerfully and more self-assertively, to display will-power, and to affirm our identity. All this results in being able to consolidate and strengthen our ego or "I," with which we identify ourselves.

Outwardly we want to appear and function as clearly recognizable individuals. We want to be as independent as possible while being considerate of others. The building up of a properly functioning and powerful ego is not automatic. In a Jungian sense, the ego is the center of our conscious; it is an inner function that we use to understand and survey life, both internally and externally. Through the ego, we make choices and receive the help to control all sorts of impulses and desires that rise up in us.

To some extent we can liken the ego or "I" to a central control room; and if it is not there or is out of order, everything goes haywire. Thus from a Jungian standpoint, it is important to develop as solid an ego as possible, so we can function in an effective and balanced way. This is definitely not the same as being egotistical or thinking of nobody but ourselves.

Therefore we should certainly not want to ignore the ego, as that would involve particularly harmful consequences for our further development. An ego that functions satisfactorily will keep a watchful eye on the self, the others around us, and on the environment. On the basis of the assessments it makes in both worlds—the world of the psyche and the external world—the ego can make choices and decisions that benefit all concerned. The more poorly developed the ego is, the more unbalanced are the choices it makes.

The Chariot represents the problems we encounter in strengthening the ego. The Chariot is being pulled by two different colored sphinxes (black and white) which are looking in different directions: an obvious representation of the often conflicting contents of our unconscious, which tends to jolt the chariot of the conscious.

It is the charioteer, or our ego, who must dare, or learn, to take the reins in his hands, who must realize what is tugging at him inside, and how this can work out in him and in the outside world. By driving his chariot alertly, he is able to spot undermining impulses in good time and to handle them in such a way that they do not disturb his functioning in the outside world, and (which is even more important) he does not repress them, but lets them lead a life of their own.

The paradox of The Chariot is that we must attend to the development of a strong ego, while battling with unconscious drives and impulses which can disturb or deform ego-development. The ultimate inner goal of The Chariot is to set the ego firmly in the saddle, so that the personality is able to capture a place in the outside world by virtue of its good qualities, insight, and will-power.

However, if we linger in The Chariot phase, the impulse to develop a strong ego can go too far and lead to egoism and hardness. Exaggerated self-expression and boastfulness, thinking too much of oneself and misunderstandings come to the fore, and we see an ego that (to use a figure of speech suggested by the card) wants to be in control and thinks that its horses are reined in, when in fact they are bolting. Attempts to remedy the situation can give The Chariot a very bumpy ride that may shake it to pieces or overturn it. In this case ego-development is undermined instead of being supported.

The Chariot phase reveals, in the process of ego-development, how powerful our unconscious impulses are. The next step is that of learning to cope with them.

STRENGTH—CARD VIII

Represented here is the urge to make effective contact with the conflicting forces in our unconscious that are experienced in The Chariot phase. We wish to get to know these forces and impulses, and to learn to manage them. Generally speaking, they have had no opportunity to express themselves when we were growing up, because they were not socially acceptable, or because we repressed them. But they may also be hidden talents stirring in the unconscious while trying to make contact with the ego.

In the phase of Strength we are open to messages from the unconscious; we learn to listen to our instincts, and take notice of the images that come to us out of the unconscious. The woman on the card depicts receptivity, and she has a firm hold on the mouth of the lion (our instinctive world). She can open it when she wants to listen, and close it when she does not.

This is a well-balanced mechanism. For although it is usually good to listen to what the unconscious has to say, there are a number of situations in which it is better if it remains silent. For example, if you have just been through an upsetting time, the unconscious may want you to come to terms with it by having a good cry. But if you are looking after young children who need constant care, or perhaps you have other responsibilities, there is not always an opportunity to retire for a period of assimilation. Certainly you need to be aware that you will have to do so at some time, but to satisfy the demands of everyday life, it is sometimes necessary to close the lion's mouth. It can be opened again later.

Strength is a powerful card, but not in the sense of being imposing. Strength is more subtle and restful than that. Will-power is present, it is true, but there is receptivity at the same time, and a combination of the courage to look at oneself and the calm determination to learn to understand oneself. Strength is therefore a process of self-discovery and a consequence of the projection mechanism. We learn to recognize the role of the unconscious in our psyche, and start to discover that our actions are more or less determined by unconscious impulses, not by conscious convictions, even though we may have thought that our decisions were wholly rational. In the phase of Strength, one learns to make contact with one's less acceptable traits, such as anxiety, grief, and insecurity, or even passion, malice, nagging, or sloth.

Making contact with these things and accepting that even they, however much they have been repressed, do belong to your own psyche, gives a certain inner stability and, with it—strength!

In everyday life, Strength often goes hand in hand with tasks requiring positive but not undue action. Both discipline and application are demanded; and when you put your whole heart into doing something that appeals to you, you can derive a great deal of pleasure from it, especially when you have a deep understanding of all the forces acting on the matter or question. Strength often brings psychological confrontations, too. Having regard for the whole picture, it may be clear that the time is ripe for working on yourself—especially if you use symbols rather than words.

If we hang back in the phase of Strength, this can lead to extremes. For instance, the lion's mouth can no longer be shut and we are flooded with conflicting impulses and their attendant (often violent) emotions. Instincts that then break through, do so in an ethically and morally uncontrolled form. The consequence can be objectionable behavior which lands us in a lot of trouble. On the other hand, the unconscious can also assail us with fears which, for example, can lead to very regressive behavior, or can produce all sorts of flight and defense mechanisms that hinder rather than facilitate our contact with the unconscious.

In that event, there is no longer any chance of self-acceptance. Strength degenerates into overprotectiveness, and the unconscious seems to become inimical to us instead of being its usual helpful self.

When Strength works positively, we stand on the threshold of new developments—in the first place, we experience humility in the realization that there are forces greater than those of the will or the conscious mind. And this can inspire us to set out on a quest—The Hermit. Also we can come to see that, through these unconscious mechanisms, we are regularly inclined to operate in fixed patterns— The Wheel of Fortune.

Last but not least, we can also make an honest assessment of our role in the outside world—Justice. Thus Strength sets the scene for the following cards of the Major Arcana.

THE HERMIT—CARD IX

THE HERMIT.

In the earlier process of ego-building and confronting instincts in our unconscious, our innate religious function, represented by The Hierophant, has been functioning in the background. In Strength, for example, we have been able to develop a sense of awe following the discovery that there are forces in our psyche that are greater than that of the ego—forces that need not be seen in terms of good or evil.

This sense of awe, and the feeling that there is something *more*, induces us, in the phase of The Hermit, to go on a personal search for universal values and laws, stripped of external rituals or any dogmatic approach. In some ways you can say that The Hierophant seeks personal fulfillment in the phase of The Hermit. Therefore, The Hermit chiefly represents our need to experience the spiritual and the religious in an individual, wholly personal manner, and thus to make sense of life in general, and of our own life in particular.

To some extent, The Hermit is an undemonstrative card. Outwardly nothing much seems to be going on, but inwardly there is a certain restlessness and the urge to conduct a search. Fresh interests can make their appearance, especially those that have to do with anything profound. Out of these interests there develops a different view of everyday affairs, which generally assume less importance. When you experience a feeling that you are part of a greater whole, and that life is manifesting through you, it matters less whether you are well thought of or not: your inner window becomes clearer.

Also, on the basis of what you feel, read, hear, and experience, you can move toward other goals, goals in which social success yields to making sense of life and to doing something meaningful. Internal activity is so important in the period of The Hermit that one runs the risk of paying (too) little attention to one's immediate environment, so that conflicts can arise with those with whom one lives or works.

As a psychic process, The Hermit can produce an inspiring period, a time in which we look at things more and more from another dimension. This dimension could be called cosmic, but we need to be careful in this phase. Above all else, The Hermit depicts our journey of discovery which, in The World (the final card), can result in the integration of the religious and the mundane. The Hermit, himself, scans, questions, seeks, and researches, allows himself to be borne along on the wings of philosophies and cosmologies, and in this fashion forms his own picture of his place in life, perhaps to be followed by making this concrete—his place in society. Thus, The Hermit can certainly indicate very practical social visions, but behind them there will always be a process of probing and searching.

The danger inherent in stopping at the stage of The Hermit is that of gradually losing contact with reality. Metaphorically speaking, we are walking on air. Because The Hermit naturally has little involvement with the outside world, he seems, in his negative expression, to cut the umbilical cord linking him to ordinary life and to live as a maladjusted eccentric, whose vision no longer has any plane that is tangent to reality.

In such a state, one runs the risk of becoming a phony guru with delusions of being the special mouthpiece of the cosmos; or of suffering from a decay of the ego, which becomes lost in a sea of spellbinding dreams.

Whereas the true Hermit has an open mind and is prepared to take on board positive criticism and to check it out, the negative

Hermit simply refuses to listen any more, but forces his ideas down people's throats and will not brook contradiction. He does not make room for others, and if anyone asks a friendly critical question that is meant to be constructive, he stigmatizes him or her as "ignorant" or "hostile." Discussion is out of the question. Admittedly, the true Hermit is inward-looking, but the negative Hermit settles down in this process and becomes increasingly desperate to convert the world to his own point of view. What he fails to see is that his inner uncertainty has taken such a form that only by convincing the world can he convince himself and preserve a false sense of security. Nothing remains of any crystallization of religious feelings; and life appears to be more and more enmeshed in all the things he is frantically trying to exclude.

However, the positive Hermit gains an insight into his place in the greater whole, and is prepared to put this insight into practice in everyday life.

THE WHEEL OF FORTUNE—CARD X

WHEEL of FORTUNE.

How often it happens that we enter a real-life situation that seems very like one we were in before! Maybe other individuals are involved, but the structure is the same. It is like the story of a dominating woman who tires of her husband's timidity and gets a divorce, only to take up with another man who has the same characteristics. The picture stays the same.

The repetition, with minor variations, of certain patterns, is the result of projections we have still not seen for what they are. It is the result of the influence of our complexes, through which our behavior and our expectations are not the same as we consciously perceive them. It seems as if life is playing a game with us, and we are constantly the victim of what it pulls out of its bag of tricks.

The Wheel of Fortune confronts us with the following mechanism: we encounter the workings of "fate" and can now come to see that there is a connection between what strikes us apparently out of the blue in the outside world, and our own psychic dynamics. If we can understand how we, ourselves, are involved in the processes and situation in which we find ourselves, we shall be able to change them: we can get off The Wheel.

But wrong conclusions or creeping away into misplaced guilt feelings simply increases the effect of The Wheel, and we end up sitting on still more sharp points in constantly repeating patterns. In many cases we encounter resistance and setbacks as The Wheel of Fortune turns. The things we would like to do are unsuccessful, or are obstructed on every hand, no matter whether we want to pursue work or hobbies. Things can even reach such a pass that we start to feel that fate has really got it in for us. Questions such as, "What have I done to deserve this?" are quite common in this phase, and we have to be prepared to deal with them. A good response is to look at ourselves, our situation, and the problems, as objectively as possible, or at any rate to stand back a little, watch what is going on and, above all, study our own reactions, emotions, hopes, and fears. That is where the key to insight lies. Once we see, for example, that specific anxieties have led to a defensive attitude, however subtle, and that this attitude is provoking the very reactions we are trying to avoid, then we have found one way of tackling The Wheel.

Reverting again to "the woman who likes to wear the pants," when she sees that she behaves like this because she is mortally afraid that otherwise she will have no control, and because she probably also does not know how to relax, she will be able to explore some other way of looking at life. For instance, she could undergo relaxation therapy, or something of that sort. Then she will change on the inside, and begin to resonate differently with the outside world. The timid man will no longer cross her path so frequently, for she is no longer the same. The Wheel of Fortune can also repeat decidedly positive situations!

If we continue in this process for too long, we often become the victim of mistaken guilt feelings. And then we can hide, or, to put it more strongly, we can passively accept what happens in life as the "due punishment for our crimes."

In fact, certain ways of seeing the concept of karma can be traced back to getting stuck on The Wheel of Fortune. Fatalism and a negative attitude toward oneself are the consequences.

Another from of clinging to The Wheel of Fortune is to become increasingly angry with the world. With an attitude of, "I deserve better than this," or "I am too good for this world," or "they owe me something," we create, as it were, a justification of the negative spirals in which we keep finding ourselves. We become more and more petulant and sulky, and sink more deeply into feelings of resentment against the world and those around us.

And that is a pity, because the real purpose of The Wheel of Fortune as a drive is to confront us in such a way that we can take a big step toward maturity in order to be better able to take full responsibility for our own lives.

JUSTICE—CARD XI

Again we are faced by choices, but very differently from the way in which we were faced by them in The Lovers. As we have seen, The Wheel of Fortune asks us to look at ourselves as objectively as possible, and Justice does so, too, but at the same time she asks us to examine fairly and squarely what we are and where we stand.

Justice confronts us with the knowledge that life contains a succession of pleasures, obligations, and problems. We need to accept that it imposes restrictions which have to be accommodated. The less we have done this in the past, the more traumatic the confrontation with Justice will be.

For, following on from The Wheel of Fortune, Justice teaches us that our life at this moment is the result of all the psychic processes of the past—the choices we have made, and those we have shelved (depending on our disposition).

To some extent, Justice continues the process of The Wheel of Fortune; but whereas, in The Wheel, patterns in society and in the outside world are still important, Justice is a more inward-looking card, which gives the desire to be in the clear with all the mutually opposing inner forces.

Here is the sword of discrimination, enabling us—through critical analysis of ourselves—to gain a more balanced picture of how we have functioned in the past, and of how and at which junctures, we have put a spoke in our own wheels by wrong attitudes and faulty expectations.

Justice tries to establish a balance between the forces of the unconscious and the postures of the conscious. Once again, the question of ethics does not enter into the matter. Take responsibility for your actions and see the connection between your inner conflicts and those in which you are embroiled in the outside world. And jettison superfluous ballast.

Justice cannot abide dishonesty. Evasions and excuses are automatically unmasked because they disturb the internal equilibrium and trigger unbalanced reactions in the outside world. The process of Justice leads us to adopt a more humble demeanor, knowing that even if, in some ways, we may have "arrived," we still have much to learn. This humility has nothing to do with masochism or an inferiority complex.

People who settle down in the phase of Justice often develop a very biased opinion about who they are and what is happening to them. Those around them are always entirely to blame; but they themselves are spotlessly clean, and full of good intentions. In their eyes, others are good for nothing and, what is worse, are deliberate offenders. Therefore, we often see the people signified by this card threatening legal action, or taking it.

Conversely, being repeatedly the victim of legal action by others is the other side of this complex: then once more the world is experienced as blameworthy, with the added indignity that these others are trying to prove that it is you who are legally in the wrong. It will be obvious that, in lawsuits of this kind, tremendous amounts of emotion are generated, usually by both parties.

While Justice as a process has a certain cleansing effect in the sense that one's reactions and expectations lead to a better understanding of oneself, and to greater clarity and soberness, negative

Justice supervises a build-up of obscurities, incriminations, emotions, and difficulties, which can produce a sense of alienation—as if nobody wants anything more to do with you.

The fact of the matter is that this feeling flows from a widening gulf between the conscious and the unconscious. The unconscious is no longer able to reach you with helping forces, and the conscious feels isolated and left in the lurch—feelings that are then projected on the "wicked world."

One feels repudiated, and this can make the next phase, of The Hanged Man, very difficult, whereas simplification and positive and constructive humility are what are required to add a new dimension to this phase.

THE HANGED MAN—CARD XII

In all aspects of your daily and social life, you feel as if you are sitting in a waiting room. You do not even know what waiting room it is, or where you are supposed to be going. Things forming under the surface now break through: a reorientation is taking place in yourself and in your life.

The gloss seems to have worn off the pleasant things of life; they have lost their appeal. There is a tendency to stagnate in whatever is not going well. Affairs are not prospering in the world outside: your business is not doing so well, you are less motivated at work, and at home—for no reason at all—you feel rather like a displaced person. In short, you are at loose ends, and don't know what to do about it.

Nevertheless this is not a negative period—far from it. Part of the religious function has been reactivated, and in this phase we simply cannot keep on toiling and moiling. The Hanged Man is the desire to retire into ourselves and to experience, realize, and above all, to integrate, the humility acquired in the previous phase. It is also the willingness to accept the ups and downs of life as a natural rhythm.

In Justice, we saw the dawning of the mental realization of life's rights and obligations; in The Hanged Man we see the emotional acceptance of the sun-and-shadow side of life.

As a result, defeats and sorrows must now be given their due: they belong to the rhythm of life—there is no escaping them. Their acceptance enables us to tap another source of energy in ourselves: a voice deep inside which whispers that, in one way or another, we are always going to survive.

It is not some great trumpet call in us, but a subtle knowledge that can help us to build up a new, deeper, and more heartfelt confidence in life and in ourselves, while allowing for the fact that things do go wrong, that we sometimes take a tumble, and that we simply cannot do everything we would like.

This attitude of acceptance can produce a state of peace and calm in which you observe that you have become more tolerant toward yourself and others. Your religious sentiments can be broadened by this experience. By withdrawing a little from the hustle and bustle of the world, you are in a better position to perceive the delicate feelings which would otherwise never have attracted your attention—feelings which enhance your sense of union with the world of humanity, with nature, and with the universe. You no longer have so much need to fight, to compete, and to exert yourself: you can more easily let things take their course.

Quite often, this card puts in an appearance at a moment in your life when everything is against you. You are in a situation in which you do not know which way to turn; perhaps you have lost your job and all your plans have fallen through. Disruptive experiences of this sort belong to The Hanged Man. The art of The Hanged Man is to learn to accept that life is like that, and to draw strength by quietly retreating in order to be able to advance again later.

If (figuratively speaking) you stay suspended in the phase of The Hanged Man, feelings of self-pity can predominate so that you become more and more of a grumbler. Or (usually unconsciously) you undermine your own position in every possible way by inappropriate behavior. The Hanged Man is certainly not naturally provocative; in a negative sense, he is rather lax, slovenly, unenthusiastic, and dependent on guidance from others (which may mean foolish reliance on the so-called horoscopes in newspapers and magazines!).

In this unsettled condition, our personal emanations have a very demotivating effect on those around us, who react negatively toward us, and we become further removed from the inner repose that belongs to the positive action of the card. Internally we become more and more restless and confused, and therefore even more inclined to withdraw from the world of responsibilities and to take refuge in a world of Utopian dreams. Sitting every day, early and late, in front of the TV set, and no longer doing one's own thing is a prime example of this aspect of The Hanged Man.

If we give heed to the true message of The Hanged Man, we shall imperceptibly be refined—more thoroughly than we might imagine. We shall start to feel differently as we take a fresh look at ourselves and at life—not in the sense of becoming more mature, but in the sense of experiencing a growth toward wholeness. Our imperfections may begin to show, and we may start to worry about losing face. We are being prepared for laying aside our masks and defense mechanisms in the next phase.

DEATH—CARD XIII

Say goodbye to those things that have served their purpose, give up attitudes that are no longer helpful, and discard whatever is superfluous. That is the message of Death, the inner drive to have done with attitudes, behavior, things, and situations that will hinder us if they continue to be a part of our lives.

In a positive sense, this also means removing the masks behind which we like to hide. If we now confront the insecurity that these masks allow to build up, we will observe that we need to adopt a more sober, unaffected, and unceremonious attitude, without airs and graces.

DEATH.

Although, initially, this seems to be a big step in the dark, it will give greater confidence at a later stage. But the beginning of the process is difficult.

Whether we want to or not, we have to abandon tried and trusted behavior and quit a familiar situation, and we just do not know what will take its place. How are people going to react to us now? What response will we get? Will something new really come along? Such questions reflect the anxiety and insecurity that activate the tendency to creep back into old behavior, or to maintain some safe but no longer useful situation. "A bird in the hand is worth two in the bush," might seem to be applicable here, but it does not hold good for the card Death. Death indicates the end of one situation and the advent of some other situation that is still under wraps; we do not see the latter clearly yet—only its faint outline.

Clinging to the old brings out every negative thing that Death can produce; by which I mean internal deadlock, increasing petrifaction in (for example) frantic dogmatism, while all mobility and vitality gradually ebb away. The work you must do requires more and more effort, because more energy is required to overcome inertia. You lose your sense of proportion and although you try to stay cheerful come what may and to behave as if nothing is the matter, life becomes hollow and empty.

With this card, you are being told that it is high time for an end or a conclusion; and the more sensibly and calmly you come to terms with this fact, the better it will be. The card does not say whether you will find the closing of a chapter in your life painful and sad, or as a relief and a liberation. Go along with this development; then at a later stage, as you look back on its consequences, you will surely experience a sense of contentment, emancipation, or joy.

In practice, this card is often associated with straitened circumstances or (substantial) difficulties. It seems as if nothing that is done can improve matters. When it is a question of work, the drive in your own psyche represented by Death asks you, "Are you really doing the work you are cut out to do?" Or it asserts, "A change of occupation or another place of work is necessary for your psychic development."

This is significant, because Death does not always imply an absolute end. If you draw the card in an inquiry about work, then certainly something in the latter is going to have to change; but it need not mean that you will lose your job. A radical alteration in your behavior, the termination of certain activities, the evaluation of your functioning, and the drawing of far-reaching conclusions all belong to Death, as does dealing with any overly fixed ideas and opinions you may have. The form in which you work, live, or function, must now change. Everything can feel dark and somber for a time, depending largely on the extent to which you have been living selfishly, or have always played safe.

In a deeper sense, Death is saying, "Come on and throw your ballast overboard, for you are sailing toward further self-development and it is time to steam ahead."

Through fear of the future and of the menacing blackness that looms ahead, you can easily turn tail and cling more tightly still to what you should be leaving behind. And in addition to the fading of gladness and magnetism from your life, you will notice an unconscious tendency to walk up dead end streets. Nevertheless, with this card, you can certainly win through, provided you work hard and do not have high expectations. If you quit or give up, even more life energy flows away, and then the danger with this card is that it brings with it depression, mental deadlock and, quite probably, physical symptoms, which often commence with increasing tiredness and apathy, but can develop into some illness (which need not be serious) that compels you to rest for a while. I have more than once seen broken bones when those who drew the card remained at this stage and would not take a single step forward, but preferred to keep playing at hide-and-seek with their real feelings. They opted for the safety of what was familiar, even though their lives were full of conflict, and wound up breaking a leg.

Yet, if you lay aside all masks and forms of artificiality, adopt a more open and receptive attitude, and take a step in the dark on the way to the new and improved life that certainly will come, you will be rewarded even during this process with an increasing sense of comfort and will "feel good" even though nothing definite has come along yet.

TEMPERANCE—CARD XIV

If you are investing less energy in masquerades and in play-acting of the sort that puts on a bold front and makes out that you are different than you really are, and if, in the previous phase, you have jettisoned all or most of your ballast, you will be in a much better position to restore balance now. After all the problems and uncertainty in the phase of Death, Temperance chiefly gives a sense of relief and contentment. It is the calm after the storm. But the calm does not last long, and Temperance is usually an intermediate stage which quickly passes.

Although we have taken off our masks in the previous phase, and are now looking for a fresh stance, the confrontations we experience, and the problems we encounter, are enough to be going on with. We are still undergoing an inner change while learning to cope, and that is what we see in Temperance: a placid frame of mind in which we review current conflicts and problems of every variety in order to resolve them. So there is still some tension in Temperance, but a feeling of unruffled peace prevails, and we are able to relax.

As a psychic drive, Temperance reveals herself as the desire to reconcile opposites and to find a new, dynamic form of harmony. Not one of binding compromises, but one in which viable solutions (that do not lead to rigidity) can be reached by contemplation and insight. Therefore this card is apt to appear when a wholly new and open approach leads to a sudden breakthrough in deadlocked negotiations. This breakthrough is not seen as a goal by Temperance, but as part of a process (even if it has resulted in a reward). And this is how Temperance always operates.

Often everything seems to run smoothly even though considerable effort is required, because Temperance, as an inner urge, has little need for distractions or adventures. This new and peaceful mode of functioning can create space for deeper feelings, such as a love of life and of others. And sometimes we see a movement toward what has been called cosmic consciousness. In every case, the positive aspect of Temperance gives us the equipment with which to confront, in a balanced way, our deeper and more troublesome instincts. And she shows us how good it really is to tackle all kinds of situations in a peaceful way instead of being emotional and aggressive.

However, if we remain too long in the Temperance phase, she imperceptibly flows into her reverse mode. While you continue to identify with almost "divine calm" and complacently gaze on the masses with the idea that (unlike them) you understand everything, you fail to observe that in the meantime various drives and impulses have been reactivated inside you and are having an increasing effect on what you do. Eventually this leads to a situation in which your actions are completely at variance with what you say or think.

In the extreme case, you fall into utterly unethical behavior while preaching to others in honeyed tones, and this inevitably leads to complications and intrigues of all kinds, or to becoming enmeshed in the very things you hope to avoid. The confrontation with The Devil as an inner drive then becomes hard and involved, whereas Temperance, when positive, can meet him calmly.

THE DEVIL—CARD XV

In principle, the energy of The Devil has to do with the instinct of self-preservation. However, this easily gets out of hand. Hidden away in each of us is the ego-oriented drive that encourages us to satisfy our personal wants. The Devil has no interest in the consequences of his activities: he is concerned with his own interests, not in others' interests. There are cultural and moral values that can keep this drive in line and channel it, but it will always be present as a general human trait.

In some situations, The Devil can be life-saving: if you are in the middle of a severe crisis in which you will either sink or swim, then it is the strength of The Devil which, without more ado, can go all out to save you. In wartime, you can stay alive by doing things you would be ashamed of in a time of peace. The same instinct is involved.

Think again of teenagers who want to be different from their parents and their background. They display egocentric behavior that often has a provocative side, knowing that it can be hurtful to the older people. But this does not seem to matter; the behavior wells up instinctively in response to the life situation: they feel that the time has come to make a break and will not take advice. There is a wanton indulgence in a whirl of pleasure, dancing all night, having unsafe sex, or getting caught up in group activities that may not be very mature. All these things are expressions of The Devil. But The Devil can also be a "sharply dressed dude" who well and truly sets to work with selfish motives and lots of elbow-work to gain an advantage over others. Enjoying oneself to the detriment of others, enriching oneself at the expense of others, and, in fact, any short-sighted pursuit of personal gain and power is the danger of this card, irrespective of your position on the social ladder. The instincts that can be life-saving can also trip us up badly.

Sooner or later we are going to stand face to face with the less ethical sides of ourselves. We may not be very aware of it, but there are numerous occasions when The Devil raises his head. For example, why have you such a need to meddle with certain affairs? Is it always from pure motives? Or is there a power-devil lurking in the background, and the temptation to be manipulative? Not very pleasant questions to ask oneself, but necessary if one is to keep clear of troublesome complications and problems.

When The Devil raises his head, he does so in the shape of internal questioning, or "chances" in the outside world that are very tempting but are taken on the backs of others. Are you in a state to resist the temptation? Or do you put on a fair show while working underhandedly? In short, The Devil confronts us with our Shadow, with all those things that we would rather not see or know about ourselves (anymore), but which we simply must pass under review if we are going to be able to integrate them. Only then will they no longer be able to insinuate themselves into our behavior so strongly, and, above all, so stealthily, to land us in complicated problems, so that we find ourselves being blamed without fully realizing what it is all about.

The pursuit of power and pleasure is not only alluring but gives us pseudo-satisfaction for a long time. What we do not appreciate to begin with is that it introduces a certain hollowness into our existence so that we need stronger and stronger kicks to maintain the same level of enjoyment. At the same time we form a completely false picture of ourselves and of the world, and project all our Shadow properties on others. In our own eyes, they bear the blame for everything, and we feel justified in fighting them verbally or even physically.

We become set in this way of seeing, becoming increasingly emotional, and more and more quickly involved in confrontations with the reflection of our Shadow in the outside world. Our psychic growth stops and our true self is imprisoned in the desire world, until the storm breaks with The Tower.

The Devil is always a risk card and signifies confrontation. It is possible to face this confrontation fairly and squarely. It is good to come to terms with what you discover in yourself, and also to realize that you are once more changing your attitude and your opinion of yourself—The Tower.

THE TOWER—CARD XVI

THE TOWER.

If you are floundering in the desire world, in headstrong behavior, or in an accusatory attitude toward the outside world (either toward a single individual or toward society as a whole), then sometimes only a great fright or a shocking experience can break through this attitude. That is the essence of The Tower: the sudden thunderbolt striking the "upper storey" so that your entire way of thinking and point of view are upset in an instant.

The Tower represents the inner urge to release ourselves from the fetters of our fretfulness, which, in this case happens through fierce confrontations, which need not necessarily come from outside. Deep depressions also belong to the domain of

The Tower. The character of suddenness is central—The Tower brooks no delay.

Death can produce a rounded personality gradually; The Tower can do so in a more explosive manner. Quarrels, nasty surprises, the unexpected failure of a plan one has been hatching—these are The Tower. Fright, disquiet, and nervousness are its usual characteristics. It is like an earthquake: the solid ground under foot trembles and one does not know whether or not it will open up, and, if so, where.

Externally we often see far-reaching changes take place under the influence of The Tower. Only one thing is certain: everything is changing and nothing will go on in the same old way any more. It is not easy to keep up with all this. Nevertheless, in a positive sense, The Tower finally provides the opportunity for those breakthroughs you have secretly had in mind for a long time, but have not been able to make.

And The Tower also provided opportunities for suddenly getting behind your projections of yourself, and for seeing through your own conduct and correcting it. If you study yourself honestly and do not shy away from the confrontation with your Shadow, The Tower will guarantee very rapid psychological growth and strengthening of your character, even though this is often associated with turmoil, and perhaps even with painful circumstances. The Tower can make life sparkle again as soon as you burst the bubble of illusions and false hopes.

However, if, in the phase of The Devil, you got bogged down in self-centeredness, then the phase of The Tower is distressing. Your contact with reality is far from gentle: it is a very sharp encounter, and in a negative sense could even involve being picked up by the police. Life gives you such a knock that you come face to face with the consequences of your previous behavior, and with the knowledge that there is only a way through and no longer a way back. This creates an explosive situation, which can also produce great inner stress. (The Tower often comes with insomnia.)

In The Tower, also, you can stagnate in two ways. You may either become increasingly reclusive and set yourself against any form of change, in spite of the fact that you are having to sail through choppier seas and increasingly difficult circumstances; or you play the part of The Tower in the lives of others—shocking behavior, complete maladjustment, or hysterical tantrums in which you lash out at everything within reach.

In both cases there is stagnation of inner growth and a strong alienation from the world, which, ultimately, with The Tower leads to inner tension and stress that blow your fuses. Those who have already cut themselves off from society tend to be even chillier in their response to others and to shut out all feelings. However, The Tower would not be The Tower if, even here, it did not, through some fright or shock, give the individual an opportunity to wake up to reality.

If we have put in motion the inner changes prompted by the sudden breakthrough of insights in The Tower phase and, in spite of all the unrest, have grasped our creative side, then we are in a position to maintain a much better internal equilibrium than we experienced in Temperance. Where Temperance was a first resting point after a crisis, the next card, The Star, is a second such resting point at a deeper level.

THE STAR—CARD XVII

The Star denotes a period in which you pull yourself together after a turbulent time. You renew your hope and regain confidence in the future. As a result of going through the phase of The Tower in a positive way, you feel inwardly that everything that cramps you flows from fear—fear of life, fear of being yourself, fear of what others will think of you.

At the same time, you see that this cramping drains all the life out of you and makes you still and unapproachable; which in itself provokes confrontations and shocks. The Star refuses to put up with this any longer. You now have the psychic need to be yourself and to obey your own internal dictates, whatever others may think. You now have the urge to do the things that are essentially "you."

The Star, as an inner drive, has no need to struggle or fight hard for something. What you aspire to is peaceful resignation. Not that you withdraw entirely, but you do not want to be pestered by others now that you are busy discovering the most important thing in life for you.

You can now much better gauge and keep in proper perspective the outside influences from your employer, society, and your family. Also you are less afraid of the consequences of your attitudes, opinions, and behavior, and you feel calm and relaxed. This radiates out of you, and you are able to function more agreeably and more adaptably in your environment, while paradoxically enough you "do your own thing" more freely than you did before.

Nevertheless, The Star definitely takes others into account, and will certainly not engage in anything solely out of self-interest. It is important to begin to feel stronger in the emotional arena in the phase of The Star. We can develop a calm and level-headed form of self-confidence, which enables us to accept ourselves more readily. In a positive sense, The Star is associated with the desire to discover and distinguish between what belongs to us and what does not, and also with the desire to be occupied with what concerns us in the light of a better relationship with our inner world, without being thrown too far off balance by the intervention of the outside world.

By knowing that life opens doors only when we try as much as we can to develop our own potential creatively, we find in the optimum case that the things we start under this card often take a positive direction and even lead to success. This can have to do with our work but also with problem solving, entering into a relationship, or beginning a new hobby. Success has a psychological meaning here and is therefore good for the development of the personality.

However, genuine social success is often only part of the picture. The Star is not purposefully involved in external affairs, but is directed inward in order to plumb more of the depths of the psyche, to gain a better understanding of the drives and paradigms buried in the unconscious.

If we linger in the phase of The Star, its energy is slowly converted into its opposite. The restfulness is only apparent, and by dodging important issues, we encourage a retreat onto safe terrain. This strengthens the need for confirmation and acceptance by those around us, and forces us to rely on them for our peace of mind. In the negative Star, I have often seen that, being uncomfortable with ourselves, we do everything we can to be liked, and we are dissatisfied with our bodies, and unable to appreciate our health, and tend to measure ourselves by external standards at the cost of downgrading our own personality.

Another manifestation of the negative Star is unapproachability. We may seem self-sufficient but, in reality, we are only encasing ourselves in armor to ward off the outside world. This is a false calm, and substitutes for the inner peace the positive Star can bring. This peace is essential for confronting deeper-lying factors that can surface if there is genuine openness to the unconscious.

The onslaught of the unconscious world, its images and anxieties, and also its ultimate helpfulness, are seen in the next card—The Moon.

THE MOON—CARD XVIII

THE MOON.

When the unconscious gets the opportunity, given by an irruption of complexes, or by the fact that we open ourselves to them, it will speak powerfully to our conscious in picture language, and will show, through symbols, what is living and burrowing deep inside us. This language comes in dreams and fantasies, daydreams and visions, doodles, free dance, and in all other activities where spontaneous expression can flow freely.

In The Moon stage we desire to contact the unconscious in a positive involved way in order to understand ourselves at a deeper level and to grasp the impulses and activities of our instincts. In response to this approach, the unconscious will reveal itself as a friend and helper, and we shall be in a much better position to shape our course. The result will be a more profound and abundant confidence in life.

But the unconscious is very different from the conscious. We have only to look at dreams to see that. Often we can make neither heads nor tails of them, even though they are conveying a message. We try hard to approach and analyze this interior world of unconscious pictures and messages with the rules of the conscious. We need to learn to speak the language of the unconscious, to accept its capriciousness, and to gain a fresh feeling for, and understanding of, symbols.

In The Moon stage we open up to these inner images, which obtrude themselves on us much more strongly than in the Strength phase. Whereas in Strength we were prepared to listen to and accept the unconscious, in The Moon it is as if the unconscious, itself, takes the initiative and floods us with pictures, emotions, and feelings. We can no longer hold it back, and we react very sensitively to people, objects, and religious ideals, and to everything that arouses our feelings. We cannot circumvent it and it takes most of the matter-of-factness out of us. Now it's easier to dream, and easier to fall prey to nebulous atmospheres.

To begin with, it's hard to see where the images, fantasies, feelings, and atmospheres fit in. They seem to be erratic and unfathomable, but at the same time reveal any deep-lying problems that need to be solved, and show us hidden gifts and talents that should be given an airing.

The best way to restore our sense of balance and wholeness is to convert the stream of images (we often find that we have entered a period of vivid dreams when this card is drawn) into something creative and artistic.

Although socially this may seem to be a "waste of time" or "quite pointless," it is now the lamp of the nightside of life that is shining, and that means that we must devote ourselves to things that society may not consider very productive. However, they are vitally important for our inner growth and development. Some people play musical instruments and spare the time to improvise in a dreamy way, some go for nature walks and give thoughts free rein, some people draw or paint without paying too much attention to technique or performance, and notice something liberating that results from these activities. What we are doing is providing the unconscious with a channel for communication; if we do not understand its messages, do not fret: the increased sensitivity will eventually enable us to decipher them without too much trouble.

When, in The Moon, the unconscious comes to the fore, it often gives the conscious a severe testing. Fears that we did not know were bottled up inside us can suddenly make their presence felt. Complexes we thought we had integrated long ago can reveal a hitherto undisclosed face. Past experiences which we had come to terms with, and which were no longer a problem, can suddenly make themselves well and truly felt in a final convulsion of every element we overlooked when assimilating them.

All this can evoke a horde of emotions, so that The Moon can inaugurate a very unsettled period. The conscious mind must now accept that it cannot govern everything and that our psyche harbors dark corners from which awkward and unpleasant things can jump out. The Moon signifies a psychic situation in which, first and foremost, we realize that we are human. However calm we may feel after a crisis, our development always continues—a development that invariably includes a nightside or dark side.

In a positive sense, we are fully receptive in the stage of The Moon to what the unconscious wants to tell us, and this gives us access to tremendous help and power. The Moon is the urge to learn to cooperate with the depths inside us that contain both constructive and destructive energies.

In a negative sense, however, we can allow ourselves to be inundated by tides of emotion and confusing projections, and we may not have the wit to recognize that these are our own feelings, or that the key to dealing with them lies in ourselves.

If we linger in The Moon stage, the unconscious will force some unavoidable issue and, in trying to defend ourselves, we shall activate stronger and stronger emotions, anxieties or phobias, while landing ourselves in increasingly tangled emotional situations.

In order to escape from our own chaotic feelings, we are inclined to lean more and more heavily on others, to the extent that they may feel we are stifling them. This produces rejection or dislike in others. In this case, too, we have to deal with greater sensitivity to and accessibility of the unconscious. Our attitude will determine whether or not we turn the unconscious into an ally or into an adversary.

THE SUN .

THE SUN—CARD XIX

The desire to reach out from within in order to enjoy life to the full and cheerfully be yourself is represented by The Sun. The keynote of the phase of The Sun is that you are in a position to accept yourself totally. You have become aware of your dark sides and have given them a place. You accept the consequences of your actions and have forged an identity that is not rigid and dogmatic, but able to adapt to tomorrow's changing circumstances.

Lively flexibility is combined with an inner firmness, and expresses itself in an enormous love of life because you have learned to love yourself. This must not be confused with egoism. The Sun shows how, by simply accepting and liking yourself, you are able to value and like others. You radiate happiness and warmth due to the inner power and joy you have accumulated. There is something youthful about you that is certainly not immaturity; on the contrary, in this phase, you realize your responsibility as a human being.

In a positive sense, you are not so quick to take offense in The Sun phase. You have come to know and accept your weak points, and acknowledge that you can have awkward traits that are still not discovered. Disparaging comments made by others do not bother you unduly: you are not apt to feel you are under attack and can more easily spot when people are projecting their own deficiencies on you. And when slurs or criticisms have a grain of truth, you are able to acknowledge the fact and do something about it. You are less likely to become involved in mutual recriminations, and your behavior in conflicts and quarrels will become much more balanced without being weak.

And so The Sun is paradoxical: you have the inner strength to enable you to stand up for your rights, and to some extent it is natural for you to hold center stage; but at the same time, you are able to retire, to let others take precedence, and keep yourself in the background, because you do not have the same need to prove yourself. You have a very flexible attitude toward such things as fame and honor: if they come your way, this is fine; if they do not, then that is fine, too. For you realize only too well how brittle they are and how many obligations they create. Fame and honor are hollow if you have no opportunity for self-expression, which is what you want. You are happiest now just to be yourself.

The Sun represents warmth and mirth, and in a certain sense it also represents rest. Not in the same way as in The Star, where the general direction is more introverted; here you share life gladly with others. Owing to the enthusiasm of this energy you see that everything you now undertake has a great chance of success provided you adhere to the straightforwardness, animation, and honesty of The Sun.

If you remain too long in the phase of The Sun, the inner joy will gradually drain away, to be replaced by the need to prove yourself and to elbow your way to the front. This can degenerate into a bombastic display of your own importance which robs others of their opportunities.

Whereas the positive Sun takes its place almost automatically and with charisma, the negative Sun often becomes embroiled in various conflicts over such matters as power and authority. And instead of stimulating people, it tries to make them docile and compliant. Your light alone is allowed to shine—that of others may no longer do so. In this situation, the joyfulness and self-confidence vanish, and you become a "big noise" shouting down your insecurity.

Another side of The Sun can also make its presence felt: that of the eternal youth. You become like one of the "perpetual students" who defer accepting responsibility, insisting that nothing should be expected of them at present, although they always talk about what they will accomplish someday. You will never realize your potential as long as you stay at this stage. All you will want to do is to enjoy life, and to have everything done according to your own wishes. This produces the remarkable contrariness of onesided immature behavior, and a very demanding attitude toward others and toward life in general. True vitality is lacking and there is no fun in anything. But the positive Sun imparts enormous pleasure to everything you do.

JUDGEMENT.

THE JUDGEMENT—CARD XX

The joy of living, such an integral part of The Sun, becomes deeply anchored in the psyche with positive encouragement, and awakens new feeling. Although we can interpret this as a religious feeling of sorts, words are inadequate for expressing its ambiance and depth. Regardless of the circumstances in which you find yourself, you feel great gratitude for life and a deep sense of fulfillment.

It is not only with the mind that we know that we are part of a greater whole: we now experience inside that Mother Earth and the cosmos belong to one another—that we are all one. This releases us from the chains of everyday trivialities, but does not impede our functioning. On the contrary! Because we have found a way of keeping the conscious and the unconscious in a state of living interaction, and have learned to understand the language of the unconscious, we are like the child's toy known as "Tumble Baby Surprise": that is to say, however much you are knocked off balance, you quickly regain your composure.

Judgement represents the desire to preserve the flexible link between the conscious and the unconscious, and automatically creates the need for a much more broad outlook. In addition to the joy of living, and thankfulness for your own life, you also feel a deep respect for everything that grows and thrives, for the Earth and for the Universe. You are part of it and are aware of that fact. One obvious consequence is that you become more of an environmentalist. You just know that whatever damages your surroundings and the world, damages you, even if your pocket does not suffer directly.

This feeling of wholeness releases a store of energy: even though you know that you are still human and must always keep working on yourself, you see how to tackle your complexes and problems more effectively. It also gives latent talents the chance to break through: they are less and less held back by complexes in the unconscious.

In everyday life we see the phase of Judgement paired with changes in a positive sense. These can occur in many different areas, from promotion at work through fresh views on life. But there is more in hand than run-of-the-mill improvements. Internally, you have been going through a long process, and what is happening now has been slumbering all the time below the surface without your being aware of it. Life seems to be in closer contact with what is inside you. Also new hobbies and activities can come along, and these are very meaningful to you and give you a great sense of fulfillment. Frequently little events trigger breakthroughs that are highly significant. Now it is possible for small matters to have large consequences when things are waiting to happen and the time is right. And this is the time—the time of Judgement.

If you linger in the phase of Judgement, then the sense of relief originally felt can peter out, and you tend to mistrust breakthroughs and opportunities instead of greeting them with open arms. Judgement is a review by life of what you have done so far, and your reward consists of getting your inner just deserts.

In a negative sense, you, yourself, start passing judgments as if you had a monopoly on wisdom. You pontificate on morals, on good and evil, and run the risk of becoming increasingly dogmatic. What was very liberating and spiritual turns into pressure and anxiety. You project your discontent on the outside world, and condemn it as bad, sinful, or immoral; and do not see that your own deeds of commission or omission have very harmful consequences for others.

Another negative expression of Judgement is that you refuse to change. When Judgement puts you on the path that is right for you, you appear to have no inclination to take that path, but do your best to step off it. You are determined not to alter, and you want nothing to do with any mystical-sounding union. Or else you take things out of proportion because of some dogma, or explain them away "logically" and fall into a life-denying attitude that cuts you off from any sense of union with heaven, earth, or even other human beings. A limited vision and a narrow outlook on the world are then unavoidable.

Whereas the negative expression of Judgement gives us the illusion that we know better than anybody else, and we take our stand as "Big Father" or "Big Mother" who is beyond criticism, in its positive expression we know that we are being acted through by Mother

Earth or Father Sky, of which we are a unified part. We are no longer judgmental, because the relationship is based on reverence and on an inner tolerance and moral sense that we know each must discover for himself or herself.

When you reach this point, the important question is, "Dare you import this new dimension into everyday life?" If so, you will observe that you and life are whirling round in a cosmic dance—the card of The World.

THE WORLD.

THE WORLD—CARD XXI

This card depicts an androgynous individual (male and female at the same time) dancing to the rhythm of life. An individual who is complete and who knows what is meant by having its own place in the scheme of things; an individual, too, who does not allow success to go to its head but remains unassuming, yet refuses to be driven from the field by sorrow and reverses. The World takes life as it comes and calls it good. To everything there is a season: twenty-four hours encompass both night and day, and life has its gloomy and its bright times, its hard and easy times. They must all be accepted—they all have their place.

In the phase of The World, we no longer take for granted that everything ought to go easily. Life is flowing, yes, and we are part of it, but not everything we want is good for us, and we have experienced that getting things at any cost doesn't make us happy. Maybe we have reached some external goal, but his has not guaranteed that the needs of our inner, true personality or of our true path have been met.

The World is able to take life in its stride and to pick up and pass on life's rhythm (yet without becoming lost in it). In the phase of The World we know, or simply sense, when to take the lead and when to keep our hands off, when to engage in active planning and when to bide our time; we are guided by what "feels right." This is not fatalism, but a positive and deep involvement in life. We have been learning that there are more powerful forces than those of the ego and its will-power, and that life sometimes has other players, at present unknown to us, waiting in the wings.

Because we are at one with life, we do not experience it as a surprise attack or as a defeat when something unexpected happens; we feel that we are being borne along on the flow of events by a higher Wisdom. Life is in full flood, and even when we are carried into wretched circumstances, we are able to feel the grief and cry openly without losing touch with our deeper source.

It does not matter so much now whether you are a man or a woman. Given positive cooperation with The World, a man can make useful contact with his female side (his anima, in Jungian terminology) and can give the world of the emotions and the intuitive a natural and self-evident place in his life. Moody and irritable behavior disappear.

A woman in this phase is able to give shape to her own identity and independence, and to feel whole without overacting and without being hard. She experiences her creative power, but does not feel that she has to square up to the male world in a spirit of rivalry. Her creative power and independence are her heritage as a unique individual, and she can mold them in her own way. Insecurity, fault-finding, and harsh judgments have quit the field. In a Jungian sense, there has been a conjunction with the animus.

With this card you can sometimes have a very poignant feeling of unity, which can perhaps best be described as cosmic consciousness. The feeling is so powerful that it can continue to inspire you after it has disappeared.

If we insist on staying put (which would be misguided, for The World is not an end-phase), our initial adaptability will change into a lack of initiative and the tendency to let well enough alone. We avoid doing anything about our situation by refusing to take any responsibility for it, or we blame it on circumstances beyond our control. "That's the way of the world," is one form of cop-out.

Other manifestations are laziness, the inability to see the point of starting a new venture or of doing anything creative. At various times I have seen this card drawn by children who are addicted to computer games: they live in a fantasy world (in a world of virtual reality, as it is so aptly called), they no longer do anything creative, and are unable to resist the allurement of passivity. Their addiction leads them further and further away from a satisfactory contact with everyday life.

If you are stuck in this phase, trivialities become important and you can become involved in gossip and intrigues. Another negative expression of The World is a selfish pursuit of pleasure, in which the trait of positive unity is turned into its opposite. We become quite capable of preaching pious sermons while embezzling the funds from our religious organization.

The World completes a cycle. We can dance cheerfully through life. The World card is also indicative of the drive behind our need to be independent of external stimuli and to find happiness, fulfillment, and wholeness inwardly. It is the urge to find and to be ourselves.

Chapter Eight

THE TAROT AND ASTROLOGY

CAN WE USE TAROT cards in an astrological sense? In many tarot books, and on the cards themselves in some decks, certain cards are assigned to a planet or sign, and sometimes to a planetary aspect or to a planet in a sign. There is no agreement over how this should be done however, and doubts have been raised about whether it is feasible to translate the tarot and astrology into each other's languages.

In order to compare them, we shall make a list in which the elements of the two mantic systems are put side by side.

Astrology

ASTROLOGY PRESENTS US with twelve signs, which serve as a background for the planets. They show the capacities in which the planets are working. The planets themselves are patterns of psychic (of the psyche) predispositions and reactions. In the astrological chart they are connected by aspects (angles between the planets). The circle of the zodiac is also divided into twelve sections called "houses." These denote the areas in life into which the energies of the planets are channeled or, in other words, the predisposing patterns (planets) we are using to give shape to specific domains (houses).

The twelve signs of the zodiac represent twelve successive stages of development, and their nature is entirely different from that of the planets, which express powerful energies and desires. The planets initiate action, which is hardly true of the signs and even less true of the houses.

The horoscope as a whole reflects our potential and our unique individuality. The elements of the horoscope do not have the same significance and dynamics as the cards of the Major and Minor Arcana.

The Tarot

THE TAROT IS DIVIDED into the Major and Minor Arcana. The Major Arcana represent our inner dynamics and processes which, as we have already seen, are comparable with the mythical Way of the Hero. All the cards of the Major Arcana are dynamic and mirror both life processes and some of the associated phases of life. The Minor Arcana reveal how these processes are working out (or have worked out) from day to day. They concretize the Major Arcana. The Minor Arcana are divided into four sets, the four suits, each of which reflects a specific aspect of human life. Each suit is subdivided into ten number cards and four court cards, and these in turn have their own meaning. This is a very different division and a very different picture from the one offered by astrology. We have only to put under the magnifying glass a few astrological attributions to the tarot to see the problems involved in trying to combine the two systems.

The following list shows how different authors have looked at the astrological correlations with the Major Arcana cards. We will use Banzhaf (see Hajo Banzhaf, *The Tarot Handbook*), Crowley (see Aleister Crowley, *The Book of Thoth: A Short Essay on the Tarot of the Egyptians*), Masino (see Marcia Masino, *The Easy Tarot Guide*), Muchery (*La Tarot divinatoire*), Papus (see Papus, *The Tarot of the Bohemians*), Thierens (see A. E. Thierens, *The General Book of the Tarot*), and Wirth (see Oswald Wirth, *The Tarot of the Magicians*). As you will see, not everyone agrees.

0—THE FOOL

     1. Banzhaf: Uranus/Mercury
     2. Crowley: Air
     3. Masino: Uranus
     4. Muchery: Moon/Cancer
     5. Papus: none
     6. Thierens: Pluto
     7. Wirth: none

I—THE MAGICIAN

1. Banzhaf: Sun and Mercury
2. Crowley: Mercury
3. Masino: Mercury
4. Muchery: Sun/Leo
5. Papus: none
6. Thierens: Aries
7. Wirth: Taurus

II—THE HIGH PRIESTESS

1. Banzhaf: Moon
2. Crowley: Moon
3. Masino: Moon
4. Muchery: Moon/Cancer
5. Papus: Moon
6. Thierens: Taurus
7. Wirth: none

III—THE EMPRESS

1. Banzhaf: Venus in Taurus
2. Crowley: Venus
3. Masino: Venus
4. Muchery: Mercury/Gemini
5. Papus: Venus
6. Thierens: Gemini
7. Wirth: none

IV—THE EMPEROR

1. Banzhaf: Sun in Capricorn
2. Crowley: Aries
3. Masino: Aries
4. Muchery: Venus/Taurus
5. Papus: Jupiter
6. Thierens: Cancer
7. Wirth: Virgo

V—THE HIEROPHANT

1. Banzhaf: Sun in Sagittarius
2. Crowley: Taurus
3. Masino: Taurus
4. Muchery: Jupiter/Sagittarius
5. Papus: Aries
6. Thierens: Leo
7. Wirth: Aries

VI—THE LOVERS

1. Banzhaf: Venus/Jupiter and Venus/Mars
2. Crowley: Gemini
3. Masino: Gemini
4. Muchery: Mercury/Virgo
5. Papus: Taurus
6. Thierens: Virgo
7. Wirth: Sagittarius

VII—THE CHARIOT

1. Banzhaf: Aries
2. Crowley: Cancer
3. Masino: Cancer
4. Muchery: Venus/Libra
5. Papus: Gemini
6. Thierens: Libra
7. Wirth: none

VIII—STRENGTH

1. Banzhaf: Leo
2. Crowley: Libra
3. Masino: Leo
4. Muchery: Mars/Scorpio
5. Papus: Mars
6. Thierens: Scorpio
7. Wirth: Libra

IX—THE HERMIT

1. Banzhaf: Saturn in Aquarius
2. Crowley: Virgo
3. Masino: Virgo
4. Muchery: Jupiter/Sagittarius
5. Papus: Leo
6. Thierens: Sagittarius
7. Wirth: none

X—THE WHEEL OF FORTUNE

1. Banzhaf: Saturn
2. Crowley: Jupiter
3. Masino: Jupiter
4. Muchery: Mars/Scorpio
5. Papus: Virgo
6. Thierens: Capricorn
7. Wirth: Capricorn

XI—JUSTICE

1. Banzhaf: Jupiter/Mars and Venus in Libra
2. Crowley: Leo
3. Masino: Libra
4. Muchery: Mars/Aries
5. Papus: Cancer
6. Thierens: Aquarius
7. Wirth: Leo

XII—THE HANGED MAN

1. Banzhaf: Pisces and Sun in 12th
2. Crowley: Water
3. Masino: Neptune
4. Muchery: Jupiter/Pisces
5. Papus: Libra
6. Thierens: Pisces
7. Wirth: none

XIII—DEATH

1. Banzhaf: Saturn in 8th
2. Crowley: Scorpio
3. Masino: Scorpio
4. Muchery: Saturn/Aquarius
5. Papus: none
6. Thierens: Saturn
7. Wirth: none

XIV—TEMPERANCE

1. Banzhaf: Venus
2. Crowley: Sagittarius
3. Masino: Sagittarius
4. Muchery: Saturn Capricorn
5. Papus: Scorpio
6. Thierens: Mercury
7. Wirth: Aquarius

XV—THE DEVIL

1. Banzhaf: Pluto
2. Crowley: Capricorn
3. Masino: Capricorn
4. Muchery: Venus/Libra
5. Papus: Sagittarius
6. Thierens: Mars
7. Wirth: none

XVI—THE TOWER

1. Banzhaf: Uranus/Saturn
2. Crowley: Mars
3. Masino: Mars
4. Muchery: Venus/Taurus
5. Papus: Capricorn
6. Thierens: Uranus
7. Wirth: Scorpio

XVII—THE STAR

1. Banzhaf:	Jupiter in 11th
2. Crowley:	Aquarius
3. Masino:	Aquarius
4. Muchery:	Mercury/Gemini
5. Papus:	Mercury
6. Thierens:	Venus
7. Wirth:	Pisces

XVIII—THE MOON

1. Banzhaf:	Moon in Scorpio and Sun in 8th
2. Crowley:	Pisces
3. Masino:	Pisces
4. Muchery:	Moon/Cancer
5. Papus:	Aquarius
6. Thierens:	Moon
7. Wirth:	Cancer

XIX—THE SUN

1. Banzhaf:	Sun in 5th
2. Crowley:	Sun
3. Masino:	Sun
4. Muchery:	Sun/Leo
5. Papus:	Gemini
6. Thierens:	Sun
7. Wirth:	Gemini

XX—JUDGEMENT

1. Banzhaf:	Jupiter/Uranus and Sun in Aquarius
2. Crowley:	Fire
3. Masino:	Pluto
4. Muchery:	Mercury/Virgo
5. Papus:	Saturn
6. Thierens:	Jupiter
7. Wirth:	none

XXI—THE WORLD

1. Banzhaf:	Jupiter in Pisces in	
	harmonious aspect with Saturn	
2. Crowley:	Saturn	
3. Masino:	Saturn	
4. Muchery:	Sun/Leo	
5. Papus:	none	
6. Thierens:	Neptune	
7. Wirth:	none	

This is merely a sample of the various ascriptions we can find. There are other writers and still more differences. Agreements occur, too: thus the ascriptions of Masino are nearly always the same as those of Crowley. However, where Crowley was not tied to a system, Masino was. He, like Thierens, wished to match the twenty-two cards of the Major Arcana to the twelve signs and the ten planets. Crowley assigned the meanings of astrological elements to three of the cards.

In these places Masino diverges from Crowley in order to preserve the correspondences between the signs and planets. Other authors, such as Papus, give no attributions at all in some places. No satisfactory explanation is offered. They either leave a blank, or write "no affinity."

As the reader will observe, the business of making attributions is obviously complicated. It we take a closer look at some of the them, we shall gather why there is no consensus of opinion.

• Example 1: The High Priestess

In our review there seems to be a fair measure of agreement over the attribution to The High Priestess: one author gave no attribution, one author gave Taurus, and five authors gave The Moon.

The High Priestess passes for a perfectly serene yin card. She represents deep receptiveness and total passivity, and throws us back on our own emotions: not our passing feelings, but the depths, the infinity in us. There is no movement in this card except that of the water flowing from her skirts. This waster is connected with the sea hidden behind her veil: that is her secret. She is an infinite yin principle, who stands at the beginning of our emotional development and makes the promise that if we are prepared to give our receptive yin side a place in our lives, we shall eventually come into harmony with infinity and with the unconscious: the sea.

How different is the sign of Taurus, attributed to this card by Thierens (and also by others not mentioned in our review)! Admittedly, a Taurean can display a certain amount of passivity, and popular books state that he or she is born tired (though capable of working very hard and long); but the basic meaning of The High Priestess is in no way represented by Taurus.

Hajo Banzhaf gives, as the astrological counterpart of The High Priestess, "the Moon, as the expression of our lunar consciousness, the intuition and power of our unconscious forces." I doubt that his description of the Moon fits the usual astrological interpretation. In chart readings the Moon has mainly to do with unconscious patterns of behavior, which are unconsciously adopted to make us comfortable again when we feel ill at ease.

Intuition is usually ascribed to other horoscope factors, such as the element Fire, when it is intuition of the Jungian type, or Uranus where flashes of pure insight are concerned. But the Moon is no flag that covers the cargo of The High Priestess card. Although the Moon represents yin qualities, and reflects the light of the Sun, she also has certain active sides and forms of expression, and that is a facet completely absent from The High Priestess. What is more, unconscious behavior patterns are not part of The High Priestess.

• *Example 2: The Devil*

The tarot card, The Devil, stands for an almost irresistible urge to indulge in appetites of all kinds in the most diverse areas. These can range from sexual cravings to a lust for power, from greed to a love of display; the central theme is a concentration on satisfying one's own longings without regard to the consequences for others, and these "others" can be sacrificed in the process if necessary. Often this happens unintentionally, because as a rule we take no pleasure in such behavior, nor in the extent to which we display it.

Our behavior can be an overcompensation for the past. It can connect to a certain phase in youth (puberty!) in which self-assertion and egoism can, within reason, be normal psychic mechanisms for demarcating ourselves, and through trial and error we learn to explore and maintain our identity. The Devil is always a confrontation with the self, and above all with things we do not yet see or would prefer not to know about ourselves. Our repressions and less ethical character traits force their way to the surface in the phase of The Devil in order that we confront them, set them right, and integrate them.

Looking now at the astrological attributions in our list, we see Pluto once, Capricorn twice, Venus in Libra once, Sagittarius once, and Mars once. Wirth has no attribution to suggest.

Anyone who knows anything about astrology will see that there is a world of difference between Pluto and Venus, and between Capricorn and Sagittarius, to mention but two examples. Where a confrontation with the Shadow is concerned, The Devil can certainly share one aspect of Pluto. But, in astrology, Pluto as the god of the underworld is the force that loads one with problems through a powerful outburst or crisis. Pluto is a transforming force, the phoenix that rises from its ashes. He is on a scale that is beyond human control.

To use an illustration: if Mars is a common burglar, then Pluto is the Mafia. Psychologically, Pluto is the image of a volcanic eruption: a great deal of disorder is violently created, and there are scenes of destruction, but deep in the earth in these very areas, the most beautiful gems are formed.

Therefore Pluto is much more than a confrontation with our Shadow. To be sure, he is a mechanism that helps to bring the latter out into the open, but we fail to do justice to Pluto if we equate him with The Devil. That card has nothing to do with crises; I have known people who have drawn it and have had "the Devil to pay" for years without any signs of a crisis. With Pluto this would not be possible.

Thus Pluto has traits that The Devil does not have, but equally The Devil has traits that are not possessed by Pluto. For in itself Pluto does not represent our desire nature!

Essentially, Pluto is a powerful urge toward growth and transformation, and actually confronts us with the inhibiting effect on our psychic growth of seeking nothing but self-gratification.

The sign Capricorn is not an urge or psychic energy but a background for the planets in astrology. Capricorn encapsulates an idea, the idea of identity, arrangement, and structure, such as are encountered in rules and regulations. It is also the sign of methods and obligations, or perseverance and the way up the social ladder. To be honest, I see little in common between Capricorn and The Devil, unless we are supposed only to look at the picture of The Devil as a goat.

The same problem of a lack of consistency in the meanings crops up with Venus/Libra and with Sagittarius. Mars is something of a better prospect: the planet does encourage thoughtlessness in doing what we enjoy without noticing that we are treading on the toes of others. But whereas Mars exhibits a pioneering spirit, initiative, and action, these characteristics are not signified by the card of The Devil. And Mars as the planet of competitive sport is even less like The Devil.

Whichever way we look at it, The Devil cannot be matched with any of the above astrological indicators. Attempts to match it with other astrological factors are even less satisfactory.

We can examine all the cards of the Major Arcana in the same way and hold the astrological attributions up to the light. Only one conclusion can be reached: astrological concepts do not run parallel with those of the tarot; sometimes there is a partial overlap and sometimes there is none at all. Some astrological indicators seem to have been suggested by the design of the card, as we saw when assigning the sign of Capricorn to The Devil because both have goat symbols. If we look at the Tarot de Marseilles, we will notice on the card of The Sun two children who look like twins. So in this card we seem to encounter an astrological reference to Gemini as well as to the Sun!

Some authors also attribute various astrological factors to the cards of the Minor Arcana. We find, for example, the Ace of Pentacles astrologically linked with Venus in the 2nd house, and so on. Although I can sympathize with attempts to combine astrology and the tarot, I must object to this way of working.

In the first place, when attributions are made indiscriminately to both the Major and Minor Arcana (for what difference in importance is there between the Sun in the 5th house for the card of The Sun and Venus in the 2nd house for the Ace of Pentacles?) one receives the impression that the Major and Minor Arcana have an equal weighting in interpretation, since there is no difference in the weightings of the astrological factors.

In the tarot, the cards of the Major Arcana are essentially more penetrating (more archetypal) than those of the Minor Arcana—as their very names suggest! A further objection is that even in the Minor Arcana we do not get complete coverage of the meanings.

However, the Minor Arcana are connected with astrology in another way. The fourfold division, the four suits, seem to be just asking to be coupled with that universal quartet, the four elements. This has been done in various ways; so even here there is no general agreement.

Thierens offers the following attributions:

Wands	=	Air (connected with Clubs);
Pentacles	=	Fire (connected with Hearts);
Swords	=	Earth (connected with Spades);
Cups	=	Water (connected with Diamonds).

Elsewhere we often find these attributions:

Wands	=	Fire;
Pentacles	=	Earth;
Swords	=	Air;
Cups	=	Water.

Only Cups remain the same; the rest differ considerably. Needless to say, this has important consequences for the interpretation and meanings of the cards. Who is holding the right end of the stick? It is only to be expected that an author's opinion is always his own projection. For Thierens, who had a known Theosophical background, the theme "earth" and "solid matter" had to do with heaviness and problems, and was something that could easily trip us up on our journey to spirituality.

But others see an analogy between Pentacles (or Coins), and the concrete physical world. Making a connection between Coins and the element Earth, which is associated with the senses, is then a logical step. Speaking for myself, I have obtained excellent results by applying the second series, in which Wands (Rods) reflect a Fire idea, Swords an Air theme, Pentacles have an affinity with Earth, and Cups are related to Water.

I am careful to think of these as "relationships," because even here we have no complete agreement between the characteristics of the astrological elements and those of the suits of the Minor Arcana.

For instance: Swords have a predominantly "difficult" feel and frequently go with problems. A contentious atmosphere surrounds them, and usually it is a sign that matters will be hard to resolve when Swords appear in a layout.

Astrology knows no difficult or easy elements. Each element represents a certain function of consciousness (which may be linked with the four functions of Jungian psychology), and each function has its advantages and disadvantages, its opportunities and its hazards. Thus, to be sure, there are substantial agreements between the four suits of the Minor Arcana and the four astrological elements, but we must not consider this as an identity!

To date I have not seen a successful attempt to merge astrology and the tarot, nor have I seen anyone able to interchange the symbolism so that it "works." Perhaps we should take an entirely fresh look at the matter.

A very fruitful angle from which to tackle this problem is offered by the psychology of C. G. Jung. Practitioners of astrology, the tarot, or other systems employing symbolism, speak highly of the archetypes of Jung. It is commonly thought that archetypes are, so to speak, latent pictures in the unconscious, which can be developed in different ways. There is a widespread misconception that the archetypes are neatly organized, and, like separate "little boxes," each labeled with its own name and waiting to be opened.

From this—incorrect—point of view it seems logical that each mantic system must ultimately depend on the same "little boxes" and that somehow it must be possible to translate these systems into one another's languages because their symbolism must be interchangeable. Not only has it been found so far that this leads to insuperable difficulties and usually does not work in practice (as I have already demonstrated in regard to the astrological attributions to the tarot), but Jungian psychology does not support such an idea. We have no little pictures or boxes in our unconscious arranged in a neat little row. A wealth of experience is tucked away in our unconscious; we have an incredible fund of "knowledge" enabling us to meet widely differing situations instinctively in the right away. The archetypes in our unconscious act as regulators. They are best described as our innate manner of perceiving, conceiving, and understanding. Just as the newborn infant immediately "knows" that it must suck its mother's breast as soon as it sees and feels it, so do we "know" unconsciously and instinctively what to do in general human situations of all kinds.

This can be crucially important. In the baby in our example we speak of the "mother archetype," which comes to life in the child as soon as it sees and feels its mother. The child projects its inner knowledge on the mother and responds "automatically."

But the archetype also forms images. Archetypes in dreams adopt the appropriate symbolism, that is to say, the symbolism that fits our situation and helps us to gain a better understanding of ourselves and our circumstances. The symbol expresses the archetype in certain pictures, and each archetype has a tremendous range of possibilities in this respect. Thus, in a dream, the mother archetype can appear literally as a mother, perhaps as our own mother, but also as a well, as a cave, as water, as a fruit-bearing tree, as a witch, as the Virgin Mary, and so on. The choice of image by the unconscious completely depends on our psychic situation at the moment and on what the unconscious wants to say with this image in the context of the dream as it unfolds.

Many people think that a given image can belong to only one archetype. But this seems not to be the case. A tree, for example, as an erect object, can have a phallic or male significance, but as the bearer of greenery and fruit, it can also have a female significance. Much depends on the context.

But we also have to bear in mind that there are still more incomprehensible things in the unconscious, and a single image can belong to several different archetypes. The archetypes can also be interconnected and influence one another. Guggenbühl once wrote that our dreams are like theaters in which the archetypes put on performances and communicate with one another.[1]

It may even be that a complex symbol implies an association of several archetypes. Especially in such things as the tarot, where each card presents a tapestry of symbols, there is a good chance that we have to deal with the interplay of just as many unconscious facets, the archetypes. And the interplay of archetypes in a single card certainly

---

1. Adolf Guggenbühl-Craig, *Eros on Crutches: Reflections on Amorality and Psychopathy* (Irving, TX: Spring Publications, 1980), p. 79.

need not be the same interplay that we encounter in a given astrological factor.

I, myself, have the impression that the astrological factors, the components of the horoscope, are less "mixed" than the tarot cards are; and I say this without feeling that one is "better" or "worse" than the other. In my view, the tarot and astrology are essentially different: they are projections of different contents of the unconscious which, whether or not they emerge in combination, are not for that reason interchangeable.

The same applies to the different forms of astrology: Aztec and Western or Hindu astrology are not interchangeable concepts either, but the results of these distinct systems do point in the same direction. That is why, after twenty years of research and experimentation, I have stopped trying to translate the tarot and astrology into one another's languages.

What remains is the possibility of combining two particularly valuable methods while allowing them to speak for themselves. The very fact that they are so different allows them to complement one another splendidly. On numerous occasions, when someone has turned to horary astrology for the answer to some question, I have also asked them to draw tarot cards, and it has regularly happened that the tendencies in the horary chart were paralleled by those in the tarot spread.

But, because of the differences in the composition of the symbols, the tarot cards can provide supplementary information where astrology is silent, while astrology can reveal connections and timing that will put the tarot reading into perspective.

Chapter Nine

WORKING WITH THE CARDS

SOME READERS MAKE a great mystery over working with the cards. We are warned never to allow anyone else to use our cards, or we are told that the cards will not work unless they are kept wrapped in a piece of silk. This tends to give the tarot a magical aura, but this is usually nonsense in practice. Anyone is welcome to hold and examine my cards, and I carry the deck around with me in various ways—sometimes in a handkerchief to keep them clean, sometimes in a plastic bag if it is raining. After use, they are left lying about on top of my desk. In short, they are no more than tools, like the pen with which I write. I have never had any unfortunate repercussions from treating the cards in this manner.

However I can appreciate the thinking behind the obsolete rules. It is certainly important when working with the tarot (and with any other mantic methods such as the I Ching, geomancy, etc.) to be in a quiet and relaxed, yet concentrated, frame of mind. By treating the cards with respect, and observing a little ritual, one can often enter a state that feels quite different from the hurry and scurry of everyday life. So, if you feel the need, you can develop our own rituals for handling the cards; but, again, let it be said, there is absolutely no need to keep hard and fast rules. Treat your deck in the way that is most comfortable for you. This is the most important piece of advice that can be given on the subject.

Whether or not everything runs smoothly in the laying and interpreting of the cards depends largely on your psychological state. If you are in the grip of some strong emotion, you will be unsettled, and this will show in the cards. Frequently at such times, you will draw cards that are not so much an answer to the question as a measure of the intensity of your emotion. Also bear in mind that if you force yourself to sit down and ask a question, this can have the same effect. In other words, when laying the cards, it is good to think about what you are doing and why you are doing it. But go about it in a relaxed manner. If you "do your best" to concentrate on the question to the absolute exclusion of every other thought you will cramp your style. The laying of the cards usually turns out best when you take a playful interest in the subject and are therefore absorbed in it without getting uptight. Rage, fear, and also the state of being head over heels in love, are frames of mind that are best avoided. The problem is that these are your frames of mind when you most feel the need to discover "how things will turn out." It is better to calm down first, and to leave the cards alone until you feel more at ease with yourself.

And this brings us to another point that is often a cause of misunderstanding: what questions are permissible? In principle, you can ask any question in which you have some involvement with the subject or the person. Questions about yourself are always valid. Questions concerning others can give rise to complications, although they do seem to be possible in practice. It is important to remember this: if you ask a question about some third party with whom you have absolutely nothing to do in daily life, you run the risk of getting an utterly meaningless or even a misleading answer.

The chances are that the answer will be a reflection of the motives behind your query. Questions about celebrities who are not personally known to you (such as, "Is film star X having an affair with so-and-so?") are none of your business and will not receive a satisfactory reply. A man once asked me to answer a question of this sort and he drew The Devil. And that was precisely his motive for putting the question: an ego-drive which expressed itself in opposing whatever came on his path, rather provocative behavior in the sense of "you can't do that," and "show me." Thus the card had nothing to say about the subject of his question.

But if you are involved with the person about whom the question is being asked, and if you are directly or indirectly implicated in the activity or situation concerned, then there is a much better chance of obtaining a meaningful reply. But do be aware that what can also come through in the cards is the relationship in which you stand to that person. Say you have taken a dislike to someone who has opened a new business which is obviously thriving, and you want to know how this business will do in the future: you are quite likely to draw The Devil or some such card, and this card will probably not be saying how the other person is going to get on, but that you are hoping he or she will run into all sorts of problems. In other words, it will reveal the hidden motive behind your question.

The tarot usually works best, as a mirror of the unconscious, in the presence of honesty. Therefore always take care when you ask questions about third parties, and be conscious of your motives.

Laying Out the Cards

IF YOU WANT to ask a question, and have decided what layout you are going to use, you begin by shuffling the cards. There is no rule for this. You, yourself, can do the shuffling. If you have a client for whom you are doing the reading, you can let the client shuffle. What we have said above applies here, too: do whatever seems best at the time. It makes no difference whether you are good at shuffling cards or not: there is no need to riffle them dexterously as if you were in a casino or card club. If you cannot manage a hand shuffle, then lay them face down on the table and slide them through each other. The only thing that is important is that the cards should have a new order "of their own" in the deck.

After shuffling, tap the cards into a tidy pile. When you are shuffling or sliding the cards, one of them can fall from the deck. In the Middle Ages there was a well-known saying: "What falls comes." And that applies here, too. But there is the little problem that the fallen card does not come within the chosen layout pattern, so its "place" may not be easy to interpret. A rule of thumb is that this card imparts a certain atmosphere to the whole spread, and is a tendency which has to be taken into account as the other cards are laid.

Push the card back into the deck and proceed with the layout in accordance with the method of your choice. If the card that fell out reappears, the place it occupies is very important! Allow extra weight to it in the interpretation.

In general it is best to draw the cards "blind." This means that when you (or your client) are taking them from the deck, you should not be able to see the faces of the cards. Therefore fan them out with their backs upward and pick a certain number (depending on how many are required for the layout) one after the other. Only after all the necessary cards have been drawn are they laid face up in the order of succession of the spread.

Some people lay each card face up as soon as it is drawn, even though there are other cards still waiting in the deck. This is very inadvisable because the imagery of the card has an influence on the psyche of the person concerned, and emotions can slip in that affect the drawing of the following cards. Just imagine how you would react if you were madly in love and caught sight of the Eight of Swords (or Three of Swords). Involuntarily your heart would have a spasm of fear! Usually, when you are in this situation, you cannot respond objectively to the pictures or see the positive aspects of the "difficult" ones. And so you draw the other cards with a thumping heart and trembling hands.

Therefore it is better to keep the pictures hidden during the entire process of drawing the cards. Even in the case of a card falling accidentally from the deck, it would be wise, when reading for a client, to screen the picture from the client—if the client has not already caught a glimpse of it. If you are laying cards for yourself, this is not possible, of course, but you should pay close attention to the emotions you experience at that moment.

Many tarot readers cut the cards. When the cards have been shuffled and restored to a tidy pile, you (or your client) will separate this big pile at random into two, or often three, smaller piles. Some tarot readers will even look at the undersides of the piles to obtain two or three cards they consider to be significant. But most consultants place the three small piles on top of one another in a new order before commencing the draw.

However, there are many tarot readers who do not cut the cards. Speaking for myself, I have never found that it hurts to neglect cutting them. Whether or not you cut the cards depends entirely on your own attitude toward the matter. If it appears to be a good idea, do it. If it strikes you as pointless, leave it alone.

Is the Future Fixed?

LIFE IS A PROCESS, it is a stream of movements. The tarot cards can help you to decide the nature and characteristics of what is going on around you, and what things are playing a part in it. The processes depicted have their own legitimacy and mode of development, and you will surely meet them in the real world. Let us suppose, for example, that the total picture presented by the cards is that a certain situation has reached its limits as far as you are concerned, and that changes are now required; you may be sure that some such situation will materialize in everyday life and will set you thinking along exactly the same lines. What is more, your contacts with those around you, and their reactions to you, can make it clear that something will have to change.

To that extent the future is predetermined. But—and it is a very big "but"—by identifying the processes at work, you can handle them constructively and turn them to your advantage. This is also the reason why it is hard to "predict" whether or not something will flare up into a drama or crisis: it depends on the individual.

In any case, the cards reveal basic trends, but certainly do not provide a detailed analysis. So there is room to maneuver. Each tendency can materialize in any of a variety of ways. Finally, when you are consulting the cards without being in the grip of some strong emotion such as anxiety, the insight you get into the situation can influence its further course, not to mention the way you tackle it. In fact, during the laying of the cards you are already changing the outcome of the spread, although not necessarily in its main features.

Suppose a relationship has entered a crisis and you wish to know what will happen. You draw The Tower and see a thunderbolt smashing it, and two people falling to the ground. A logical first reaction can be, "Oh dear! There's going to be a dispute, a fight, and a separation." But take a good look at the symbolic meaning of the card and at its role in the whole individuation process, and a completely different light will be thrown on the situation. The card warns you that if you have rusted onto certain ideas and attitudes and have not noticed, or have turned a blind eye to, signals telling you to make changes, there will come a moment when the unconscious is under such pressure that "the dam bursts." Thus The Tower need not be prophesying that your relationship is going to fall apart.

What this card is in fact saying is: take a look at the places where you have become too encapsulated in set patterns and convictions in regard to yourself or the other person. These have now outlived their usefulness. If you are able to deal with them, then the relationship can continue on a wholly new basis. The only thing The tower is saying here is that it is high time for fresh input, and that you will see it being made in your relationship in one way or another—either through a shake-up or through a terrific outburst of emotions—or in some other way.

The core of the matter is that the tarot, as a mirror of your unconscious, reveals what is now ripe for experiencing. In my own practice I have been able to go as far as this, but I have not been able to predict what the client will do, or if the course of events will be constructive or destructive. And this brings us to another essential factor in the laying of the cards: questions that have to be answered by "yes" or "no" do not belong to the tarot. This ensemble of cards full of symbolism gives insight into processes and dynamics. It reveals backgrounds. And that debars any short and simplistic "yes" or "no." Therefore it is preferable to avoid questions of black or white.

What Is the Best Layout to Use?

ALTHOUGH, GENERALLY speaking, books on the tarot describe a few standard methods of laying the cards, new methods are constantly being published. The range of possibilities is simply endless, and this has its advantages and its disadvantages.

What I am about to say may sound strange, but it makes little difference what method you use. The main thing is that it should be a method that appeals to you, and one with which you are conversant or can become conversant. That is what is most important. Some traditional methods are widely advocated, such as the Short Question, the Cross, and the Celtic Cross, and these can be found in most books on the subject. I shall be giving them further on, but by working with the tarot you can spontaneously discover new methods, or the analogy of certain symbols or myths can put you on the track of new methods.

It is obvious that people who work with astrology will quite spontaneously think of laying the tarot cards in the form of a horoscope circle with its twelve houses, only to discover that various authors have already had the same idea. Laying the tarot in a Tree-of-Life pattern in an analogy to the Kabbalah is another example. There is great scope for inventiveness in this area. For instance, you can take The High Priestess card and say that the Tora she has in her hand is a significant point, as is the crown on her head, the Moon at her feet, and the pillars that flank her. In keeping with the symbolism of this card, you can assign a special meaning to each of these places and can associate the meanings with the cards that happen to occupy these places in your layout. In this way layouts are produced on the basis of symbols of all sorts, from the Grail through the signs of the zodiac.

But myths, legends, and fairy tales also lend themselves to pictorial representation. Each myth packages a symbolic message. The successive stages of the narrative can be treated as successive places for your cards, so that each position is linked to a given circumstance or situation in the myth or fairy tale. The card that is laid in that position has to be interpreted in the light of that part of the myth. Admittedly, this requires practice, but it is a very creative manner of working with the tarot. You will discover that the longer you work with the tarot, the greater will be your desire to extract more out of it, and you will want to do different things with it. It is a good idea to develop your own layouts.

What it all boils down to is that there are a few methods that are very widely used, but actually you can fit in all aspects in your spreads. Remember that laying the tarot amounts to working with the unconscious. The language of the unconscious is pictorial, creative, and definitely not logical. Handling images and symbols has an inspiring effect and, if you venture to employ them creatively, you will keep on seeing new dimensions in them, especially in this set of designs which one cannot praise enough.

Nevertheless, if you are just a beginner, it is usually a good idea to have something to go on. Therefore in the following chapters I shall give a few tried and trusted methods. But do feel free to vary them to your heart's content as and when required!

Chapter Ten

BASIC LAYOUTS AND READINGS

T HERE ARE A NUMBER of layouts or spreads you can use to learn about your life using a tarot deck. We will start with the simple ways of reading the cards. You can draw one card, or a number of cards, and you can use very complicated spreads.

The Short Question

A VERY SIMPLE and direct method of reading the tarot cards is to concentrate on your question or situation and to draw one card out of the Major Arcana. This card typifies the (psychic) situation involved in the theme of your question. Insight into the card and its symbolism brings with it further insight into the development of the situation. You can also draw a card without asking a question, in order to see what sort of day or week you will have; the purpose being to learn how to translate the cards into everyday terms, which is a very educational way of working!

For example: a boy had to choose which secondary school to attend. He had the options explained to him and could enter either a big prestigious school with a wide range of instruction, or a small special school which offered only those courses in which he was interested. His classmates were going on to the big school. He was interested not so much in the teaching at the two schools as in what sort of life he would lead in them.

He drew The Devil for the big school and Temperance for the small special school (figure 13, page 202). The Devil is the card of ego drives and obeying the instincts. Translated into the situation of

Figure 13. The Devil (Card 1) and Temperance (Card 2).

a child at the start of the secondary school period, The Devil can point to confrontations with macho behavior and the need to fight for acceptance—by putting on a bold front and the like. Temperance conveys nothing of all this, and (in terms of the schoolboy's situation) suggests a mind at rest.

Not so much on the basis of the cards, as on his impressions of the two schools, the boy chose the small special school. He has been very happy, in spite of the fact that he is the only member of his old class to go there. He feels mentally relaxed and accepted, and has absolutely no need to "act big" in order to get a place in the group. Judging by what they say, his old classmates, who have gone to the big school, have had to put a lot of effort into holding their own.

The Two-Card Spread

As a variant of, and an extension of, the Short Question, we can have a two-card spread. First of all, we take the situation and draw a card from the Major Arcana to signify that, and then we inquire as to how the situation will develop, and for this we draw a second card from the Major Arcana. Card 1 paints the problem and how we ought to approach it, and Card 2 reveals how these things are going to develop, or what we shall encounter one way or another.

The Three-Card Spread

THE THREE-CARD spread is an extension of the two-card spread and allows for the past as well. Concentrating on the question or situation, draw Card 1 for influences from the past, Card 2 for present developments, and Card 3 for future developments. Here again, only cards from the Major Arcana are employed.

The Four-Card Spread or The Cross

IN THIS FINAL layout of cards taken exclusively from the Major Arcana, four cards are drawn and laid in the form of a cross (see figure 14 on page 204). The order of the cards is:

Card 1 = The theme and what is at work
unconsciously or in the background;
Card 2 = What you ought to do;
Card 3 = What you should refrain from doing;
Card 4 = What the consequences will be, or how
the matter will develop.

A series with a somewhat different set of questions can be:

Card 1 = How are you at this moment? or,
What is your situation?
Card 2 = What do you really want? (That need
not always be consciously!)
Card 3 = What are you going to do about it?
Card 4 = How will it go on? How will it develop?

One disadvantage of the second series can be that it contains no caution like that of Card 3 in the first series, which tells you what you should definitely not do. However, in the second series, Card 2 hints at a warning of its own: what you want on the quiet is not always what you think you want. And this card can also give a warning glimpse of some unconscious motive. For example, in cases in which you are actually out to harm somebody, but cover this up with a display of noble motives or decent behavior, Card 2 can suddenly bring you face to face with what is really behind it all.

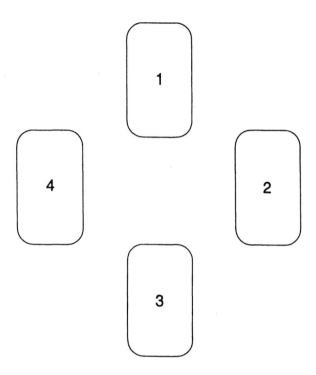

Figure 14. The Four-Card Spread (The Cross).

This four-card layout can also be done using the whole deck, that is to say, with both the Major and Minor Arcana. But then it is important to note that when a card from the Major Arcana falls on one of the four places, that is the main indication. If we are laying The Cross according to the first series and a card of the Major Arcana falls on it, then the following is the significance of the place where the card of the Major Arcana falls:

Place 1 = The theme is extremely important for you;
Place 2 = It is essential to handle the matter with great care; much depends on the way in which you do it;
Place 3 = You are inclined to make wrong decisions. Beware that you do not walk into a trap set by this card!

Place 4 = Developments to do with this theme will
be important for you.

The more cards of the Major Arcana there are that appear in
The Cross, the more emphatically will the theme come to the fore,
and the more important it is for your present and future situation.
The cards of the Minor Arcana carry less weight and are more limited in their effect.

Improvisation

YOU CAN ALSO improvise a short layout on the spur of the moment,
either with the Major Arcana alone, or with the Minor Arcana in
addition. Make sure that you always include the Major Arcana in
your method, because if you use the Minor Arcana on their own you
will miss important details, and the interpretation will have much less
depth.

Here is an example of a spontaneous layout to show how it
works. It concerns a woman in her 30s who suffered from being
overweight. She had tried one diet after another, but had achieved
no more than short-term results in which she lost a reasonable
amount of weight, but quickly put it on again, and in most cases she
could not keep to her diet. As far as her place in the community was
concerned, she was a successful business woman who seemed to
have few problems; her affairs were always in good order, she knew
what she wanted and worked energetically to achieve it. She combined forcefulness with good humor, and those around her did not
see how much she worried about her appearance and her inability to
eat more sensibly. "What is stopping me now from sticking to a
good diet?" she would ask. She was not really looking for a cause,
because she already suspected that the strict upbringing she had
been given by her parents could be a part of it, and this was not
what was bothering her. In further discussions about how the question should be framed it emerged that she sought an explanation
that would help her to understand the phenomenon and also a way
out of the problem.

On the spur of the moment we decided to draw two cards from
the Major Arcana to reflect the background: one to show what was
involved in the problem, and the other to point out the direction in
which the solution lay. We also decided to draw one card from the

Minor Arcana to show what she had been doing wrong so far. The cards she drew are shown in figure 15.

We did not look in books for an interpretation, but set to work on the pictures ourselves. I quickly told the woman the stages occupied by Cards 1 and 2 on the Way of the Hero. It is striking that they present two faces of the feminine: the mysterious-passive one with

Figure 15. Card 1 is The High Priestess; Card 2 is The Empress; Card 3 is the Eight of Swords.

primeval knowledge (The High Priestess) and the creative one who revels in life (The Empress).

It was safe to say that the shoe pinched. I asked her if she was prepared to do absolutely nothing, even if there was nothing to be gained by it. The High Priestess likes to sit quietly and become absorbed in utter stillness, in order to maintain contact with nature, with receptivity, and with femininity. The woman replied that she was not able to do so: she always had an overwhelming desire to be busy and, above all, to be usefully busy. "The Devil will find work for idle hands to do" was something she had learned early in life, and her parents had always taken good care that their children's days were occupied as usefully as possible. The woman said that she was very grateful for this, because it had enabled her to carve out a good career for herself early in life and she was well off.

I asked her to look at the card of The High Priestess and to try to relate to it and, above all, to pay attention to her feelings. The card made quite an impression on her and she thought it was very beautiful. It reminded her of the distant past, of fairy tale times, and of unreality. At the same time she came up with a judgment: "It is not right to remain so passive—unless there is good reason for it." That was an important signal: the imagery of the card had impressed her, it had resonated with an item of knowledge in her unconscious, whereas her upbringing led her to firmly reject the atmosphere of the card. This provided a reason for returning to the theme of "doing nothing."

But first the second card: The Empress. We followed the same procedure. It was not so much the picture, itself, that the woman found repugnant, as the interpretation that it betokened a surrender to life, to enjoyment, and to creativity, regardless of whether this would be productive. When challenged, it appeared that she did not know what enjoyment was. "I enjoy my work," she said, "but if I have no work, I do not know what to do and I feel empty. I cannot enjoy other things."

Even things such as gardening were pleasurable only if they were profitable, and she was able to plan them. I made her look at how comfortably The Empress was leaning back on the cushions. She reacted emotionally when I asked her if she could put herself in the place of The Empress in this picture. Instead of relaxing, she sat up straight, and said that she sensed the very disapproving look of her father, and heard her mother sigh. "You are incorrigible and ungrateful, after all the pains your father and I have taken with you."

She was terribly frightened by this reaction; it had never got through to her that her incapacity for enjoyment and her urge to keep busy doing something useful was fastened to her neck like a chain from the past. She was not living to do what would make her happy, or what she was cut out to do, but she lived the wishes of her parents. It also became clear that this was why she projected the passivity of The High Priestess so far away and had condemned it so roundly at the outset.

She looked at the two pictures again, and carefully started to muse a little: ". . . it would be nice to be like these tarot cards . . . they feel really good . . . but could I manage it? I'm afraid I would go mad if I had nothing to do." And she tried to enter into the atmosphere of these two cards. It was as if they were speaking to her, and she began to be fascinated by them, a sure sign that she needed to do something about their message.

So the problem that, unknown to her, was involved in her obesity, could be couched in some basic questions. Where is your yin component? Why can't you relax properly? Are you prepared to release things and let them go? Are you able to have fun? Do you feel comfortable with your body? Are you enjoying life? The woman had to answer all these questions in the negative and felt very emotional. She did not know whether to weep or if that would be wrong, but she said emphatically that she felt that it was very important for her to be still.

The we dealt the Minor Arcana card: the Eight of Swords. "That's exactly how I feel," she exclaimed, and then more crossly, "And I never know what is going on, but I feel all knotted up. I don't know which way to turn anymore, I see that now. And I also see that I am trying to escape from this sense of oppression by eating!"

The Eight of Swords was drawn in answer to the question, "What have I been doing wrong to date?" At first sight what is going on outside the woman seems to be implicated, but I have known various women to draw this card when they were trapped in a "Cinderella complex," a complex that made them subservient to others. They neglected their own interests in order to pull other people's chestnuts out of the fire. They worked all out for others, if necessary until they dropped, and even when they knew that they had been overdoing it, they refused to take care of themselves. Whether or not they were successful socially depended on their behavior; but in either case they had a fundamental mistrust of themselves, their identities, and their bodies, as if to say, "Don't you see? I am not fit to be alive!" In my own experience, this attitude is often associated with strong opinions on how one should live and act. And one erroneous lesson that had been hammered home to them was that they must treat themselves remorselessly because self-pity is childish.

In practice, it seems that women of this type can fight and work for others very well, but are extremely hard on themselves. As an odd compensation of the unconscious, they have less and less control of their own affairs. They seem to attract the wrong advisers, are unable to persevere with their diets and, in short, their personal and inner lives are frequently the very opposite of their social success.

Nor was this lady any different. I asked her to take another look at the card. The woman on the card is blindfolded and can no longer perceive reality well. What is more, she is unable to move her arms because they are tightly bound. Only her feet are free; she can run away from the situation, but needs the help of others to release herself. Behind the swords we see a castle, a symbol of settled values. She must run away from these, through mud and water—or, in other words, through her problems, her Shadow, and her unconscious desires—in order to emerge from the morass. She must discover her own values.

The swords are grouped in three on her right hand, which means: "Revise your fixed ideas!" There are five on her left hand, pointing to movement of another kind—the springing into life of Lilith, or suppressed femininity. This means: "Dare to relate!" So the card is not really so bad; it reveals that there is a way out.

But the underlying attitude that everything in her life was predetermined, plus the lack of yin (The High Priestess and The Empress) which expressed itself in a Cinderella complex (one possible effect of the Eight of Swords), was her real problem and it had materialized in her overweight.

She wrestled with the situation for a time, and was eventually able to decide not to be so hard on herself, or to punish herself so much. Little by little, she learned to relax, although in the beginning there were considerable withdrawal symptoms. But she felt that her attitude had to change. And she was more flexible in regard to her diet, too. She no longer went in for demanding on strict diets, but watched what she ate now and then. Very gradually she has shed a few pounds, and she knows that she can lose more in the future.

However, she is not bothered about it, and has even managed not to set a target weight. In complete agreement with the two yin cards, she knows intuitively that a moment comes when you just feel good, and then you must not push yourself any further. The entire process has taken years, but she feels considerably better. Her cheerfulness is now genuine, and no longer a mask in order to help her to "belong," as she once described it.

So here was a layout that arose spontaneously, and we worked mainly with the pictures. Of course, the meanings of the cards entered into the reading, one cannot ignore them; but the treatment was open and creative. This is an example of associating and connecting the client with the cards and observing how she reacted from deep within herself. When you are very familiar with the tarot, this method is a marvelous help in therapy and support.

Chapter Eleven

THE CELTIC CROSS SPREAD

For the Celtic Cross, ten cards are drawn and laid in the pattern illustrated in figure 16, page 212. Each position has its own significance, and the card that falls on it must be interpreted in the light of that position. The meanings of the positions are:

1. The situation of the querent or the question being asked.

2. Whatever tends to interfere with the situation, or whatever is experienced as some form of resistance. This need not always be actual resistance, it can also be help that is misinterpreted!

3. What is prominent in the querent or the question. In other words, the causes or forces clearly affecting the question. It can be treated as whatever influences the question or situation as seen by the conscious.

4. Things that are fundamental to the querent or to the question, or are applicable to the situation, or are so firmly anchored in the unconscious that they make themselves felt time after time, even when we have forgotten about them. These can be pleasant, but also unsettling because, again and again, whatever we do, they seem to step out of nothing. At this point I must observe that often I have seen the card signify some inconvenience at the start, even when it is one that the querent regards as positive. I believe that what happens, in this position, is that a number of cards that bring hidden talents or creative potential to light, do so at awkward moments, or with the help of mechanisms that we do not particularly appreciate. For exam-

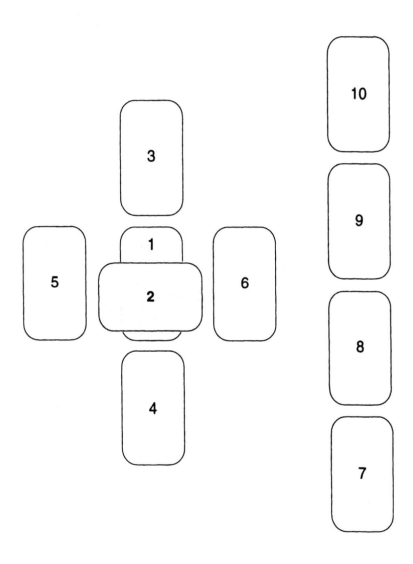

Figure 16. The Celtic Cross.

ple, if you are subject to lapses of concentration and you find The Empress at Position 4, your unconscious is almost crying out that the time is ripe to enjoy yourself or to give free rein to your artistic skills, but in any event, it refuses to dwell any longer in hidebound patterns. If you are very busy in your job, this call for a change can be absolutely irritating, but it is really a move in the direction of inner wholeness. Position 4 is not easily pushed aside.

5. Those influences from the past that are at work in the current question or situation.

6. Developments that will become apparent in the short term.

7. The querent as far as he or she relates to the question or situation; that is to say, his or her position in regard to it, and the character traits that play an important role in what has been going on.

8. The part taken by others in the question, or the nature of the environment; in short, any influences that have to do with the role of other people who are involved in, or occupied with, the matter (the active part) and or the role of the actual place where the things concerned are occurring (the passive part).

9. What the querent is looking forward to and/or what the querent fears.

10. Different descriptions are possible here, depending on the way in which the question is put, or on the aspect that is emphasized. Position 10 represents the conclusion of the entire matter if there is something to conclude. It can also reveal developments in the more distant future (Position 6 always has to do with the near future) if we are dealing with a process or evolution of some sort. Thus Position 10 shows us in which direction or sphere the question will end up.

The Celtic Cross is an easily grasped method which provides a great deal of background information, and therefore is much employed when the tarot cards have to be laid for a complete stranger. The cards give many starting points for a consultation.

A method mentioned earlier applies here, too. Wherever a card of the Major Arcana falls, that position should receive extra attention, because this card will play a prominent part in the whole affair.

• *Example 1: A New Life*

A man going on 50 drew the following cards for The Celtic Cross without really asking a question (see figure 17 on page 215). The situation in which the querent found himself was shown by the Six of Swords in Position 1. Outwardly his life was running smoothly and seemed to have little in common with this card: he had a career, a fine family, was reasonably healthy, and very little of the Six of Swords was visible to others. Inwardly, however, the man was worried out of his mind. He was having more and more difficulty with fears which he had always struggled to hold at bay, yet which had always affected his functioning in the outside world to some extent. A lack of self-acceptance had given him, on the one hand, an attitude of "at all costs avoid attracting attention" and, on the other hand, boyish behavior in order to avoid the things mentioned. And whenever, in spite of himself, he had to stand in the spotlight, he immediately became very defensive, and was sharper and more forceful than he really felt, especially in the way he spoke. He wanted to change this conduct and to make a fresh start. The Six of Swords showed that he had already embarked on a new behavior and new attitude. But the swords are still in the boat—he was taking his old self along. Looking for a new attitude meant a confrontation with this own swords in order to throw them out of the boat one by one. The promise of a fresh start beckoned, but there was still much tidying up of things left over from the past to be done.

The Magician lies across the first card and occupies Position 2. Because it is a card of the Major Arcana, this position is heavily emphasized—so there is a lot of obstruction! Normally, The Magician is a strong yang card, full of male energy, and ready for action, for new undertakings and fresh starts, in order to reach new understandings and results. When it lies across, there can be problems with male identity, or an inability to take action, or some kind of overcompensation in these areas.

In Example 1, the man admitted that he had great difficulty with himself. He did not know what it meant to take a stand. Yes, he could stand up for impersonal things, but not for himself. The consequence was a feeling of insecurity in himself and with regard to the outside world, and a lifelong denial of his ability to do anything, of his executive ability; therefore he withdrew as much as possible from situations in which he would have to do some decision-making. He

Figure 17. The Celtic Cross. This example is discussed in the text.

also avoided confrontations outside his small circle. The change of attitude that he sought with the Six of Swords, centers here on the problem of his sense of personal worth in the area of masculinity and decisiveness, and that is strongly accentuated.

With the Ten of Cups at Position 3, he knows that, whatever else may be amiss, he is supported by his family. A measure of emotional comfort and security is present, which he rates very highly. In fact, much of his motivation is provided by his children. This has both its positive and its negative sides. The positive side is that here is a first step toward knowing he is secure and accepted. The negative side is that his domestic environment supplies him with an escape route, a safe place where he can go into hiding and take no further steps into the outside world, or at least no more than are absolutely necessary. Also this retreat into a small circle can accentuate the lack of initiative and action represented by the "at-cross-purposes" Magician.

The Three of Wands at Position 4 keeps acting on the querent from the unconscious, and colors the problem in which he find himself. Frequently we see the Three of Wands putting in an appearance when someone is at a turning point, or a point of intersection. You have achieved something and can reap the benefit of it, yet at the same time you realize that you want to do more. There is a search for a new fulfillment, or for an improvement in the old fulfillment, because some of the turmoil of building a career is over. In itself, this is a friendly card. In the case of this man, it was immediately clear that he also wrestled with the idea that he was now "unemployable," by which he meant that if he were to lose his job, he would fall into the category of job-seekers employers automatically turn down. He was too old. And this troubled him a lot. Now there was not the least sign that he would lose his job—far from it. But the mere idea that he could be called unemployable filled him with anxiety. In the light of what we have already discovered, that is understandable. Naturally, if one has already been struggling with low self-esteem, unemployability is not an encouraging thought. Behind the thought (and this explains his sensitivity to it) really lies the problem of the cross-lying Magician and the central Six of Swords. The man also mentioned that in the past he had had various jobs, which he had found enjoyable in themselves, but now he was utterly unable to summon up any enthusiasm for them. Nor did he have any sense of being able to benefit from them or to build on them, even though this is a feature of the Three of Swords. And yet that theme was at work in another way. After reviewing and pondering on his life, he concluded that there were a number of things he simply could not do any more. Some dreams had flown, which grieved him, but many dreams had faded, probably because he had become more mature. And he realized that as he had altered, he had obtained inner help to find a new attitude to life. Out of his unconscious came the conviction that he had reached a turning point and was searching for new fulfillment in life, and clearly he would have to do something about it.

The King of Swords at Position 5 reveals that a very hard frame of mind has persisted from the past, from which emotions have been excluded, possibly in the interests of keeping a cool head. So the King of Swords can often get the right end of the stick—but not always. The man responded at once by describing the cruel way in which his mother used to tease him, and how when she saw him at a loss, she would deliberately rub salt into the wound to make him feel even more insecure. She had had her fun with him for years, and he had suffered immensely and had become very shy and withdrawn. What is more, her treatment of him made him very defensive against the outside world. He also reckoned that this card reflected his very hard, negative judgment of himself, which gave him such a lack of self-confidence.

The King of Wands at Position 6 represents short term developments. Hopefully that is the man's problem; this is to say, he has a great need to come to terms with certain issues, or actively seek self-development. However, he does not want to do this in a childish and unconcerned way, but with more maturity and independence. And that is precisely what the King of Wands shows. His inner conflict should lead to a changed attitude, although he still has a fight on his hands with the cross-grained Magician.

The Two of Pentacles at Position 7 is the querent, himself, in this situation. It reveals the inconsistency between what he expects of life and the way he goes about trying to achieve it. The issue here is whether or not he is prepared to commit himself to life and to derive enjoyment from what he does. In the light of what has gone before, this card underlines the attitude he has already built up—which he is now going to experience as a problem—and it asks him what he is going to do about it.

The World, another card of the Major Arcana, at Position 8, informs us about the role of others in this reading, and also about the influence of the place where the man lives. The World is a card that gives way and dances, which might indicate that the environment does not make things difficult for the man as he is. He is accepted by it; but then The World also shows that his environment has little hold on him. Even the place where he lives has no real influence on his process. In a positive sense, The World here suggests that he is not being harassed by the people around him, and that he is permitted to be himself. In a negative sense, this can mean the absence of any incitement to get busy, leaving him to motivate himself. The World in this position appears to reinforce the role of the Ten of Cups at Position 3: his positive family life supports him, but can also provide him with an easy way out.

The Four of Pentacles at Position 9 represents the fear of making a move. Position 9 shows what one looks forward to or what one dreads. This seems somewhat paradoxical: dreading the fear of making a move. But you can look at it this way: the man is expecting that "nothing will come of it again," wholly in keeping with his negative self-image. He always feels a strong inclination to stay put. Because Pentacles are involved here, this affects his functioning in the material world mainly. Although he does not derive much satisfaction from his job, he has been taking no steps to look for anything else. So there are few concrete impulses. We saw with the King of Wands at Position 6 that he will, in fact, be taking some initiative. With the Four of Pentacles here, this is going to create one or two problems for him, but the King of Wands promises he can certainly carry the day. He reacted to this information with a mixture of joy, surprise, and a pinch of disbelief.

And finally, the Page of Pentacles at Position 10 indicated that he would undertake new activities, as well as throwing himself into current activities with renewed enthusiasm and a fresh approach. And that confirmed, "in conclusion," something of the message of the King of Wands, namely that he ought to be taking some initiative. But the Page of Pentacles is a stripling, and has a youthful outlook. Pages can find it difficult to handle responsibility, and the Page of Pentacles is in a certain tension-field here. Pentacles are oriented toward a concrete result of some sort, but Pages are still rather inexperienced and feckless. A possible compromise is for the man to start doing things that interest him, to get involved in them, and to enjoy them. It does not matter too much whether the things in question are certain activities in his job or are hobbies, as long as they are practical.

Without the man having to put a question, The Celtic Cross exposed the deeper-lying problems with which he had been wrestling for some time, his attitude toward them, and the reasons for this. It was amazingly appropriate, as he was quick to recognize; and it demonstrates how useful this spread is when nothing specific has been asked.

Chapter Twelve

THE TREE OF LIFE SPREAD

T HE TWENTY-TWO CARDS of the Major Arcana are associated by various practitioners of the tarot and the Kabbalah with twenty-two paths linking ten Sephiroth in the Tree of Life, a key symbol in Kabbalism.

The Kabbalah, which had been passed down by word of mouth for centuries, began to be committed to writing in the present era. Important sources are the *Sepher Yetzirah* (The Book of Creation) and the collected writings of Rabbi Simeon ben Yochai, in the Zohar (*Sepher ha-Zohar* = The Book of Splendor).[1]

In essence, the Kabbalah discusses the nature of God and the divine emanations in our world, and is a mystical and symbolic account of Creation. The Kabbalah states that God permeates the whole universe, that He *is* the universe. Nevertheless, His presence is apparent only when He activates His creative power, and as a medium for this, He uses the ten Sephiroth or intelligences that stream out of Him like light from a light-source.

---

1. Students who want to explore the Kabbalah can read numerous books published on the subject. The *Sefer Yetzirah* was edited by Rabbi Aryeh Kaplan (York Beach, ME: Samuel Weiser, 1990), and the most common edition of the Zohar is edited by Maurice Simon and Paul Levertoff (New York: Soncino Press, 1934). In addition, see William Blank, *Torah, Tarot & Tantra* (Boston: Sigo Press, 1991), Alexandra Gabrielli, *Kabbalah* (Wassernaar, Holland: Mirananda, 1981), and Gareth Knight, *A Practical Guide to Qabalistic Symbolism* (York Beach, ME: Samuel Weiser, 1978).

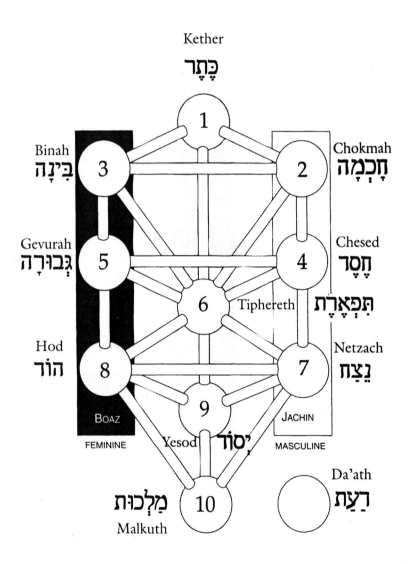

Kether
כֶּתֶר

Binah
בִּינָה

Chokmah
חָכְמָה

Gevurah
גְּבוּרָה

Chesed
חֶסֶד

Tiphereth
תִּפְאֶרֶת

Hod
הוֹד

Netzach
נֵצַח

BOAZ

JACHIN

FEMININE

MASCULINE

Yesod
יְסוֹד

Da'ath
דַעַת

Malkuth
מַלְכוּת

Figure 18. The Kabbalistic Tree of Life, with the Three Pillars.

The Sephiroth are also described as dynamic energy sources, and as fields of action within the human soul. The first Sephirah is the desire to become manifest. It contains the nine remaining Sephiroth, which issue from one another in numerical order. See figure 18 on page 222.

1. KETHER: THE CROWN

The center that crystallizes out of the Limitless Light. The will or the desire of the Godhead, the germ of creation: therefore, the germ of individual consciousness. Although there is no agreement in the literature over its sex—some say that Kether is male, others say it is male or female—Kether is often symbolically regarded as paternal.

In tarot readings, Kether can be seen as the pattern that totally underlies your current development. It is the dynamics from which everything flows, but at the same time it is the goal toward which (if you lack insight) everything is unconsciously heading.

A confrontational card at this position can reveal a fixed pattern that has held you in its grip over a long period of time. However, because the card has landed on this place, the pattern will now be transformed.

2. CHOKMAH: WISDOM

The Crown becomes conscious of itself and projects an image of itself in Chokmah: standing face to face with the Godhead. "The Word was with God and the Word was God" (John 1:1). The universe was created by the attendant Wisdom, also known as primeval form. Symbolically regarded as the Son, also divine creativity.

3. BINAH: UNDERSTANDING, INTELLIGENCE

From the above-mentioned pure force arises the idea of form. Binah is still a force, but a form-idea slumbers within it. Understanding implies that there is something to be understood, whereas Wisdom, the previous Sephirah, is more abstract. Binah is female, and symbolically she is the mother. Also discerning insight and reason are ascribed to Binah. Binah is the written Torah (in contradistinction to the oral Torah). In the capacity of the written Torah, Binah belongs to the physical world, which is why Binah is often called prime matter.

In tarot interpretation: where do we need insight? What dynamic has become involved without our having been aware of its significance? Just as a mother is always present as a factor in the background, and her role is usually taken for granted, so can a card in this position point to a powerful influence of which we may not be fully aware.

Are you able to yield to this energy and to integrate it without coercion (that is to say, in a yin manner)? A self-evident way of doing things, which is striking to others, though not to you, yourself, can also be indicated by a card at this place.

These first three Sephiroth form, as it were, the thought behind reality: they lie at a very deep level. They represent the world of ideas (or of emanation). The next three display a much more material activity and together form the world of creation, also termed the ethical world. They may be regarded as a condensation of the first three Sephiroth.

4. CHESED: MERCY, KINDNESS, LOVE, GRACE

The latent energy of the universe; virgin energy. The experience of luck and favorable conditions. You are especially aware of this when you are heading toward a goal that suits you, and this, in turn, affects your personality.

In tarot interpretation: what influence have your attainments had on you (regardless of whether we are talking about parenthood or high earnings)? Such successes set the tone for your further development. What direction looks hopeful?

With confrontational cards there is a warning that we run the risk of forfeiting luck and favorable conditions if we persist in the attitude signified.

5. GEVURAH: SEVERITY, STRENGTH, AND JUDGMENT

Also called "fear," it is connected with the inexorable law or the inexorable course of life. It is in this light that we have to see the attribute of "judgment." It is no ordinary fear, but is more akin to the "fear of God," the feeling of awe when in the presence of a mighty power.

In tarot readings: what have we to fear concerning our development? What must we be on our guard against? What is bound to come upon us through the law of cause and effect, or through some course of events that we are unable to change? What makes us full of will-power and assists our motivation? Gevurah seems rather negative, but is not so in reality. It reveals what we are about to encounter because the time is ripe for it, irrespective of whether it is pleasant or unpleasant. The experience, negative or positive, can strengthen and motivate us. Of course, with confrontational cards, the process is more testing.

6. TIPHERETH: BEAUTY, ORNAMENT

The central point of the Tree of Life and the center of gravity of everything that has been and of all that is to come. Tiphereth is also called the liberator, and represents balance. Beauty and balance are the result of grace and law together. But Tiphereth is also the balance between Kether (1) and Malkuth (10).

In tarot interpretation: how balanced are we inwardly? Are we sufficiently balanced psychically to be able to cope with life? How do we stand in regard to ourselves?

With confrontational cards, the whole Tree of Life will be affected, because then the capacity for being flexible and balanced in one's approach is reduced.

The next triangle is considered to be the invisible side of the entire physical, or natural, world.

7. NETZACH: VICTORY, FIRMNESS, ETERNITY

The balance of Tiphereth has become divided into different aspects or energies. This is an active Sephirah. Netzach is also the power of creative imagination, or imagination in general, and of the emotions. Dominance is another attribute of Netzach, but then in relation to its antipode Hod. Netzach indicates fixed patterns that are successful or useful.

In tarot interpretation: what dynamics or energies are available to you for redirecting your creativity into successful patterns? Or, with confrontational cards, what energy is obstructing this redeployment and therefore needing to be overcome?

8. HOD: GLORY, SPLENDOR

The energies of Netzach now take form. Hod is the power of the concrete imagery belonging to mental concepts; submission in regard to Netzach; in a positive sense, our life gains luster when we are prepared to make a sacrifice in order to bring our creativity to the surface. The sacrifice is to cultivate "submission." We are no longer completely free. But the creative facet that comes into view now is able to shine and can become increasingly conspicuous.

In tarot interpretation: what has to be sacrificed before further progress can be made? Or: what will brighten our life?

9. YESOD: FOUNDATION, BASIS

In this basis all the powers of the previous Sephiroth come together, and Yesod forms the source of all that exists, and everything perceptible and palpable on Earth. Yesod is like an architectural drawing, or blueprint, of what is going to be expressed in the following Sephirah. The world of instincts is also included in Yesod.

In tarot interpretation: what is slumbering below the surface, but is at the point of breaking through, both psychologically and in concrete reality? Also: what path can help us to move inward (thus from Malkuth to the highest Sephiroth)?

10. MALKUTH: KINGDOM

In this Sephirah we behold the total of all the foregoing Sephiroth; Malkuth is correctly seen as Earth, but it is better to treat it as our whole physical universe, of which Yesod is, so to speak, the subtle body. Malkuth is the world of paradoxes: here contraries encounter each other as conflicting forces, and male and female oppose each other, whereas on a higher level of the Tree of Life they are harmoniously united. Malkuth is the world of the human individual in which one has to struggle, and must do one's best in daily life to restore harmony to the primary polarity. (It is generally accepted that we can gain access to the last seven Sephiroth, but that the upper three are beyond our reach.)

In reading the tarot, although the card that falls here implies immediate and direct confrontation with reality, this card cannot be seen in isolation from all the preceding cards because they demonstrate the process of construction, of which this one is the result.

Not only does the figure of the Tree of Life have special places for each of the ten Sephiroth, but it is constructed according to a profound pattern. Thus the Tree of Life has three pillars:

- The middle pillar is nameless, but is termed the pillar of mildness; this pillar symbolizes balance and union, and is androgynous;

- The left hand pillar is called Boaz, and is the pillar of Justice; it is the female pillar, and its color is black;

- The right hand pillar is called Jachin, and is the pillar of Mercy; this is the male pillar, and its color is white.

The ten Sephiroth are distributed among the three pillars: four on the middle pillar, three on the left, and three on the right. Each of the Sephiroth on the three pillars are also linked both directly and indirectly in a pattern known as the paths. As mentioned above, there are twenty-two paths regularly associated with the twenty-two cards of the Major Arcana.

The Sephiroth Kether (Crown), Chokmah (Wisdom), and Binah (Understanding), the first, second, and third, together form a triangle with the point up. Numbers four, five, and six, Chesed, Gevurah, and Tiphereth, form a triangle with the point down. What is more, the two triangles are so arranged that these Sephiroth combined together form a circle (see figure 18, page 222).

Underneath these are four further Sephiroth, which can be joined by lines, but can also be made into a three-dimensional figure: the tetrahedron, or four triangular surfaces which form a unity. Here the numbers three and four are joined together in a way that marks the entry of solid, material form.

Although there is much more symbolism in the Kabbalistic Tree of Life than this, we are concerned mainly with symbolism we can use for a tarot reading. Once you become familiar with the combination of the tarot and the Tree of Life, I can whole-heartedly recommend dipping deeper into the Kabbalah. The Tree of Life layout (shown in the next section) will gain more perspective and an extra dimension, and will become a real adventure! It will no longer be a spread that you use "just" to answer questions. The Tree of Life is concerned with more spiritual and mystical matters; not least with your own development as a unique individual, your individuation process as Jung would call it.

So how can the Tree of Life be used as a tarot spread? Actually in any way that appeals to you, but the following can serve as a guide.

The Tree of Life and the Major Arcana

IN ORDER TO GAIN insight into your psychic (of the psyche) state, you can lay cards of the Major Arcana on the diagram of the Tree of Life, preferably on the places of the ten Sephiroth. The spread has then to be interpreted in the light of the meanings of each place. Room can also be made for the so-called eleventh, hidden, or veiled Sephirah, Da'ath. Some people locate it between the second and third Sephiroth (which, when taken together, represent the marriage between man and woman), but if there is no room for it in the layout, you can set it by itself, at the side of (or under) the Tree of Life. From a symbolic point of view, it is better not to put it above the Tree, because that is the place of God.

The Tree of Life and the Major and Minor Arcana

HERE WE SET to work in precisely the same way as described above, except that now the whole deck is employed. More depth is attached to any interpretation whenever cards of the Major Arcana are dealt, for the places where they fall are accentuated, and attract a part of the interpretation to themselves.

The Comprehensive Tree of Life

FOR THIS WE TAKE the Major and Minor Arcana and lay the cards face down, one after another, on the ten Sephiroth from 1 through 10, starting at 1. In total, you can go around seven times so that each Sephirah gets seven cards. The remaining eight cards belong to the secret eleventh Sephirah, Da'ath.

The art of the reading is to associate the meaning of each Sephirah with the cards that fall on its place. These cards reveal inhibitions and stimuli, needs and problems in the manifestation of this divine emanation or theme. Thus we have to find a connection between the seven cards on each Sephirah so that they present a coherent picture or story. Initially it may not be easy to do. The method is quite complicated and requires experience to handle successfully, but it is worth the trouble.

• *Example 1: A Male Client*

A middle-aged man dealt the following cards on the ten Sephiroth of the Tree of Life in order to gain some insight into his current situation. Although there was a lot going on, and his situation was turbulent, he was coping well and was not letting things get him down. These were the cards (see figure 19 on page 230):

1. Kether: Nine of Swords
2. Chokmah: The Emperor
3. Binah: Ace of Wands
4. Chesed: Seven of Wands
5. Gevurah: Page of Cups
6. Tiphereth: Judgement
7. Netzach: Temperance
8. Hod: Ten of Swords
9. Yesod: The Fool
10. Malkuth: The Chariot
    Da'ath   Three of Pentacles

There are five Sephiroth that stand out because a card of the Major Arcana has been dealt on them: 2, 6, 7, 9, and 10. Sephirah 6 is particularly important: Tiphereth indicates how the man looks at himself, and how well balanced he is and if he is able to cope with problems. Judgement is positive here and confirms the impression he has already made. He is fairly optimistic and able to accept the turmoil in his life (both inside him and outside him) and can see the reason for it without rationalizing it. With this combination we can view the remainder of the layout with greater confidence.

The Fool is about to put in an appearance: he is still dormant, but is on the point of breaking through, at Yesod. It is a step into space, into the new and unknown. A new direction in life, or some great inner changed combined with a new attitude is on the point of manifesting itself. The man has known for some time that his life ought to be different, but has not been able to say what the difference should be, or how it might come about. This impression has been quite strong.

Figure 19. The Tree of Life Spread.

Malkuth has The Chariot. This signifies taking oneself in hand, and is an impulse toward the (further) development of the ego. It also signifies an awareness of the opposing forces in oneself which have to be mastered (the black and white sphinxes that are supposed to be pulling the chariot). In combination with The Fool immediately above, it presents him with the task of taking a fresh look at himself and, at the same time, of dealing with his inner drives in a new way, without losing sight of them or failing to keep control of them. With Judgement on Tiphereth, he should be able to face this development confidently.

However, the Nine of Swords on Kether shows that the man's inner problem goes back a long way. Kether is called the father, and although this is meant metaphorically, the man is in no doubt that his own father's harshness and lack of affection in the past had done him a great deal of psychological damage. He observed that the thought "father" still bothered him, in spite of therapy, and his own efforts to work on it. The Nine of Swords is a depressing card with apparently nothing much to offer. We can find the cause in the patterned quilt. If you take a close look at it, you will see various astrological symbols. The one classical planet that is missing is Venus! Venus, as you may know, is the planet of relationship—the energy directed to, and holding out a hand to, the other person. It is the security provided by the love between oneself and others. All this is missing from the bed quilt and is a contributory cause to the depression of the Nine of Swords. When thinking is taken too far without any communication with life and with a partner, it falls apart. Kether is, so to speak, asking for Venus to be embroidered on the quilt, or in other words, for the man to be prepared to relate more.

The Emperor on Chokmah reveals that every effort is being made to deal with concrete issues efficiently. But rigidity and inhibition and dullness, and the desire to control too much, can obstruct the attainment of the inner goal. Since the card in question belongs to the Major Arcana, the warning is all the stronger.

The Ace of Wands on Binah shows that the man has no (or almost no) idea how much various thoughts and initiatives play a role from his side. What sort of role? Their practicality can rescue this man from problems of all kinds. While he does whatever is necessary right away, the combination of The Emperor on Chokmah, indicates too much control, and some of what he does, when added to his holding on to things, may possibly thwart his inner goal. For there are no ventures that the Nine of Swords facilitates in any way. Even though taking charge and being active can sometimes help when he is feeling down, it is really important to get involved in the outside world and in life itself when the Nine of Swords enters the picture. The Ace of Wands can reveal strong self-involvement, because it represents a naive flow of possibilities and ideas, but The Emperor is definitely not a friendly card.

The Seven of Wands on Chesed lies in the same line. What help may we expect? In itself, keeping busy can give a good feeling. But the seven is paradoxical, and carries with it the danger that whatever is done will readily create and aggravate strife. A war of attrition with oneself is another risk of the Seven of Wands. He must look out for this in case it spoils things.

However, the Page of Cups on Gevurah comes irrevocably on his path, with a budding emotional life or some premature emotional response—and the Page, being only a Page, is still uncertain as to what to do. Now, uncertain or not, this is definitely something which he needs in order to counter the Nine of Swords on Kether. It is important for him to do something with his burgeoning feelings, for what he does will bear fruit.

Netzach has Temperance and Hod has the Ten of Swords. Netzach asks what energy we can expend in order to express our creativity in a better way. Temperance is a dynamic that we encounter in our psyche after a difficult time or crisis, when things have calmed down and we are no longer putting on an act, but have laid aside all masks, all artificial behavior. In this state of tranquillity we are trying to become more balanced—that is what Temperance is saying here. If the man is able to preserve his inner calm (and with Judgement on Tiphereth there is every chance that he will do so) his creativity will break through of itself. However, he must take care that he does not relax into a state of pseudo-rest and imagine that he has already arrived. For with the Nine of Swords on Kether, this is a distinct danger. The Ten of Swords on Hod gives clear notice that he must give up his opinion of himself if he wants to avoid inhibiting his creative processes. A light glimmers on the horizon in the Ten of Swords, but with this card one often sees strongly negative thoughts or fears which hamper the life. The man will have to give up these before he can go further, before he can make his life brighter.

On Da'ath falls the Three of Pentacles. His work is not yet done. He must keep pressing on to reach his goal. Da'ath's "knowledge" can best be interpreted as a reassurance that, if he makes due allowance for the insights gained from the rest of the reading, the path he is now on will lead to genuine results.

The picture that emerges as a whole is that the man, himself, is well balanced (Judgement on Tiphereth) in spite of the difficult time he is having. He will keep regaining his composure. His inner problems have mainly to do with negative judgments and situations from the past, in which he was deprived of affection and did not feel a part of life—the Nine of Swords on Kether.

The man can set to work systematically (The Emperor) and make every effort to overcome the problems, but runs the risk of setting too high a standard, falling back into his old pattern, and remaining negative about himself.

He may not realize how active he is, and how many new things he is devising with the unconscious intention of providing himself with some form of security (the Ace of Wands on Binah).

This pattern of activities can obstruct his emotional ties with the world. He is far too busy, and with the Seven of Wands on Chesed, even runs the risk of setbacks from excessive activity, or from fighting a long battle with himself.

Situations will arise in which he will come in contact with his feelings, although he will not feel entirely comfortable with them (the Page of Cups), and he needs to realize the contact is vitally important for his further development (he will be judged on it at Gevurah!).

Although he is in a position to live and work tranquilly, he has to guard against developing this into a sort of mental detachment, or the Page of Cups will not be able to make itself felt.

What is more, he must do something about his low opinion of himself—the Ten of Swords on Hod. Thus he must make room for his emotions and must abandon his negative thoughts. Then The Fool on Yesod will be free to take a positive step toward a new life, with fresh responsibilities and an identity that is in the course of changing (The Chariot on Malkuth).

The fact that the Middle Pillar has a card of the Major Arcana on three out of four positions indicates that the man is standing at an important point in his life, a period in which there is a great deal of activity and inner turmoil on the way to a new equilibrium.

Chapter Thirteen

THE ASTROLOGICAL
TAROT SPREAD

FOR ASTROLOGERS, interpreting the twelve houses of the horo-scope is a tried and trusted method. Certainly experienced prac-titioners of astrology, who have the meaning of the twelve houses at their fingertips, will soon master the art of laying the tarot cards on the places of the twelve astrological houses. Even non-astrologers can do well, but of course it will take them longer to understand the finer points that will be apparent to a good astrologer right from the start.

The Layout

WITH THIS METHOD it is not usual to ask a question, because the extensiveness of the spread provides insight into the total situation, and the question that may concern you is part of this. By paying too much attention to a single question, you can easily muddle the inter-pretation.

Allow yourself plenty of space and imagine a circle; begin on the left and lay the circle counter-clockwise. Or you can use a ready-made astrological chart. Your circle has to be divided into twelve compartments: these are the houses. Each house is of the same size and has its own meaning. The house on the left under the middle line is the 1st house, and next to it (in a counter-clockwise direction) is the 2nd, and so on (see figure 20, page 236).

You can now set to work in one of two ways: either you can deal the Major and Minor Arcana separately, or you can deal from a deck in which the Major and Minor Arcana have been shuffled

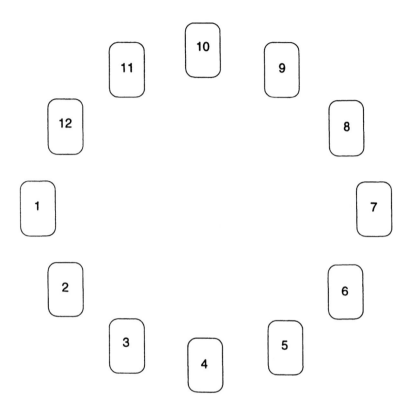

Figure 20. The Astrological Tarot Spread.

together. In either method you may choose how many rounds to lay. For example, you may make do with one card in each house, but you may also lay four or five cards in each. The latter practice makes interpretation a much more complicated affair, and I advise the beginner against it. Later on it will be well worth the trouble to experiment with two cards in each house; for my own part, I have generally found three cards per house is enough. Then everything remains clear, because the cards supplement one another and map out a course. Bear in mind that what comes in the houses in the first round is what is the most significant, and that the following cards are less important. They refine the meaning of the first round and show what can develop out of that round in the course of time, or else they show what requires attention.

The advantage of using the whole deck—the Major and Minor Arcana together—is the certainty that when a card of the Major Arcana falls in a house, that area of life stands in the foreground for you or will quickly do so. The cards of the Minor Arcana relate to it in a subsidiary manner.

It may well be that, when you lay several cards per house, one house stand out because it contains more than one card belonging to the Major Arcana. Indeed, it is a common experience that a certain area of life becomes more prominent during a particular period, or perhaps the other areas retire into the shadows for a time. With this method you automatically identify the different areas plus whatever is going on inwardly.

If you decide to use the cards of both groups separately, you first of all take twelve cards from the Major Arcana without looking at them and lay them face down on the houses of your choice. Thus you may easily lay your first card on the 9th house. The sequence does not matter; what counts is that, without taking too much thought, you just lay each card where you feel or intuit it should go. Having laid your twelve cards, you still have ten cards of the Major Arcana left; which means there are not enough for another round, for there are twelve houses. Put the deck aside; perhaps you can use it later.

Now take the Minor Arcana and lay one or more cards from this on each house. This can be done in various ways. You can keep on drawing one card per house. You can also draw one card per house at random in the first round, and then draw cards one after the other from the top of the deck in a subsequent series. If you want to know more about a certain house while giving a reading, you can draw a card at random for that house from the remaining Major Arcana in order to see any further trend or development.

Of course, you can use up the entire deck and lay several cards everywhere; it does not matter if there are more cards in one house than in another. Just follow your feelings and be creative. But do be aware that, because of certain fears or uncertainties, you will be inclined to pile cards in a certain house in order to have something solid to hold on to, and the sheer number of these cards is bound to be confusing!

For example, when a love affair hits problems, you will tend to stack extra cards in the 7th house just to discover how it will turn out in the end. These cards represent not only the process that is taking place inside you, and how the love affair is getting on, but also your actual worrying. And if you are too eager for a solution or an answer, you psyche is usually so biased that it is easy to make mistakes when reading the cards. Sometimes it is better to treat that house normally when making the layout, and to wait until you are in a more calm frame of mind about that theme before venturing into an interpretation.

As it will already have been gathered, the layout is a circle of twelve compartments, each containing one or more cards. Each compartment or "house" represents an area of life, a terrain in everyday existence through which (and in which) certain experiences are acquired. The houses also have a psychological import and are associated with specific predispositions. Therefore a house may have a number of interpretations.

The cards or cards dealt into a house indicate(s) what is happening in that area of life, the experiences that are taking place there, what is coming on your path, what you, yourself, are doing, and what needs and responses are forcing themselves on you. Some skill is required in order to make a meaningful combination of card and house and to interpret this correctly. To give you something to go on, I shall briefly state the meanings of the astrological houses.

1ST HOUSE

Psychological: Our immediate attitude to the external world and the impression we make in it and on it. Our way of reacting (mentally and physically) to any kind of external stimulus. The beginning; the tackling of something new; the personality; vitality; stamina; self-regard.

External: The external characteristics of the person in question; gestures; appearance; the public image of each thing or person; outward form, with its beauty or lack of beauty.

Personal: The querent, the newcomer, someone who is just arriving, traveling companions.

Physical: The head.

2ND HOUSE

Psychological: Our attitude toward wealth and objects that offer security. Feelings of satisfaction, dissatisfaction, and the motivations arising from them. Skills for maintaining our existence; i.e., abilities that enable us to earn an income. The need for material security and the way in which we express it; economic sense.

External: Money and property; everything that has to do with possession; spending habits; sources of income; debts, wealth; profit and loss.

Personal: Ancestors, jewelers, bankers, investors, cashiers, brokers, valuers.

Physical: Throat and nape of the neck.

3RD HOUSE

Psychological: Practical thinking, the urge to examine and classify all facts and matters that come before us. Consequently: analytical thought; the connection of facts; the connection of people with one another through communication and contact; also the connection of people and things, as in trade (in which people exchange goods with one another for money); practical analytical thinking; classifying, arranging; brief communications and quick, short but not very profound contact; thirst for news; exchange of information.

External: Letters, mail, announcements, every form of publicity; short journeys; means of transport; documents; the text of agreements and contracts; telephone; neighborhood and the immediate environment; numbers and mathematics; broadcasting.

Personal: Neighbors, brothers, sisters, merchants, postal workers, representatives, traveling salespeople, teachers, journalists, speakers, visitors, translators, writers, publicists, and broadcasters.

Physical: Lungs; air passages; hands.

4TH HOUSE

Psychological: The need for emotional comfort and security; inner emotional basis; attitude to and experience of domestic circumstances; desire to cherish and care for others, both active and passive; feeling for the source of things—thus tradition, family and ancestry; youth and how we remember it; final solution or conclusion.

External: Houses, land (building sites), hotels, antique property, inherited goods.

Personal: Parents, family, the farmer, horticulturist, or builder.

Physical: Breast and stomach.

5TH HOUSE

Psychological: The need to make our mark through things we enjoy, such as sports, games, pleasures, entertainment, and love; desire to be ourselves, to develop self-reliance and to place ourselves in the center of things. Our creative urge, and the need to be productive for our own delight and inner satisfaction, without regard to any consideration of usefulness. The creative drive in such things as love and art, or in "procreative" love-making where we surrender to sexual desire and may become involved in the creation of children.

External: All places of entertainment: cinemas, theaters, casinos, the circus, concert halls, places where (pop) festivals are held, theme parks, golf courses, football and baseball fields and other sports grounds, etc.

Personal: Children, entertainers, lovers, hobbyists, speculators, gamblers, sometime speculative brokers (in combination with the 2nd house), sportspeople.

Physical: Heart and back.

6TH HOUSE

Psychological: The need to ponder, analyze, and understand, in order to be able to apply in a clear, useful, and concrete way, what we have learned. Our attitude toward work and the work environment, especially where subordination and menial tasks are concerned. The enjoyment or frustrations arising out of our work. The care we take of our bodies, especially as this affects our health: thus what we do about diet, disease, and related matters. The way we react to objective everyday reality.

External: Conditions at work; the office, factory; doctor's surgery; shops; restaurants; police stations; military camps. In addition: injuries inflicted by animals, such as bites and scratches. The harvest.

Personal: Manual workers, storekeepers, dietitians, clerks, assistants, physicians, and anybody who is of service to others.

Physical: Intestines.

7TH HOUSE

Psychological: Attitude toward the partner, what we have come to expect of our partner and our experiences in the partnership (marriage or living together). Approach to teamwork with others and experiences in this; need for harmony and beauty; need for equilibrium and a friendly atmosphere; enemies and how we treat them.

External: Marriage license, contracts, peace treaties, the fine arts.

Personal: Partners, companions, diplomats, open enemies; contract partner(s), other party in lawsuits, sometimes the foreigner or refugee, "the other person" in general.

Physical: Kidneys and lower back.

8TH HOUSE

Psychological: Fondness for taking risks; digging to rock bottom in order to get the truth; talent for psychology, parapsychology, occultism; unconscious attitude toward partners and working with others, which is the consequence of the relationship we have with our unconscious here. Consequently—anxieties and repressions brought into play by the urge to employ and exhibit our creativity. Fear of death and love of life; intensity; power of psychic recovery; sexual attitude (and yieldingness to our partner).

External: Legacies, bequests, funerals, death, mental illness, (life) insurance, wills, shared finances (with partner or companion), taxation, post-mortems, cemeteries, the abattoir, the sewers.

Personal: Undertakers, surgeons, underwriters, archeologists, deep-sea divers, sometimes also miners (in combination with the 6th house), psychologists, psychiatrists, detectives, tax inspectors, investigating officers, researchers, butchers, murderers, the suicide.

Physical: Reproductive organs.

9TH HOUSE

Psychological: Need for expansion and wider vision; thirst for travel (both in the flesh and in the spirit); our attitude toward further education, studies abroad, and toward religion and philosophy; ideals and sense of justice.

External: Long journeys (well beyond familiar surroundings), foreign countries, anywhere remote from our own place of residence, textbooks, embassies, worldwide contacts, the supreme court, exports, publications, universities, high schools, international transport.

Personal: University professors, clergy, judges, explorers, ambassadors, couriers, travel agents, strangers, grandchildren, sisters-in-law and brothers-in-law, jurors, philosophers, and writers who specialize in metaphysics, travel, religion, science, law (as far as dispensing justice is concerned). [Law in the sense of maintaining order belongs to the 10th house.]

Physical: Liver and hips.

10TH HOUSE

Psychological: Need to demarcate our "I" and form a clear picture of ourselves and of the outside world; pursuit of a recognized social position; conscious mask we wear in order to feel that we are functioning in the outside world; the desire to define and pigeon-hole ourselves and others so that everyone knows their place; the first impression we create.

External: Government buildings, career, fame or infamy, social position, reputation, law, all rules and regulations, status and place in society.

Personal: Heads of state, prime ministers, presidents, monarchs, people with power and authority, employers, legislators, executives, ambitious individuals; often—one of the parents.

Physical: Bones, teeth, hair, nails (thus the hard parts of the body), knees and other joints.

11TH HOUSE

Psychological: The urge to break through rigid boundaries and to get to know others as equals (i.e., neither as superiors nor inferiors); attitude toward friends and friendship and what is expected and experienced in this area; the need to associate with like-minded people and to be able to discuss matters freely with them.

External: Clubs, the premises of societies and political parties, legislative assembly and democracy; organizations with a specific aim; law-givers (especially when carrying out political programs); international treaties.

Personal: Friends, confidential advisers, union members, club members, sons-in-law and daughters-in-law.

Physical: Calves and ankles.

12TH HOUSE

Psychological: The need for isolation and detachment in order to break free from the trammels of the world of everyday cares. Secret fears and inhibitions that may cripple us, but can also supply the incentive to seek for a mystical inner union which transcends the personality. The absorption of the personality in the collective, the masses, or the unconscious (at some risk), on the one hand, but on the other, the gift of being able to communicate with the unconscious; understanding the meaning of dreams, symbolism, and the whole inner life, and being able to integrate them in daily life.

Here is a mechanism which threatens to "liquidate" personal development, but at the same time has the capacity for lifting the personality out of the world of opposites to a higher level in a well-nigh religio-mystical manner. Confrontation with everything that is working away in our personal psyches as a result of unconscious experiences in early childhood (the mythic phase) and of our reactions at that time to the atmosphere, susceptibilities, and repressions of and around our parents and care-givers, and to hard circumstances.

This house signifies our need to express a more profound feeling of union with life, for example in prayer and religion, but also in music and art, or in helping the underprivileged. Our oneness with life can also find an outlet in clairvoyance or psychometry.

External: Cloisters, institutions, prisons, hospitals, sanatoria and similar places, concealed places, isolated regions, the sea, secret societies, drugs, poisons, impediments, pain, suffering murder, suicide, scandals, defamation, bribery. But also: meditation, charities, social work, sleep, and hypnosis.

Personal: Monks, nuns, yogis, social workers; but also secret enemies, thieves, confidence tricksters, kidnappers, displaced persons, fugitives, and drug addicts. Widows and orphans, people who have been institutionalized or are in a reception center, and all people who are in need of help, or who stand on the fringe of society. Prison guards, nurses (also in the 6th house as a service career), anesthetists. The clandestine love affair. The medium, but also the sleepwalker, hypnotists and alternative practitioners, such as homeopaths. Sailors, artists, and musicians.

Physical: Feet.

When you have prepared the astrological layout, try to let the pictures on the cards quietly work on you. Do not worry about what you view as "negative" cards, and at the same time do not be gleeful over what look like "positive" cards: each card has two sides and, as a matter of fact, it is unfortunate to be locked into either of them. Treat the cards as a description of your current situation and see if you can gather from their symbolism what is the way out of the given problem.

• Example 1: A Female Client

A young, enterprising and active woman felt tense and restless. A number of marital problems had arisen and, in her work, she felt motivated and demotivated at one and the same time. Her children were fine, and she had a good relationship with them.

She drew the following cards from a deck which included both the Major and Minor Arcana. In the first round the cards were fanned out and drawn at random; but in the second and third rounds they were dealt from the top of the deck (see figure 21, page 246).

1st House:	Six of Swords	(1)
	The Moon	(2)
	Ten of Pentacles	(3)
2nd House:	Ten of Cups	(1)
	The World	(2)
	Eight of Cups	(3)
3rd House:	The Magician	(1)
	Two of Pentacles	(2)
	Seven of Swords	(3)
4th House:	The Devil	(1)
	The Fool	(2)
	Seven of Wands	(3)
5th House:	Seven of Cups	(1)
	Wheel of Fortune	(2)
	Queen of Pentacles	(3)
6th House:	The Hanged Man	(1)
	Ace of Wands	(2)
	Page of Pentacles	(3)
7th House:	Page of Cups	(1)
	Queen of Cups	(2)
	Eight of Pentacles	(3)
8th House:	Ten of Wands	(1)
	Three of Pentacles	(2)
	Nine of Pentacles	(3)
9th House:	Three of Swords	(1)
	Nine of Cups	(2)
	King of Pentacles	(3)

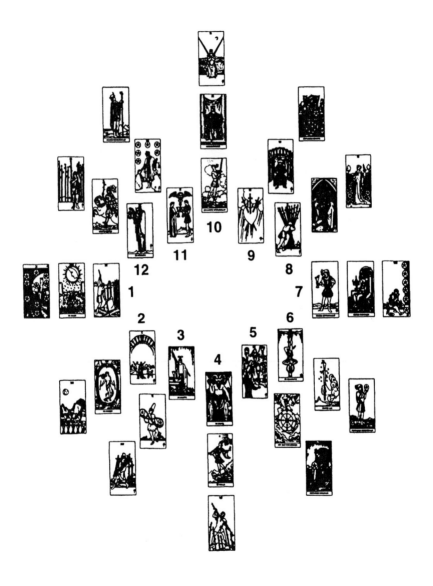

Figure 21. The Astrological Spread. This is the layout that we discuss in Example 1.

10th House:	Page of Swords	(1)
	Justice	(2)
	Two of Swords	(3)

11th House:	Two of Cups	(1)
	Six of Pentacles	(2)
	Page of Wands	(3)

12th House:	The Hermit	(1)
	Knight of Wands	(2)
	Nine of Wands	(3)

There is nothing intrinsically wrong with working systematically through the houses to ascertain and combine the meanings of the cards; but you may prefer to see if anything stands out, such as houses where a card from the Major Arcana fell in the first round. Quite often the story seems too revolve around these themes. In our example we see that, in the first round, Major Arcana occupy houses 3, 4, 6, and 12. In the second round, houses 1, 2, 4, 5, and 10 also contain trump cards, but these have a supplementary significance. Nevertheless, they do accentuate the houses and alert us to the fact that their supplementary significance is important.

The 4th house has cards of the Major Arcana from two of the rounds, and therefore receives a heavy emphasis! That was precisely the core of the problem with which the woman was wrestling. Although she described her problem as a feeling of unrest and of conflict between motivation and demotivation, it appears on closer analysis that she was in a very turbulent period.

Harsh juvenile experiences in the form of ill-treatment, emotional abuse, and endless domestic quarrels obtruded themselves on her during this period, and she could no longer ignore them. She observed that she could be very bad tempered, was tearful and angry, and could hardly refrain from screaming: "It is my turn now, MY turn!" She admitted that she did not always care about how her uptightness and behavior affected her family. It was hard to control herself, she said.

Look at The Devil as the Major Arcana card in the 4th house. Nothing could be plainer: in the house of youthful experiences we see the energy that has to do with impulse, aggression, and self-assertiveness. This instinct to stick up for oneself, which begins with The Devil but then has to be taken further, was suppressed in her youth, and now explodes into view. What is more, the atmosphere in which she lived as a child is well described by the card.

The supplementary cards are The Fool and the Seven of Wands. The Fool here calls on her to enter the emotion and to live through it, and to confront this experience even though she does not know what to do about it. But, at the same time, The Fool was asking her to adopt a totally new attitude to the past and a new way to handle feelings and emotions. The legacy of the past was tension, aggression, and egoism in the childhood home. The Fool indicates that the woman now faces a turning point if she does not want to become trapped. However, she does have to make contact with what these experiences and energies have released in her. The Seven of Wands is a card that takes action, but runs the risk of being enmeshed in the consequences. It is very applicable to this woman, who has always partly tried to forget her emotional condition by engaging in various activities. Whether in employment, hobbies, helping others, voluntary work, assisting in the establishment of organizations, or whatever—she was always busy. The number seven here should alert her to the presence of a paradoxical mixture of good and evil. It conveys a reassurance and a warning: it is good to be busy just as long as she is not using this to crowd out any consideration of her problem. The Fool is crying out for a radical change, and she must not let activities stand in the way of it!

The other houses containing a card from the Major Arcana in the first round are 3, 6, and 12. Embroidering this problem we see the internalized cards, The Hanged Man and The Hermit, in houses 6 and 12 respectively, and a very active card, The Magician, in the 3rd house.

What was at stake? Everything was in full swing at work; there were no insuperable difficulties. The Hanged Man in the 6th house, the house of work, clearly indicated what she was feeling: she had a tremendous need for time out, for a "sabbatical year." But that was impossible. She noticed that going to work was becoming more and more of a struggle, which she did not understand, because she enjoyed her work. This was where the conflict between motivation and a lack of motivation came in. "I am bursting with new ideas!"

she exclaimed, "I see all sorts of novel ways of doing things and have even been asked to arrange business courses and give lectures."

Thus new jobs of all kinds were hers for the taking, and each and all of them were challenges that would normally delight her. Only something she could not account for was holding her back. Suddenly she would feel very tired and uninterested and would potter about without getting anywhere. Then she would think about these things in a positive way, or she could feel out of touch and adrift in a negative way. We observe here a combination of The Hanged Man and the 6th house, which indicates a strong possibility of fatigue and the feeling that there is an enormous gap between her work and what she gets out of it.

At the same time, the presence of The Magician in the 3rd house means that she is certainly in a position to set up creative business courses. The 3rd house always has to do with the arrangement and communication of facts, and with imparting instruction. Here is a marvelous challenge that she could gladly accept; but actually getting on with the job brings her in conflict with The Hanged Man—the energy that says "First you must internalize and enter the 'waiting room.' Other processes are taking place now; external prospects must wait."

The Hermit in the 12th house reveals her mood of exploration; she seeks a deeper connection with life and wants to make some sense of it. She would like to introduce a few new age ideas into the courses she wants to set up, but is rather hazy about them. She is still searching, but cannot say for what. There is "something" in her that agitates her, that beckons her to another set of conditions, but she has no idea how to describe it.

Meanwhile she is becoming more and more interested in mysticism, mythology, dreams, and symbolism: The Hermit in the 12th house! "They will surely take me somewhere, but I don't know where," she says, shrugging her shoulders. "Funnily enough, I have plenty of energy for things of this sort," she adds.

On delving further into houses 12 and 6, we find that the 12th house, representing the deeper dimension for which she is looking, contains the Knight of Wands and the Nine of Wands as supplementary cards. Once more, these are active cards. The Knight of Wands points out the danger of impatience, of wanting to rush matters. The Nine of Wands warns against doing things on the basis of suspicion as a consequence of what has happened in the past, as this makes it impossible to be simply receptive.

This is a paradox: in the house where she should be releasing her hold on things, in which the demands of the unconscious take precedence, it is impossible to retain everything in her grasp. The Wands cards in this 12th house seem to have a connection with the Seven of Wands in the 4th house: there is much activity and a desire to keep busy as a defense against feelings of distress, which amounts to overcompensation. This combination of cards warns that the woman will be inclined to persist in such behavior and thus to work against her best interests in certain respects.

In the 6th house the supplementary cards are the Ace of Wands and the Page of Pentacles. The Ace of Wands is a clear reflection of the fact that she has been offered many new opportunities at work and may be offered still more. The Page of Pentacles is also an indication of fresh opportunities on the material plane. This card shows how she ought to treat the new challenges—as fun rather than as obligations. Playfulness and emotional response mix well with The Hanged Man; acting out of a sense of duty and for external results do not. So there is no harm in her accepting fresh challenges, but it is best if she does not commit herself yet, or fix dates, but occupies herself with seeing what can be done and how things will turn out. That in itself will be quite a task for her.

The 4th and 6th houses are obviously complementary to one another in a psychological sense: the resistance which enabled her to hold her own in her youth, has continued as a determination to work hard, to face problems boldly, and not to worry. The Hanged Man reveals that it is no longer appropriate for her to maintain this attitude in daily life and at work, now that the old sore is breaking out again and is making itself felt in her emotions at home. Thus she really is at a turning point in her behavior.

Now take a look at the 3rd house with the Major Arcana card, The Magician, in it. The supplementary cards are the Two of Pentacles and the Seven of Swords. Giving substance to lessons and ideas, and setting to work on them, is still precarious (Two of Pentacles) and she must beware of trying to cut corners (Seven of Swords), even if time is short. In other words, if she is unable to progress because her emotions and her psychic energy are invested elsewhere (for example, The Hanged Man in 6 and The Devil in 4), and she relapses into old patterns of behavior by working too hard, then perhaps she will feel compelled to cut corners everywhere (Seven of Swords) and risk the consequences. Or, as she put it, "I could very well start a course and work on it as I go along." That is sure to go wrong with these two supplementary cards and we must therefore advise against it.

Having interpreted the most striking features and having gotten to the core of the problem, we can take a look at the other houses. And now it will be clear why there is such a varied picture in the 1st house, the house of public appearance.

The Six of Swords allows her sense of alienation to show in her attitude toward the outside world; here is her sense of needing to make a fresh start, because she is still carrying a lot of old baggage. In fact she does have the feeling that she would like to go and work somewhere else in her immediate environment but, as she says, everything is still so unmanageable. Strong emotions, fears, grief, and mood-swings are liable to break through (it is striking how closely this is connected with the cards in the 4th house), and she could be put off her stride and most probably become withdrawn.

On the other hand, she could suddenly be cheerful and outgoing again, glad to be alive and grateful for everything that comes on her path. She does not fully understand it, but if we look at the one side: the confrontation with the past, and the other side: the search for a spiritual dimension in which achievement is less important (The Hermit in 12), we shall see that she is in the process of adopting a new attitude (the Six of Swords).

Of course she is still having a struggle with her old attitude (as shown by the Wands in 4 and 12) and in the process she is experiencing her past pain in all sorts of forms (The Moon). But because she has already assimilated and come to terms with it, she has no need to dwell on it, but can experience the positive side of life—the Ten of Pentacles. Since The Moon is a stronger accent than the Ten of Pentacles, we must lay more emphasis on the emotions that immerse the querent and color her attitude to the outside world.

Another house that represents her contact with the outside world is the 10th, which, in this case, received a card of the Major Arcana in the second round. In the first place, this house has to do with the impression one makes and what one (consciously or unconsciously) reveals to the outside world. In the second place, it has to do with one's functioning in society and therefore with one's social position. The Page of Swords warns against being too brusque and outspoken, and against responding too rashly. Although she has no problems at work, she remarks that she likes her superiors less than formerly. Whereas she has always been ready to cooperate and work with their ideas, now a simple request or a straightforward question can make her so furious that she feels like saying, "Why on earth are you interfering?" Or, "Leave me to get on with it!" She feels that she had become more prickly and uncooperative.

The supplementary cards, Justice and the Two of Swords, underline the warning that she should not be too blunt. What she does will be judged completely objectively, says Justice. But this card also indicates that the woman is capable of being objective toward her own behavior and of seeing what she is doing. Therefore she can certainly revise her attitude, but with the Two of Swords she finds it hard to be emotionally involved in what she is doing and should be doing. "Sometimes I am just too tired, and no longer feel like bothering with what others want. Let them take care of it themselves. . .," she says, ". . . and above all don't bring me into it. I have enough to do as it is."

In its own right, this house has to be interpreted separately, as I have already mentioned at the beginning of our example. But this house gains perspective by being placed in the context of our earlier analysis of what the Major Arcana accentuated in the first round. Her fatigue is connected with the facts that the emotions in the 4th house (The Devil) are costing her a lot of energy and that she is looking for another angle in her work (The Hanged Man) and outside it. It is easy to see that a measure of peevishness and outspokenness can result from this if the pressure of society or of social obligations increases.

In the second round, the 2nd house also received a card from the Major Arcana, The World. The first card, which forms the starting point of this house, is the Ten of Cups. The 2nd house has to do with security, and above all with our material resources and how we manage them. In addition, it gauges our feelings of satisfaction and dissatisfaction, and the degree to which they motivate us. Strange to say, the Ten of Cups in this house often reveals a powerful motivation, and in particular an emotionally inspired attitude that automatically produces a sense of certainty. In this connection we see that the financial prospects are usually good, and that any problems are easily resolved.

This card appears to conflict with the motivation crisis that the woman described at the start of the reading. However, in further conversation with her, it emerged that her motivation problem was connected mainly with the idea that she *must* do things, that she was forced to work under the pressure of time, that she *had to* get jobs finished, that she was tied by obligations, that she must be punctual; in short, it was connected with the little word "must." As soon as this pressure is lifted, she feels she can do almost anything. And this can very well lead to a certain amount of prestige. But the core of her motivation problem is that she wants to do things out of an inner impulse and then has great difficulty coping with pressure from outside. This reactivates the pain of her past, when she was badly bullied if she did not keep in step.

So the Ten of Cups shows us that there is nothing wrong with her motivation in itself. The World, as a supplementary card, reveals that she "dances along with whatever comes on her path." She herself describes it very simply: "When things are going in my favor I enjoy myself, and when things are working against me I behave a bit more quietly. But I can't lie awake worrying about them—they are just not worth it as far as I'm concerned." And this attitude is closely related to that of The World. The Eight of Cups seems to underline it further. She is leaving full cups behind her to go in search of something new. Not so long ago she rejected a lucrative offer: work that would have been exceptionally well paid but for which she could not summon up the least enthusiasm—apart from anything else it would have been too much of a tie. She had no hesitation in turning it down, even though she had to live more carefully on her current income.

The last house to receive a card from the Major Arcana in the second round is the 5th: the house in which we must learn to like ourselves, and learn to play and have fun (and for many people that is a difficult task!). It is also the house in which we go to meet life in a relaxed and cheerful frame of mind and develop a feeling of self-acceptance and self-reliance. In this house the first card is the Seven of Cups—which warns that the young woman is standing at a crossroads: she stands, rather lightly it would seem, before a choice of either the lower row of Cups: power, possessions, honor, and aggression, or the upper row: contact with her inner being, becoming her True Self, and psychic growth. She can decide to work hard and to acquire power, money, and property—all at the expense of her spiritual development—or she can learn to listen to what her inner being has to tell her. Now in the 5th house, the upper row of cups also signifies being prepared to enjoy being herself, being ready to relax and accept herself as she is. It is remarkable that this choice occurs in the picture we have already formed of her condition.

The Wheel of Fortune seems to come into play here. According to Jung, if we keep returning to the same situation, it is high time to discover what unconsciously adopted role is consigning us to this "fate." With insight and a corresponding change of behavior we can change the "fate" and give life a new direction.

It looks as if The Wheel of Fortune here relates to the vicious circle in which the woman is going round—and will continue to go round if she chooses the lower row in the Seven of Cups, even if this choice is ever so well disguised and justified by such arguments as, "I couldn't be expected to reject an offer like that!" Or, "I'd be crazy not to seize such a good opportunity!" The unconscious does not listen to excuses of that sort. It knows precisely if you are running away from yourself again, or are doing what is right for your inner growth at your present stage. So this is definitely a parting of the ways, in which The Queen of Pentacles is, so to speak, advising her to settle for intense inner enjoyment of what she has and what there is. There is no excessive luxury in this court card, but there is a readiness to be oneself and to savor life maturely.

The woman recognizes this internal struggle. "I cannot sit still," she comments, "I always feel that I ought to be doing something useful; and for want of anything better, it has always come down to earning more money. But I cannot go on like that, and money has never really interested me anyway. It is something belonging to the past, which has to do with the way I was brought up. I have made up my mind to enjoy myself, but I am afraid that I shall somehow manage to avoid doing so. In fact, I probably don't know how. And yet I have even less enthusiasm for hard work." A plain commentary on this card combination, and also very natural in the light of what we found earlier.

At this point we have looked at all the houses containing cards of the Major Arcana, either in the first or the second round. We are left with the less emphasized houses. The processes they reflect are not so marked in the life of the querent, and will not make such a big impression on the course of events in the near future.

This does not mean that these houses may be ignored; on the contrary, they contain much valuable information. But, in the absence of a card of the Major Arcana, we must not place them in the foreground. In this instance, the houses without Major Arcana are 7, 8, 9, and 11. We shall now run through them quickly.

The 8th house is, in every respect, the house of repressions and of the assimilation of problems. The fact that there are no Major Arcana cards here, although the woman obviously has psychological problems and is busy coming to terms with them, can be regarded as a positive sign. In most cases, the absence of Major Arcana hints a problems that are already out in the open, and the fact that it is the "house of the personal unconscious" from which they are missing here suggests that there is nothing very earth-shaking going on under the surface in the unconscious. The cards of the Minor Arcana in this house indicate the instruments available to the woman for resolving and assimilating her problems. Any of them that have the nature of "warning cards" could be revealing factors inhibiting the assimilation process.

The first card in the 8th house is the Ten of Wands. This is a case in point. Her assimilation process is being impeded by too much activity and too much thinking. This is her usual style: she takes action as quickly as possible and keeps well occupied. As we saw earlier, keeping busy was a means of avoiding having to sit in misery in her youth. It was a defense mechanism then and has become stereotyped behavior on her part. But now overactivity is something that can inhibit her inner process and her reorientation. Nevertheless, the card itself is helpful, because it advises her to take stock of her activities, to be decisive, and to do some reorganization. In view of previous cards, she is certainly ripe for this advice.

It is noteworthy that the 4th house, to which many of the woman's problems are traceable, contains the Seven of Wands, and the 12th house, which seeks for internalization (especially as The Hermit falls in it), contains two Wand cards—the Knight and Nine of Wands. But the 8th house also contains one of the Wands, and Wands in general indicate action, and we see the extent to which this woman has employed action and industry as weapons in the fight against feelings and emotions. (For the astrologers among us: houses 4, 8, and 12 are water houses, and always reveal our attitude regarding the emotional world and emotional circumstances.) The Seven of Wands threatens not to calculate the consequences of what it does, the Nine of Wands threatens to go round and round in circles, and the Ten of Wands demands a review at last of all the ground that has been dug over and of all the rubble that needs to be cleared away. This is something the woman must do if she wants to normalize her feelings and resolve her problems.

The second and third cards in the 8th house are both Pentacles: the Three and the Nine. "The work is not finished yet," says the Three of Pentacles, "but carry on with it and be confident and you will surely reach your goal." Pentacles yield very concrete results, so we may expect to see a visible change. The Nine of Pentacles signifies that she should keep both feet on the ground, yet fully enjoy her union with nature, with life, and with herself. This card promises a completion of the process without becoming locked into it.

As far as assimilation is concerned, the most important thing for her to do is to bear in mind that "flight into action" is a recipe for disaster. The other cards indicate that the process will make good progress and will be helped from within herself if she continues to pursue it.

The promised help does not lie in the 8th house alone: two important relationship houses, 7 and 11, also lend support. The 7th house represents her relationship to her partner, and the 11th house represents her attitude to friends and to people on the same wavelength.

First the 7th house: although the woman stated that there were tensions in the relationship, the cards do not point in that direction. New feelings can emerge in the relationship when the Page of Cups appears on the stage, and this is usually positive. But the Page cards also indicate duality because of a certain inexperience. In the woman's situation, this may mean a new, more open, and more sensitive attitude toward her partner, but she still has no idea how to express this, and perhaps is being deliberately vague about it.

Nevertheless the Queen of Cups is a supplementary card, and indicates a much more mature and balanced expression of the feelings. It is striking that the two yin court cards of Cups are found in this house of relationships. This, in itself, shows that she is involved in a process in which she must learn to display her feelings more and just let herself go. The woman admitted that she felt that this was what she should do, but added that the idea still made her uncomfortable. She did not feel up to it yet, but she did sometimes wish she was. The Eight of Pentacles reveals that she is, in fact, still engaged in this task; it is not finished yet, but its completion is in sight. Because Pentacles are so oriented toward physical reality, we are justified in expecting that here, too, the inner process of the woman will lead to another attitude which those around her, and in this case, her partner will not fail to notice. At the same time, the card reveals that she is motivated to reach her goal, which is to display her feelings more openly in spite of her misgivings.

Can the 7th house also say something about the partner? Sometimes it does, but very often I observe that what it says is not unconnected with the internal situation of the querent. The woman remarked that her partner greatly appreciated a rapport that was more colored by her emotions and was very supportive in her process, although he did not always know what to do when she really exploded emotionally. So the Cups cards can have something to do with her husband in his longing for emotional contact (the Queen of Cups) but his awkwardness in handling it (the Page of Cups).

The main theme of the 11th house is encounter: the Two of Cups supplemented by the Six of Pentacles and the Page of Wands. The house of friendship and association with like-minded people is particularly amiable. The woman agreed that she had a number of friends of both sexes, and that although their characters were very different from hers, she got along with them really well.

The Six of Pentacles shows a merchant who is letting others—especially the poor—share his riches. He has reached a position and has to adopt a new attitude in order not to be snared by covetousness or some other craving. At first I could not accept this as an apposite picture. Sometimes the card points to a lack of balance in a friendship, so that one party is giving all the time and the other is taking.

But the woman dismissed the latter idea. However, she did say that only a few years ago she did not know how to treat friends, and she had hardly any. She was always working, or was involved in various organizations in her spare time, but she did not regard this environment as a true circle of friends. She herself clearly felt that the merchant on the card represented that part of her that business had made—in the end she had reached a good position—but now this must give way a little to another part of herself which had so far been impoverished: her social role. "I must strike a better balance," she said, "and matters will improve." She seemed to prefer people who tackled everything straightforwardly, whether hobbies or work. She was happiest with enthusiasts and stimulating "doers," and she herself was one of them. The Page of Wands is explicit on that score.

One house remains to interpret—the 9th. It represents our need to travel in the flesh or in the spirit in order to make up our minds on things, and it shows what role ideals play in our lives.

The first card is the Three of Swords, a card that literally represents a heavy heart. The Three of Swords is a process: one is on the way, and has already made a few important, and usually painful, decisions. This must now be brought into focus within the theme of the 9th house. "I am in a fight," she says. "There is so much I want to do; but I realize that I cannot manage it all, even though I am still young. I am full of ideals, would like to study and learn everything; but I have a family, and it would not be fair to make them pay for my restless aspirations."

Had she already made some decisions? To some extent, yes. She wanted to attend the necessary classes, but had drastically curtailed their number to a few which she felt really mattered. She was not taking up any extra studies. "I may be able to do so when the children leave home, but not now." But she added, "I still keep reading, and I do not concentrate simply on books relating to my profession. I have a wide range of interests and an inquiring mind." This wide range of interests did not sweep cookery books and romances into its orbit so much as financial, economic, and scientific texts. Is this the significance of the Nine of Cups, which is also found in the 9th house? Subjects that appeal to us emotionally (Cups) and in which we immerse ourselves whenever we have the inclination and the opportunity, can indeed belong to the card. The Nine of Cups need not indicate anything very profound (and can even leave one skimming the surface), but its does represent emotional satisfaction.

As far as one can see, therefore, the card may well indicate reading what interests and entertains us, and is instructive at the same time. My own impression is that she will return to useful studies.

What tends to persuade me is that the series ends with the King of Pentacles, belonging to a suit that is concerned with realization in the material world. Thus, although she has decided not to do or learn a number of things (Three of Swords), her fondness for acquiring information through light reading (Nine of Cups) will very probably lead to new concrete plans and ideals which she can achieve if she sets her mind to them, and does not allow herself to be fazed. Apart from that, the Three of Swords can also indicate some hardness in forming opinions and judgments.

On reflection, we see that what the woman had expressed rather vaguely, namely her feelings of restlessness and the feeling of simultaneous motivation and demotivation in regard to her work, not only came clearly to the fore in the layout, but were also supplied with a background and placed in context.

One thing she said did not show up in the cards: she had had problems in her marriage—misunderstandings and quarrels which had made her feel lonely and neglected. This was not discernible in the 7th house as a marital problem, apart from the indications that she was wrestling with the question of how to deal with her need to respond with a greater show of emotion and to be more open in this area of her relationship.

She admitted that she really had a good marriage, and although her husband had a fairly complex character, she always managed to cope with it. She later confessed that it was not the marriage or the relationship that was at fault, but always these misunderstandings.

On closer analysis, her own emotions, her fear of a disturbed atmosphere—which had been such a bitter experience in her youth—the fear of not being allowed to be herself and her lack of self-confidence on the home front, seem to be big factors in the marital strife.

It was not the marriage itself (the 7th house) but her emotional basis and her past (the 4th house) which were the problems in her relationship. The cards in the 7th house held the promise that the relationship itself was in no danger.

For the woman herself, this layout was one great "feast of recognition." It helped her to gain a much better view of what was going on inside her. "Deep inside me, I knew all these things already," she said, "but I did not see how they connected up. They were all loose ends and bits and pieces. But now I see their connection, I know what I have to do," she added with a sigh of relief.

And that is the big advantage of this astrological method: it gives a deep insight into the connection between internal feelings and external phenomena.

BIBLIOGRAPHY

Bach, Susan. *Life Paints Its Own Span: On the Significance of Spontaneous Pictures by Severely Ill Children.* Einsiedeln, Switzerland: Daimon Verlag, 1990.

Banzhaf, Hajo. *The Tarot Handbook.* Stamford, CT: U. S. Games Systems, 1993.

Bindel, Ernst. *Die Geistigen Grundlagen der Zahlen.* Stuttgart: Freies Geistesleben, 1975.

———. *Die Zahlengrundlagen der Musik im Wandel der Zeiten,* Vol. 3. Stuttgart: Freies Geistesleben, 1950.

Blank, William. *Torah, Tarot & Tantra: A Guide to Jewish Spiritual Growth.* Boston: Sigo Press, 1991.

Campbell, Joseph. *The Hero with a Thousand Faces.* Bollingen Series No. XVII. Princeton: Princeton University Press, 1990.

Camphausen, Rufus C. *Tarot en Kabbala.* Amsterdam: W. N. Schors, 1993.

Case, Paul Foster. *The Tarot: A Key to the Wisdom of the Ages.* Los Angeles: Builders of the Adytum, 1947.

Cavendish, R. *The Tarot.* New York: HarperCollins, 1975.

Cirlot, J.E. *A Dictionary of Symbols.* London: Routledge & Kegan Paul, 1976.

Crowley, A. *The Book of Thoth: A Short Essay on the Tarot of the Egyptians.* York Beach, ME: Samuel Weiser, 1974.

Doane, Doris Chase and Ken Keyes. *Tarot Card Spread Reader.* New York: Parker, 1967.

Edinger, E. F. *Ego & Archetype: Individuation & the Religious Function of the Psyche.* Boston: Shambhala, 1992.

Eerenbeemt, Noud van den. *Sleutel tot de Tarot.* Langenfeld, Germany: Tango, 1972.

Von Franz, Marie-Louise. *Creation Myths.* Boston: Shambhala, 1995.

———. *The Feminine in Fairy Tales.* Dallas, TX: Spring Publications, 1972.

———. *Individuation in Fairy Tales.* Zurich: Spring, 1977.

———. *An Introduction to the Interpretation of Fairy Tales.* Dallas, TX: Spring Publications, 1982.

———. *Number and Time: Reflections Leading Towards a Unification of Psychology and Physics.* London: Rider, 1974.

———. *On Divination and Synchronicity: The Psychology of Meaningful Chance.* Toronto: Inner City Books, 1980.

———. *Psyche and Matter.* Boston: Shambhala, 1992.

———. *The Psychological Meaning of Redemption Motifs in Fairytales.* Toronto: Inner City Books, 1980.

———. *Psychotherapy.* Boston: Shambhala, 1993.

Funk & Wagnalls Standard Dictionary of Folklore, Mythology, and Legend. San Francisco: HarperSanFrancisco, 1972, 1984.

Furth, Gregg M. *The Secret World of Drawings: Healing through Art.* Boston: Sigo Press, 1989.

Gabrielli, Alexandra. *Kabbala.* Wassenaar, Holland: Mirananda, 1981.

Glahn, A. F. *Das Deutsche Tarot Buch.* Freiburg: Bauer Verlag, 1958.

Guggenbühl-Craig, Adolf. *Eros on Crutches: Reflections on Amorality and Psychopathy.* Irving, TX: Spring Publications, 1980.

Hamaker-Zondag, Karen. *The Houses of Personality Development* in *Foundations of Personality.* York Beach, ME: Samuel Weiser, 1988 and 1994.

———. *Wat is toch Astrologgie?* Amsterdam: Schors, 1986.

Harding, M. Esther. *The "I" and the "Not-I": A Study in the Development of Consciousness.* Bollingen Series No. 79. Princeton: Princeton University Press, 1965.

———. *Psychic Energy: Its Source and Its Transformation.* Bollingen Series No. 10. Princeton: Princeton University Press, 1963.

Ifrah, Georges. *De Wereld van het Getal: De geschiedenis van een grote uitvinding.* Utrecht, Holland: Servire, 1988.

Javane, Faith and Dusty Bunker. *Numerology and the Divine Triangle*. Atglen, PA: Schiffer, 1979.

———. *De Goddelijke driehoek: een synthese van numerologie, tarot en astrologie*. Wassenaar, Holland: Mirananda, 1983.

Johnson, R. A. *Inner Work: Using Dreams and Active Imagination for Personal Growth*. San Francisco: HarperSanFrancisco, 1986.

Jung, C.G. *The Collected Works, Vols. 1-20*. Bollingen Series No. XX. Princeton: Princeton University Press, 1960-1985.

———. *The Collected Works, Vol. 14. Mysterium Coniunctionis*. Princeton: Princeton University Press, 1970.

———. *Man and His Symbols*. London: Aldus Books, 1964; New York: Doubleday, 1969.

Jung, Emma. *Anima and Animus*. Cary F. Baynes and Hildegard Nagel, trans. Dallas, TX: Spring, 1985.

Kaplan, Aryeh. *Sefer Yetzirah*. York Beach, ME: Samuel Weiser, 1993.

Kaplan, Stuart R. *The Encyclopedia of Tarot*. Vols. 1-3. Stamford, CT: U. S. Games Systems, Inc., 1978, 1985, 1990.

Kast, V. *Creative Leap: Psychological Transformation through Crisis*. Wilmette, IL: Chiron Publications, 1991.

———. *Fairy Tales as Therapy*. New York: Fromm International, 1995

———. *Omgaan met Angst: De Werkelijkheid van het sprookje*. Deventer: Ankh-Hermes, 1989.

Knight, Gareth. *A Practical Guide to Qabalistic Symbolism*. York Beach, ME: Samuel Weiser, 1978.

Konraad, Sandor. *Numerologie: Sleutel tot de Tarot*. Amsterdam: W. N. Schors, 1989.

Kopp, Sheldon. *The Hanged Man: Psychotherapy and the Forces of Darkness*. Palo Alto, CA: SBB Books, 1974.

Larousse World Mythology. Prof. Pierre Grimal, ed. London: Hamlyn, 1965.

Masino, Marcia. *The Easy Tarot Guide*. San Diego, CA: ACS Publications, 1987.

Muchery, Georges. *Le Tarot divinatoire*. Paris: Ed. du Chariot, 1972.

Myer, Isaac. *Qabbalah: The Philosophical Writings of Solomon Ben Yehuda Ibn Gebirol or Avicebron*. New York: Samuel Weiser, 1974.

Neumann, Erich. *The Great Mother: An Analysis of the Archetype.* Ralph Manheim, trans. Bollingen Series No. 47. Princeton: Princeton University Press, 1963.

New Larousse Encyclopaedia of Mythology. Introduction by Robert Graves. London: Hamlyn, 1968.

Nichols, Sallie. *Jung and Tarot: An Archetypal Journey.* York Beach, ME: Samuel Weiser, 1980.

Paneth, Ludwig. *Zahlensymbolik im Unbewusstsein.* Zurich: Rascher, 1952.

Papus. *The Tarot of the Bohemians.* North Hollywood, CA: Wilshire, 1978.

Pollack, Rachel. *The 78 Degrees of Wisdom.* London: Aquarian Press, 1980.

Reeth, A. Vlan. *Encyclopedie van de mythologie.* Baarn: Tirion, 1992.

Ten Dam, Hans. *Zonlicht door 78 Vensters: Praktische Handleiding Voor de Tarot.* Amsterdam: Bres, 1985.

Thierens, A. E. *The General Book of the Tarot: Containing the Astrological Key to the Tarot System Published for the First Time.* Introduction by A. E. Waite. London, Rider, n.d., circa 1930s.

Walker, Barbara. *The Woman's Dictionary of Symbols & Sacred Objects.* San Francisco: HarperSanFrancisco, 1988.

———. *The Woman's Encyclopedia of Myths & Secrets.* San Francisco: HarperSanFrancisco, 1983.

Wirth, Oswald. *The Tarot of the Magicians.* York Beach, ME: Samuel Weiser, 1986.

Zohar. Maurice Simon and Paul Levertoff, eds. New York: Soncino Press, 1934.

Zweig, Connie and Jeremiah Abrams. *Meeting the Shadow: The Hidden Power of the Dark Side of Human Nature.* Los Angeles: J. P. Tarcher, 1991.

INDEX

KAREN HAMAKER-ZONDAG is a founding member of a school of Jungian psychology, Stichting Odrerir, in Holland. She is a graduate of the University of Amsterdam with doctoral degrees in social geography and environmental engineering. Her post-graduate study of psychology, astrology, and parapsychology inspired a full-time counseling practice. She lectures throughout the world.

CPSIA information can be obtained at www.ICGtesting.com
Printed in the USA
BVOW022134200212

283387BV00001B/42/P

9 780877 288787